D0834771

GRAVEYARD DRUID

A NEW ADULT URBAN FANTASY NOVEL

M.D. MASSEY

MODERN DIGITAL PUBLISHING, AUSTIN, TX

FREE BOOK!
Go to http://MDMassey.com now to download your FREE Colin McCool
prequel novel.

Copyright © 2017 by M.D. Massey.

All rights reserved. No part of this publication may be reproduced, distributed
or transmitted in any form or by any means, including photocopying, recording,
or other electronic or mechanical methods, without the prior written
permission of the publisher, except in the case of brief quotations embodied in
critical reviews and certain other noncommercial uses permitted by copyright
law. For permission requests, write to the publisher, addressed "Attention:
Permissions Coordinator," at the address below.

Modern Digital Publishing
P.O. Box 682
Dripping Springs, Texas 78620

Graveyard Druid/ M.D. Massey. — 1st ed.

NATIONAL SUICIDE PREVENTION LIFELINE
CALL 1-800-273-8255

1

So here I was, stripped down to my skivvies and standing in a makeshift fighting ring in Rendon Park, ready to go mano a mano with a troll. And just how had I ended up here?

A few days ago, I'd gotten a call from Siobhan, granddaughter of the local fae queen Maeve many generations removed. Maeve had recently connived a way to get me under her thumb. She'd cornered the market on my mom's art pieces, threatening to ruin her career by flooding the market and devaluing her work. That was, if I didn't agree to become her errand boy and enforcer. Why she didn't get one of her fae hunters to do this work was beyond me; I supposed it had something to do with the fact that I was druid-trained, and sort of a neutral figure in the supernatural world.

Plus, you could bet that Maeve had plans and machinations spanning the course of centuries; she was fae, after all. I had a sneaking suspicion that somehow I was a key figure in those plans, at least for the foreseeable future. Her favorite chess piece. Lucky me.

After enjoying a few blessed weeks of relative peace and quiet, Siobhan had called me out of the blue, saying that Maeve had a job for me. I'd had plenty of time to recover after the huge battle I'd won against Crowley, a rogue Circle wizard who'd decided it was his mission in life to put me six feet under.

I couldn't have cared less about Crowley; I'd only been there to retrieve Maeve's magic whatzit, which turned out to be Balor's Eye. Yes, *the* Balor's eye, an artifact powerful enough to vaporize entire armies at a glance. Crowley had stolen it from Maeve in an effort to put me down once and for all. During the battle I'd killed his hired help, a mean-ass giant known as a fachen, and the Eye had put a hurt on Crowley. I won, they lost, and I ended up with a sentient magical gemstone embedded inside my skull. Temporally displaced, of course, which was the best thing I could say about the entire situation.

As it turned out, I'd also killed the son of a troll clan chief while making my way to kicking Crowley's ass. Okay, so I hadn't kicked his ass, the Eye had—but let's not get technical here. Anyway, the troll I'd killed belonged to a tribe that had served Maeve for centuries, and he'd betrayed her by turning coat for Crowley. Now, the trolls were looking to save face, or regain their honor—or whatever trolls did to make amends when they screwed up.

Apparently, that involved bare-knuckle brawling in your skivvies. Thus, my current situation. I stood in an earthen circle, roughly ten meters wide. Stones marked out the makeshift ring, spaced about a foot apart, all the way around. The dirt beneath my bare feet was hard and dry, and I fully expected to get a nasty road rash and dust in every crack and crevice before this thing was done.

Their chief, who I'd taken to calling Ookla since I couldn't pronounce his full name, patted me down to make sure I didn't have a longsword hidden in my Calvin Kleins. As he searched me I reflected on my life choices, recalling that just a few weeks ago I'd been in similar situation, but facing a werewolf. One could easily challenge my sanity and intelligence at the moment, but at least after I was dead, no one would ever be able to say I'd backed down from a fight.

It's the little things that make life worth living.

"Okay, you know the rules. Two enter, one gets schooled. Trolls get honor either way, you get killed still happy day. Okay?"

The chief's lumpy mug curled into a grin that might have been friendly, but instead came across as creepy and evil. Still, I was kind of getting to like the guy. He was in a tough spot, because his kid had screwed up royally by betraying Maeve. He was honor-bound to seek retribution for his son's death, and also to restore goodwill with the kid's former employer. It didn't seem like any of the Toothshank clan held it against me that I'd killed the kid—to the trolls, that was just the cost of crossing their employer. Their real concern was restoring their honor and reputation.

And, for some strange reason, that meant they had to prove their clan's strength by fighting Maeve's representative. Namely, me. Siobhan had conveniently forgotten to tell me all this before she'd sent me to smooth things over. One of these days, I'd put her in her place, hopefully by proving to Maeve that her great-granddaughter was plotting against her.

At present, though, I had more pressing matters. I rolled my shoulders out and nodded. "Let's get this over with, Ookla."

He smiled that creepy smile of his again, then chopped the air with his hand and shouted something in trollish that I assumed meant, "Let the kumite begin!"

———

I looked across the ring as the chief stepped out of the way. My opponent was closing in fast; trolls were deceptively quick for all their height and mass. Lean and lanky, his body was covered in long, ropy muscles under gray-green skin mottled with warts, moles, and what could only be described as tumors. But the worst thing about trolls was their smell.

The run-in I'd had with the chief's son and his buddy had been no picnic, mainly because Crowley hadn't used any magic to cover up their odor. And troll odor was bad—I mean, just awful. It smelled like necrotic flesh, feces, and foot stank, and had the same effects on the respiratory system and mucous membranes as military-grade tear gas. When Belladonna and I had jumped them, we'd nearly been incapacitated by their funk. My friend Sabine, who we were there to rescue, had been knocked unconscious by the stench. It was that bad. And I was going to have to get up close and personal with this thing.

To their credit, the trolls understood what a powerful weapon their reek was. The chief had taken countermeasures to make sure the fight was fair. The clan's witch doctor had cast a spell on me to protect me from the odor, saying it was "good juju, no boohoo you." Obviously, that cat knew his stuff, because I couldn't smell a damned thing, and I mean nothing. Besides that, my sinuses were more clear than they'd been in weeks, and with all the pollen we had to deal with year-round in Austin, that was saying something.

But still, I was going to need a magical tomato juice bath after this match. And, I'd probably have to burn anything that came into contact with the troll's skin. Meaning, my underwear were going to be buried at sea while I bathed in the river after the match.

That is, if I survived. My opponent looked like he meant business. He came forward in a low stance, similar to some Southern kung-fu and karate styles I'd seen. He had one hand in a high guard by his head, the other low and bent across his waist. His lead hand was in a fist; the other was open, fingers extended into a spear. That likely meant the lead hand was his shield, and the rear hand was his intended weapon. Good to know.

He kept inching in, closer and closer. I assumed that meant he was trying to get in range to throw that spearhand at my eyes or solar plexus. Instead of staying in place, I danced around him like Bruce Lee—and I mean literally like Bruce Lee, cat cries and all. All that showboating wasn't worth a lick for fighting, but I figured it might confuse him and cause him to make a mistake. We moved around for a minute or so like that, me dancing and making "waa-taah!" sounds as he kept edging in.

Finally, I got bored and decided to draw him out. I did a pendulum step in, rapidly replacing my front foot with my back, and snapped a roundhouse kick at his lead knee. Surprisingly, my kick connected, but it felt like kicking a steel pole wrapped in foam rubber. My instep bounced off his leg after the initial jolting impact. Before I could dance back out of the way, his spearhand darted at my face. I slipped and parried, and his fingertips creased the side of my forehead. I felt a trickle of blood run down my cheek as I moved back, out of range.

The trolls around the ring cheered.

My foot throbbed from the impact I'd made with the troll's knee. That was the thing with trolls; they were tough. Skin like leather, flesh like rubber, and bones like steel. And, they healed fast. To kill one, you basically had to behead it and then incinerate it. I had no weapons at the moment, nor was I allowed to use magic, otherwise this joker's head would have already been flying and frying. I'd just have to improvise.

I danced around a few more seconds, feigning an injury in my foot. It hurt, sure, but it was still functional. Even so, the pain made it easy to put on a good show. As I did, I allowed myself to drift just a little too close to the troll. As expected, he used that opportunity to attack again, spearing his fingers at my eyes.

As soon as he moved, I shifted my stance to face him and lowered my weight, ducking under his attack. In the same motion, I dove forward into a tackle, driving my shoulder into the troll's stomach while grabbing his legs and pulling them in close. After that, it was just a matter of leverage and forward momentum. I had the troll pinned on his back in a flash, sitting on his chest with a knee on either side of his body.

A collective gasp came from the crowd of trolls around the ring, and they began to chatter excitedly amongst themselves. The noise barely registered, though; I was busy putting a beat-down on the troll, with open-handed strikes that landed all around his face and neck. My gamble had paid off. This troll didn't know shit about grappling, and it was obvious he wasn't a fan of the UFC, either. He tried to push me off as he took the first dozen blows or so, but he might as well have been trying to move the Rock of Gibraltar. I could have used the opportunity to slap on an armbar, but the troll would just pop his elbow straight again and heal within seconds.

No, I needed something that would take him out completely. I kept striking him, waiting for him to cover his head with both arms. I continued to hammer him, aiming blows at wherever I saw an opening. A few seconds later he did exactly what I expected, rolling and covering the back of his head with his hands, guarding the sides of his head with his folded arms.

Now I had him.

I wrapped my legs around his body and hooked my heels in his groin, both for better purchase and to kick him in the balls as a distraction. I pummeled him mercilessly from his back until he gave me an opening, then quickly snaked my hand and arm under his chin and back around the other side of his head. I grabbed my biceps on my other arm and secured the rear naked choke, what the Brazilians call "the lion killer." And I squeezed, counting to twenty slowly in my head.

At the end of my count, he was out like a light. Instead of killing him, I rolled him onto his back, picking up his arm and letting it flop to the ground to show the crowd I'd dispatched their champion. I placed a foot on his chest and raised my arms in the air for good measure.

The crowd and chieftain went silent, all of them staring at me with what looked like anger and disbelief. I was getting nervous. In seconds, the troll I'd fought would come around, and then I'd probably have to fight him again. I was exhausted after the match, and didn't know if I had the juice to take him out a second time.

The chieftain shouted something in trollish, and the crowd erupted in cheers. They rushed the ring, vaulting me up on their shoulders and carrying me around the circle, chanting trollish rhymes and making one hell of a ruckus. I worried that we might draw a crowd. We were all glamoured, but the noise they made had me nervous just the same.

In the confusion, I managed to catch a glimpse of my opponent. He had sat up, attended to by the witch doctor. They exchanged a few words, but I couldn't hear what they said. He finally nodded, locking eyes with me, mouth set in a grim expression. After a brief, uncomfortable moment, he cracked a grin and placed a closed fist over his chest in what I assumed was acquiescence of his defeat. Then he stood and pushed through the crowd, joining the fray by hoisting me up on his shoulders.

I was really going to have to burn my undies after this.

2

After a quick dip in Town Lake, I spent the remainder of my time with the trolls drinking a horrendous grog of fermented giant spider milk, hashing out a new agreement between the troll clan and the fae. Conversing with trolls was always trying, because they only spoke in rhyme. Plus, they were horrible poets, and often their responses could be interpreted many different ways. I had to spend a considerable amount of time clarifying their intentions and demands, negotiating the best reconciliation I could—one that would serve Maeve's interests and also keep the trolls happy.

The chief seemed mainly concerned with restoring the clan's honor by being allowed to reenter Maeve's service. I had to tactfully point out that after his son's betrayal, Maeve would be reticent to allow them to work in their previous capacity, as security guards for her estate. This was met with considerable disappointment on the part of the trolls, but eventually I convinced them to take up the responsibility of guarding the borders of Maeve's territory. Despite their bulk, trolls were exceptionally good at slinking around and hiding. For that reason, I thought it would be a great use of their natural talents—so long as they didn't eat any humans while dispensing their duties. Sometime around one in the morning, I reached an agreement with their clan chief. After that, everything was a drunken blur.

I stayed with the trolls well into the night, getting considerably drunk on that spider milk beer they kept giving me. The first three or four mugs of it were just awful, but after that the stuff was so strong I didn't care. The troll I'd fought, whose name meant "Eats-Guts-With-Bare-Hands-And-Salts-The-Earth-After-Battle," turned out to be a decent guy—for a troll. I ended up calling him Guts since I couldn't pronounce his name in trollish. He seemed to like it so it stuck. He was the chief's nephew, who I continued to call Ookla for the same reasons. After I explained that Ookla the Mok was a fearsome creature and mighty warrior from human Saturday morning cartoon lore, the chief beat his chest and proclaimed he would add it to his many titles. Fine by me, because by that point I was three sheets to the wind and couldn't even pronounce my own name if I tried.

After a few hours of negotiation and another thirty minutes of losing trollish drinking games (the guy who puked after being punched in the gut had to drink), I had to take a whiz something awful. I stumbled outside the circle of light made by their bonfire, then tripped and fell flat on my face on top of a lounging troll maiden, which Guts thought was hilarious. After apologizing profusely, disentangling myself from the most awkward interaction I'd ever had with a female—of any species —I finally made it into the bushes to drain the dragon.

As I finished up, I heard movement in the bushes nearby, accompanied by a lot of moaning and groaning. Triggering a night-vision cantrip that I could barely recall in my stupefied state, I searched the landscape for whatever was making all that racket. Then, the wind shifted and the smell hit me.

I reached for my Craneskin Bag, which was sort of the Irish version of a bag of holding. I always kept it around, because if I didn't keep an eye on it, the bag had a way of releasing trouble-some objects from its depths at inopportune times. As I fumbled a short sword out of my bag, I yelled at the top of my lungs to warn the trolls behind me.

"Ghouls! Ghouls attacking the camp!"

A dozen trolls rushed out to join the fray, taking the threat seriously. With their surprising strength and aggressiveness, ghouls could be tough to take out. Thankfully, there were only a few of the undead in the area, so we dispatched them easily despite our inebriation. A characteristic of ghouls that worked in our favor was that they didn't reproduce like zombies did, because they tended to crack open the skulls of their prey and eat the brains. No brains, no reanimated dead. Zombies lacked the strength to crack a human skull open, which meant they spread their disease and reproduced like crazy. Even so, Guts sent some scouts out to make sure we'd killed the last of them. They soon reported that we'd killed all the ghouls in the area.

After the short battle, Chief Ookla showed up with his witch doctor, and they examined one of the corpses. The appearance of the ghouls was troubling, to say the least, and it was apparent that their arrival had put a damper on the festivities. Just as well, because the fight had sobered me up and I already felt the world's worst hangover coming on.

The witch doctor toed the corpse, then muttered gibberish and threw a handful of animal bones on the ground. His eyes rolled back in his head and his body locked up for a few moments, until he began trembling and foaming at the mouth. Since no one else seemed surprised by this behavior, I played it cool until his magic-induced seizure passed. When he came back around, he took one look at the bones and exchanged a few terse words in troll-speak with the chief. Then he spat on the corpse with a scowl and stormed off, leaving the augury bones where they'd fallen.

Chief Ookla's bumpy green brow furrowed. "Wise troll say trouble ahead. We break camp, head home instead."

I nodded. "I understand, chief, and I thank you for your hospitality. I'll relay the results of our negotiations to Queen Maeve, and let you know when your scouts can start patrolling her borders."

The chief shook his head. "We start work now for queen. Danger coming, needs to be seen."

I shook hands with all the male trolls and wished the females well, tactfully avoiding making eye contact with the troll maiden I'd accidentally "fallen for" earlier. I hiked out of the river bottom to the streets above, plopping down on a bus stop bench to review the night's events while I waited.

Having sobered more since the short battle, I had plenty of questions with no answers. What were ghouls doing wandering around so close to downtown Austin? And who the hell had created them in the first place?

The vamps were always the first group everyone blamed when lesser undead started showing up. I doubted any of the local coven members were to blame, because they weren't sloppy enough to leave half-turned victims roaming around. Even so, I decided my first order of business would be to speak with Luther, the local coven leader. Then I'd get some answers.

The following morning, I woke up under a tarp on the front porch of the junkyard warehouse, with Roscoe and Rufus curled up next to me. Actually, Finn woke me up with a light kick to my leg.

"Morning, sunshine. I figured I'd better wake you before your uncle shows up and pitches a fit. Ed's a nice guy, and he likes you, but I don't think he'd appreciate walking into his place of business and seeing his nephew passed out on the front steps."

Finn wore a set of overalls that made him look like an escapee from the county jail, and a shit-eating expression that said he enjoyed seeing me hungover. He handed me a steaming cup of coffee. I took it as I sat up and rubbed my eyes, then my head.

"Thanks. Oh, have mercy. Remind me to never get into a drinking contest with a bunch of trolls again."

"Trolls, eh? I thought you smelled a little ripe. Based on the fact that your clothes are strung all over the outdoor shower, and that you're buck naked, I'll assume that you at least had the wherewithal to clean off before you passed out."

I looked under the tarp, finding that I wore nothing more than a pair of socks. I was never going to hear the end of this.

"You could have at least brought me some clothes, you know."

"What, and spoil the show for the dogs?" The old man loved this. There had been many a time before he'd sobered up that I'd found him wandering the junkyard, or passed out somewhere in various states of undress. Whenever I'd find him, he'd always mumble something about druids not needing clothes, and I'd tell him a lot had changed in two thousand years. I guess I couldn't blame him for rubbing it in a little.

Despite the fact that Finn had seen me in my natural state before, both to patch me up after a hard fight and during our survival training, I wrapped the tarp around me as I headed to my room at the back of the warehouse. The look on his face when I came out wearing a pair of shorts with a towel over my shoulder said it all. He puffed away on a hand-rolled cigarette, maintaining a calm expression. But the tightness around his eyes and mouth said he was enjoying this whole scene just a little too much.

I decided to be a good sport about it. "Thanks for waking me up."

He nodded. "Least I could do. By the way, did you get that troll girl's phone number?"

I narrowed my eyes and feigned ignorance. "What troll girl?"

His eyes belied his mirth as he struggled to remain straight-faced. "The one that musk-marked you last night. You know that's how they mark their mates, right? They have musk glands on the backs of their ankles, and the scent is— unmistakable. I gotta say, my boy, I didn't think you had it in you."

"It wasn't—I didn't—nothing happened!"

He nodded sagely and blew smoke from his nostrils. "If you say so."

Blood rushed to my face as I wisely beat a retreat to the shower, to try to get the remainder of troll funk off me. With sandpaper and gasoline, if necessary.

Finn hollered after me as I made my escape. "I hope you used protection!" He busted out in laughter, and his ornery cackling echoed throughout the junkyard. I ignored him as I scrubbed myself nearly raw with a bar of mechanic's pumice soap, paying particular attention to my hips and thighs, where I could only assume I'd been "musk-marked" by the troll maiden during our impromptu introduction. I suspected that Finn was just playing a nasty joke on me, but a little extra scrubbing wouldn't hurt.

I walked back around to the front of the warehouse just as the morning crew began showing up. Finn was wiping tears from his eyes, but at least he'd stopped laughing.

"Something happened last night that I forgot to mention," I said, wicking moisture from my ear with the towel.

He snorted as he held back laughter. "You don't say? Finally ready to fess up about your tryst? Speaking of which, when are you going to introduce her to your mother? As you're well aware, she hates being the last to know about these things."

I sighed in frustration. "C'mon, old man, I'm serious. A group of ghouls showed up at the troll camp last night, and busted up the celebration."

He paused in mid-chuckle. "Ghouls? Does Luther know?"

"Nope, but I'm going to drop by the coffee shop to tell him. Maybe he'll hire me to take care of it again."

The last time the city had encountered a ghoul problem, it had been caused by a rogue nosferatu who was sucking folks dry without turning them. About one in four of those victims came back as a ghoul—more or less a strong, somewhat faster zombie. Luther was a friend of mine, and the de facto head of the local vamp population. He'd hired me to take care of it so his people wouldn't be blamed. In fact, that's how we'd become friends.

I didn't do that type of work anymore, or at least I hadn't for a while. But right now money was tight, and I could use the extra scratch. If Luther was hiring, I wouldn't mind putting my hunter cap back on for a few days to take out the odd ghoul or nos'. But just for a few days.

Finn nodded. "Hmmph. Been a while since you did any real hunting. Let me know what he says. And don't be afraid to ask for help if he gives you the job."

"I'm perfectly capable of looking after myself, Finn. I did it for two years while you lost yourself in a syringe and a bottle."

He winced visibly at that remark. Maybe I shouldn't have said it, but it was true. Still, I felt bad.

"I'm sorry. That was unnecessary."

He held up a hand and looked away. "No, you're right. I wasn't there for you after Jesse died." He stood and stamped out his cigarette. "Let me know if you need anything."

I watched him retreat to the back end of the yard, feeling like an ass. We'd been getting along better since he'd sobered up, and he was making an effort to reconcile our differences. Maybe it was time I forgave him for his past indiscretions. I could have followed him to make amends, but I was already going to be late for class. At least, that's what I told myself.

Entering my room, I picked Jesse's photo up from the shelf by the door.

"I know you want me to forgive him, but I don't know if I can."

I felt a soft, cool breeze caress my neck, and I could've sworn I heard someone say, *Try*. I kissed the photo and set it down, and commenced with getting on with my day.

3

I didn't get out in time to stop by Luther's, and due to my hangover and impromptu decontamination routine, I almost didn't make it to class. On arrival, I snuck in the back and crept into a seat behind all the other students. I ended up moving back a few rows after several of the students started coughing and gagging.

I guess troll funk was harder to get off than you'd think.

After class, I suffered the withering stares of my fellow students, making the lame excuse that I'd run over a skunk with my scooter on the way to class. That seemed to placate them for the most part, but I was pretty sure I wasn't going to be making time with any of the girls in class this semester.

I felt a bit guilty at the thought, and had to remind myself that Jesse was gone. I'd lost her two years prior, killing her by accident after being cursed by a very powerful witch. Jesse had been my first love, and even after all this time I still reflexively thought of her as my girlfriend. Her ghost still haunted me. Literally, in fact, which made it difficult to put the past behind. To say I was emotionally confused would have been an understatement.

I ate lunch by myself, outdoors and far away from anyone else. I sat in the very back of the lecture hall in my afternoon class, spending much of the class Googling "how to get rid of skunk smell" and taking notes.

Once class ended, I stopped by the grocery store and purchased several quarts of vinegar, a few large cans of tomato juice, six pints of hydrogen peroxide, and dish soap. Then I headed back to the junkyard and scrubbed the crap out of my skin and hair using all three at once, just in case. I smelled like pizza sauce by the end of it, but the troll funk was finally gone. I finished up by tossing my clothes in a metal drum with a stick, dousing them with gas, and lighting them on fire. A few folks pulling parts in the yard gave me weird looks. "Skunks," I explained with a shrug. They nodded and let me be.

As I finished, I realized I was late to meet Sabine. She'd quickly tired of hanging out with me in class, saying that my history prof got shit all wrong. She looked my age, but might've been much older for all I knew. Sabine was half-glaistig, so she could have been a few decades or a few centuries old and no one would have been able to tell the difference. Since we hadn't seen each other in a while, we'd agreed to meet at Zilker Park to hang out and people watch.

Zilker was a popular place for Austinites to go when they wanted to get outdoors and enjoy the fall weather. It was a huge park, close to downtown, connected with both the Town Lake Trail and the Barton Creek Greenbelt. One of the great things about Austin was the fact that we had a lot of hippies who voted, and they loved their green spaces. Environmental activists were the only thing keeping the city council from completely selling out to developers. Like many young people living in Austin, I hoped the rising cost of living wouldn't force all our beloved tree huggers out of the city.

I met Sabine by Barton Springs Pool, where we watched

people swim in the seventy-degree waters fed by an underground spring. She had prepared a simple lunch of sandwiches, fruit, and a soft cheese that smelled almost as bad as the trolls but tasted delicious. When she offered me a glass of cider I declined, citing reasons of personal health and the risk of flashbacks from the night before.

She snickered, tossing her hair back over her shoulder. "So, this troll chick thinks you're hot, huh? She'd better watch it, or Jesse's going to be haunting her lumpy green ass."

I smiled, enjoying the way the sun lit her face—although I had to concentrate to see the "real" Sabine. The glamour she hid behind often made me see two images of her, one on top of the other, unless I focused on seeing just one. I preferred looking at the natural Sabine, not the mousy, frumpy girl she wanted everyone to see. But I did understand her reasons for hiding behind her magic.

The real Sabine was supernaturally attractive, the result of her glaistig heritage. She was curvy in a pin-up model kind of way—with full lips, high cheek bones, sun-kissed skin, and freckles that dotted her cheeks. She hid behind that reverse-glamour because she was "top-heavy," and to the fae she may as well have had a third eye. Fae were supposed to be lithe and graceful, and curves like hers were a decidedly human trait that was looked down upon as a mutation.

Years of childhood teasing from both humans and fae had made her self-conscious—neurotically so, in fact. We'd met while we were both in therapy, crossing paths each week as I was leaving our therapist's office and she was showing up. Since then, I'd been slowly helping her overcome her social anxiety. Outings like this were designed to help her acclimate to being around people.

Her eyes sparkled as she laughed. I couldn't help but laugh along with her.

"Yes, Sabine, I gained an admirer last night. Just because she's a troll doesn't mean I'm not flattered."

"Dude, what are you going to do when she clubs you over the head and drags you off to her cave? You know they really do that, right?" Her expression went flat, and her smile vanished.

"Stop—just stop. I know you're bullshitting me, because if that were true you'd be dying of laughter right now. Besides, Finn already got me today with some joke about me getting musk-marked or something. Total bullshit, but he had me going for a while."

She covered her mouth with her hand, and her eyes grew big and round. "She musk-marked you? Oh, Colin—that's not good, sweetie."

I narrowed my eyes and scowled at her. "That's not funny, Sabine."

"I'm not laughing. For real, troll females like to—"

The frantic screams of a woman standing by the water's edge cut her off mid-sentence.

"Help! Someone help me! It took my baby under!"

We watched as the lifeguards dove into the water, swimming to the spot where the lady pointed. They dove down, only to come back up empty-handed.

"They can't see the kid—why can't they see the kid?" I asked aloud. I got a sick feeling in the pit of my stomach. Not only was this a favorite hangout for the local human population; Barton Springs was also occupied by a number of water fae, and traditionally water fae were not friendly. Maeve mostly kept them in check—but with the fae, anything was possible.

Sabine jumped up and down, grabbing my shoulder and pointing down the bank about fifty feet. "There!"

I looked where she pointed and saw a splash as a dark, iridescent hoof broke the water. From the looks of it we were dealing with a water horse, and they were all nasty customers.

None of the mundanes present would be able to see it if it didn't want to be seen, so it was up to me to get the kid back.

"Shit," I muttered, tearing off my shirt and sprinting down the bank to the water's edge. I ran past the gathering crowd as I hastily snapped off the words to an incantation that would increase my stamina. It wouldn't allow me to breathe underwater, but it would increase the amount of time I could hold my breath.

I dove off the bank and into the cold, clear water below. Once under, I swam as fast as I could to the spot where I'd seen that hoof break the surface. I finally spotted an aughisky diving into the pool's depths, a terrified child on its back. Aughiskies were the most vicious of water horses, with a bloodthirstiness eclipsed only by the nuckalavee. They often appeared as a beautiful horse or pony, and those who saw the steed would be overtaken by a desire to climb on its back. But once mounted, the aughisky's skin would magically adhere to the person wherever they touched it. Once the rider was trapped, the waterhorse would dive under and drown the hapless soul—at which point it would eat them.

I knew of one or two aughisky that lived in Lake Travis, outside Maeve's demesne. They drowned a few people a year; not enough to garner any real notice, but enough to warrant being hunted down... if I still did that sort of thing. Whenever someone drowned in the lake and the body couldn't immediately be found, it was likely a water horse. Why the Circle hadn't done anything about them yet was anyone's guess. I assumed they were too busy being assholes.

This one had probably gone mad from hunger or old age, and foolishly strayed into Maeve's territory out of spite. Maeve's hunters would avenge the death of any human inside her lands. Not so much due to any moral code, but because she liked to keep things peaceful so humans didn't discover the world beneath our own.

Basically, this aughisky was committing suicide by Maeve. I cared little for whether or not some unseelie fae wanted to end its miserable life. But taking out a little boy in the process didn't sit well with me at all. I put on some speed, kicking and stroking in a desperate attempt to catch them before they disappeared.

The water horse was fast, but it had paused to check its prey, turning to see if the boy had lost consciousness yet. He had. I watched as the horse nipped at the boy's arm, testing to see if he was finally out. I knew based on my first aid training that children could often survive drownings, if they received CPR in time. And the colder the water was, the more likely they were to survive. I kept low to the bottom of the pool as I swam closer, coming up to snatch the boy from the horse's blind spot.

As soon as I tugged on the kid's arm, the water horse spun to see what had tried to steal its prey. When it saw me attempting to pull the boy off, it swung its head around and snapped at me with a mouth full of razor-sharp teeth. Seeing a horse with a mouth full of barracuda teeth was more than a bit unsettling. Fortunately, I'd dealt with these creatures in the past—only on dry land, mind you, but I knew what to do.

With all fae, there were only a few weaknesses one could exploit to defeat them. One option was cutting them off from their magic by severing their connection to the Underrealms. I didn't have the juice to do that without a lot of time and preparation, so I'd have to go with option number two: cold iron.

I drew a hand-forged knife from the small of my back. It wasn't much of a knife, just a small hunting blade that I kept on me. Past experience had taught me it always paid to be prepared when dealing with the fae. As the aughisky snapped at me, I twisted and dove under its gnashing jaws, slashing it across the throat as deeply as I could. The water began to cloud with black fluid as the wound leaked blood all around us, but the water horse was undeterred. It continued to snap and bite at me, refusing to let the child go.

My lungs burned and my limbs were getting heavier by the moment. If I didn't surface soon, I was going to become the main course, and this poor boy would be an after-dinner snack. Desperate, I reversed the blade in my hand, offering my other arm up as a sacrifice. As I suspected, the horse bit down on my forearm, sinking its teeth deep into my flesh. The pain nearly made me cry out, but I resisted the urge, knowing I'd only fill my lungs with water and assure my own death in the process. Instead, I swung with all my might, stabbing the knife through the aughisky's eye and into its brain.

The creature spasmed and then went limp. The boy's body drifted away from its back as the water horse sank deeper into the silty creek bottom below. I grabbed the kid around the waist and swam toward the surface for all I was worth, gasping for air when I broke through the water.

I vaguely heard Sabine yelling for someone to help me, then other voices joined in. I held the boy's head above water as I stroked for shore, and before I knew it the lifeguards were pulling both of us out of the water. I shrugged one of them off as she attempted to look at my arm.

"I'm fine—help the boy," I said, more gruffly than I'd intended. She looked unconvinced. "It was an alligator, but it barely nicked me. Please, just see to the kid."

She relented, with an admonishment for me to wait for the paramedics so they could look at my arm. She joined the other lifeguards in delivering CPR to the child. I sat off to the side, numb as I watched them work on the boy until the paramedics arrived. They hooked him up to a cardiac monitor and continued chest compressions after suctioning him, giving him oxygen using a mask attached to a bag that they squeezed to inflate his lungs. The boy's mother was a wreck, and understandably so; she barely spared me a glance as she followed the medics into the back of the ambulance.

I hadn't tried to save the kid because I wanted any recognition. I just hoped and prayed the boy would be alright. As I watched the ambulance lights trail off into the distance, Sabine wrapped my arm in a piece of red and white-checkered tablecloth, the same one we'd been sitting on earlier. I allowed her to bandage me up, hoping like hell that the alligator story would satisfy the local authorities and news crews.

"Fracking fae," I muttered, realizing too late that I was sitting right next to one. "Not you, I mean—shit, I'm sorry, Sabine."

She looked down at her hands, which were covered in my blood. "I know what you meant. Don't worry about it. I hate them most of the time, too."

"Still, I'm sorry. Me and my big mouth."

I glanced away from the scene for a moment, and blinked in shock. Sabine had dropped her see-me-not spell. She still had her anti-glamour in place, but the fact that she was exposed in public? I didn't know what to say.

When she noticed me staring, she crossed her arms and pulled her cardigan around her, making a small gesture with her left hand. And like that, she was practically invisible again.

"Thanks for putting yourself out there like that. I know it must've made you feel like you were exposed."

She shrugged. "Couldn't let you drown, McCool. If I did, who would I get to take your place? Not too many people are willing to look like they're talking to themselves in public, you know."

I chuckled, but my laughter died as I recalled how the kid had looked as they'd loaded him up. He had been so pale, so fragile—and his mother had cried hysterically, calling—no, wailing—for her baby. I didn't think I'd ever forget that moment.

Sabine smiled sadly and pulled me down to give me a peck on the cheek. "He might make it, you know. And if he does, it'll be because of you."

"I hope so." I looked at the makeshift pressure bandage she'd devised, which had already soaked through with blood. After refusing care several times, the lifeguards had finally left me alone. "Guess I'd better go get Finn to stitch this up. My healing magic sucks."

A smile briefly flashed across her face. "Some druid you are. Call me later, to let me know how it looks after Finnegas gets through with you, alright?"

I gestured at our picnic spread, now in disarray. "Sorry about ruining our meal."

"Hush, and go get your arm taken care of before the news crews show up. Unless you want to be on TV looking like that."

"Point taken. I'll call you later." I left her to clean up the mess and jogged to my scooter, leaving the parking lot just as the first news van arrived.

4

"Crap, Colin, you didn't tell me I'd be freezing my ass off out here. Next time, warn a fae girl so she can dress appropriately."

Sabine and I sat in the shadows of a mausoleum, taking cover from the chilly wind while we staked out the area for ghouls and the odd nosferatu, at Luther's behest. He'd asked me to help him prevent an undead outbreak, knowing the Circle would blame the vamps for it whether it was their fault or not. An uneasy truce had existed for decades between the Circle and the coven, and Luther preferred to keep it intact. Certain factions within the Circle wanted to keep the peace, while others looked for any excuse to go to war with the vamps. If I took care of the issue before the Circle got wind, it would save Luther many political headaches, and possibly prevent a war.

As for why Sabine was here, she'd volunteered. To make up for the picnic I'd offered to take her out to eat, but instead she'd asked to come along with me tonight. Mostly it was to keep me company, but she also did it out of curiosity regarding what I did as a hunter. She shivered and wrapped her arms around herself, as she only wore jeans, a t-shirt, and sneakers.

I smiled apologetically. "I honestly didn't think it'd be this cold. I mean, it's October in Austin. Usually everyone is still in shorts."

Neither of us had checked the weather before we'd headed out, and a cold front had unexpectedly moved in minutes before. A frigid north wind blew out of the trees behind us, bringing a damp mist that would soon drench Sabine's cotton shirt and jeans, increasing her misery.

I pulled off my overcoat, my arm throbbing slightly. Finn had sewn me up and given me a healing draught to speed my recovery, but it would be a few days before I fully recovered from the aughisky's bite.

I handed her the coat. "Here, take this. I'm used to the cold— and besides, if it gets too bad I'll just trigger a body heat cantrip."

She draped it over her shoulders, wrapping it around her body like a blanket. The coat was a replacement for the Army trench that had gotten shredded during my fight with the fachen. That had been Dad's old coat, and I'd hated to lose it, but it had been in tatters and completely beyond repair. This one was a similar, updated version I'd picked up at a surplus store. I hadn't had time to ward it, but it was waterproof, so it'd keep the cold and damp off her just fine.

"Better?" She nodded. I pulled a thermos of coffee out of my Craneskin Bag and poured her a cup. She took it and breathed the steam in, then sipped the warm black liquid and sniffed.

"You know what? Being a hunter sucks. And it's boring as hell, too."

She passed the cup to me, and I sipped a little and handed it back. It was Luther's special blend; I'd been getting my coffee for free since I'd agreed to take this job. So, I figured I'd go for the good stuff while it lasted. Real Blue Mountain and Kona. Yum.

I nodded. "Yeah, but you can't complain about the coffee."

"You got that right." Without warning, she grabbed my arm. "Shit, I think I just saw something moving over there."

Sabine pointed to our left, at a row of gravestones that marked some of the oldest graves in Austin. City Cemetery, also known as Oakwood Cemetery, was founded in 1839 and boasted forty acres of Texas history. Not only was it the oldest city-owned cemetery in town; it was also the spookiest. And as it turned out, Sabine was a bit of a scaredy cat.

I arched an eyebrow and gave her a playful nudge.

"Sure you're not just jumping at shadows?"

We'd been out here for hours, and besides a stray cat, a momma opossum and her babies, and a homeless guy I'd given a hoagie to, we'd seen exactly jack squat. It was getting close to dawn so I figured we were unlikely to spot any undead, and frankly I'd been about to pack it in before Sabine had gotten spooked.

"No, man, I'm serious! Look, behind that creepy statue of the angel over there—see that? There's something rooting around, digging in the ground."

Admittedly, Sabine's eyes were better than mine—what with her being half-fae and all. Even with my enhanced hunter senses, she could pick up things that I couldn't. I cocked an ear but couldn't hear anything over the howl of the wind. I triggered a night vision cantrip, but the thick granite gravestones and statuary blocked my view.

I shrugged. "Okay, I'll go check it out. Stay here—I'll be right back."

"That's a whole lot of nope right there. Uh-uh, mister, no way you're leaving me here by myself. I'm coming with you."

"Suit yourself, but if it is a ghoul I'll need you to stay behind me and watch my back. And if things go south for some reason—"

"I know, I know—hide and stay that way. Got it."

I hated reading her the riot act, but Sabine was half-glaistig, so her powers were mostly related to glamour and causing excessive lactation in cows and goats. She was hella smart and fun to have around, but in a fight she wouldn't be much use.

"Alright, stay close."

I rolled up from the ground and onto the balls of my feet in a smooth, silent motion. Sabine sprang up lightly, her alacrity revealing her fae blood. Fae were spooky when they did things that showed their true nature. Most of the time they hid it well. But when you saw the real fae, with all their alien beauty and unnaturally graceful movement, it was more than a bit unnerving. I motioned for her to follow and stuck to the shadows as I crept over to the area in question.

As we approached, the sounds of digging and grunting became more clear. My view was still obscured by gravestones, so I couldn't make out whether it was a human grave robber, a stray dog, or coyote rooting around. Or, a ghoul looking for an easy meal. We were in an older part of the cemetery, but some of these plots were family-owned, and there were still fresh graves to be found here. A ghoul might find something to feed on, even here.

The wind shifted, and Sabine's suspicions were confirmed; the stench of rotting human flesh, feces, and fresh blood was unmistakable. We were in the presence of one or more of the lower undead.

There were several types of undead. Higher vampires, like Luther and his kind, were closer to humankind but still alien in their heightened physical abilities and predatory tendencies. Most of them who survived the first few months after they were turned could control their urges and blend into society. Nosferatu, on the other hand, were a much more feral type of vampire, and physically dissimilar to humans. For the most part, nos-types weren't going to blend into anything, except in low light and wearing baggy clothes. They were instinct-driven predators, motivated to hunt by nature and unable to control their lust for blood. Nosferatu tended to exist on the edges of society, preying on the weak and isolated so they stayed off the radar of law enforcement. They were the most common species hunted by the Cold Iron Circle, and many a hunter cut their teeth by taking out a nos.

As for the other undead, you had liches—undead magic-users who had performed one too many necromantic rituals. They were extremely powerful and, thankfully, rare. Then you had revenants, who were just one step under vamps. Revs were half-vamps, humans that a vamp had attempted to turn but it just didn't take. Tons of things could go wrong in trying to turn a human into a vamp; from what I understood, the master had to keep them just on the edge of death as the vyrus took hold, and then they had to stop their heart at the exact moment when the vyrus had spread throughout their system. Only at that precise moment would it be able to shift their metabolism and transform their physiology. If death came too soon, you got a rev—a kind of dumber, much weaker vamp.

Then you had zombies and ghouls. Zombies were slow-moving reanimated corpses. Unlike the popular movie versions of zombies, you couldn't create them with a drug or lab-grown infection. Zombism was exclusively a supernatural phenomenon. Zombies were either created by higher undead, when the vyrus took a weak hold in a kill and reanimated the once living, or through necromancy. Either way, it was spread when a zombie or ghoul bit a human without killing them. Within hours or maybe a day at most, the human would become ill and die, and then reanimate as a zombie or ghoul. The difference was in how much vyrus they got; ghouls were like zombies on steroids, having enough vyrus to make them stronger and quicker than your average Zed.

Zombism could spread like wildfire if left unchecked. One zombie could cause an outbreak, and that would require the Cold Iron Circle to come out in force. That almost always meant innocent lives would be ruined. The Circle was known to be ruthless in quashing outbreaks, and they'd kill anyone they even suspected of being infected. It was a side of the Circle that I didn't care for, and I sometimes had a difficult time reconciling the fact that one of my dear friends was a Circle hunter.

Besides that, if we had an outbreak the Circle would surely blame it on the vamps. It was imperative that I locked this shit down, and fast.

I grabbed Sabine and pulled her behind a tombstone. "You were right," I whispered. "From the smell of it, we have the undead out here. Do me a favor and stay out of sight while I deal with stinky over there."

She nodded. "I'll crank up the juice on my glamour—it'll never even know I'm here."

"Alright. But stay close, just in case there are more out here. They'll still be able to locate you by smell and hearing."

Before she could protest, I pulled a short sword from my Craneskin Bag. Gripping the sword firmly, I stalked around the gravestones to take out the ghoul before it discovered us.

I peeked around the monolithic grave marker to see what I was dealing with. There were two of them—ghouls from the way they were moving, digging up one of the deceased who'd been recently interred. The artificial turf was in shreds, and they were at least four feet deep, tossing wet clods of earth out in a frantic effort to reach their goal.

One of them was taller and male—thin with dark hair, and dressed in what had once been a nice suit and tie. I imagined he'd been a stock broker or banker in his previous life. He looked fairly fresh, but absolutely like a walking corpse. The stench coming off him and his partner was palpable. The other one looked a bit rougher around the edges. I couldn't see much of her at first, then her head and shoulders popped up to reveal a heavy-set black woman with hair cropped close to her head. She had a large bangle earring in one ear, and the other ear was missing, along with much of the skin and flesh on the right side of her jaw. Perhaps she'd been undead for a while—at least that meant she wouldn't be quite as fast as the male ghoul.

Sabine did as I requested and remained hidden within her see-me-not glamour. I ducked back behind the grave marker to check her position, and to make certain she wouldn't accidentally be caught in the fray once I started dispatching the gruesome twosome. With a thumbs up from her, I headed toward the ghouls.

Unfortunately, her glamour didn't mask noise. Before I made it to the ghouls, she tripped over a stone plot marker and fell, knocking over a tin flower pot with a clatter.

The sounds of digging stopped immediately and the ghouls began growling and moaning. I edged one eyeball around the monolith to see what they were doing. The male stood up and began searching the area surrounding the grave. The female climbed out of the grave in a crouch, her face close to the ground like a bloodhound, sniffing the air with twitchy, grotesque movements. She must have smelled something, because she began creeping toward where Sabine had fallen.

Shit.

5

I didn't want to risk this ghoul sniffing Sabine out. I'd never seen her in a scrape, so I had no idea how she'd react. Plus, she wasn't armed. Well, not in the strict sense, anyway; glaistigs had limited powers of polymorphism. I'd never seen her in any other form but her current one, but it was quite possible that she could transform into a hideous and more deadly version of herself. I didn't particularly care to see that transformation, nor did I want her in a position to have to reveal it, so I dove into action.

I sprang from hiding and closed the distance between the monolith and the open grave in a few swift strides, drawing the short sword as I ran and chanting under my breath to ready a flashbulb cantrip. The female ghoul snarled and skittered away at the sound of my footsteps, but she wasn't my immediate target. I assumed that the larger, fresher ghoul would be more dangerous, so I loped up and decapitated him before he had time to climb out of the grave. His head bounced once and tumbled into the grave. I kicked his torso as I leapt over him to ensure his body followed suit. Following through with my momentum, I cleared the hole they'd dug and landed on the other side.

As I landed, I slipped on something wet and squishy and lost my footing. I soon found myself teetering on the edge of the grave, waving my arms in circles to regain my balance. No dice. I fell backward, slowly at first, then more rapidly as gravity took over. I landed at the muddy bottom of the grave on top of ghoul number one. The fall knocked the wind out of me and I bashed my head on a rock, the sum total effect leaving me dazed, diaphragm spasming in an effort to resume spontaneous breathing.

Awesome way to return to the hunter life, Colin, I thought as I struggled to get my bearings. I shook off the blow and forced myself to take short, quick breaths to relax the muscles in my abdomen. Nothing felt broken, and I hadn't stabbed myself with my sword, so that was a plus. I rolled unsteadily to my knees, grabbing the edge of the grave to pull myself upright.

Sabine's scream pierced the night, cutting through my concussed mental haze and bringing me back into focus. I vaulted out of the grave, a bit unsteady but functional, and ran in the direction of the scream. Sabine was crab-walking backward away from the ghoul, but the fat lady was having none of it. The ghoul skittered forward like a spider and grabbed Sabine's ankle, pulling her away from the tree that had been her destination. Sabine grabbed onto a root and began kicking the ghoul in the face with her high-top Vans.

"Let—go—of—my—fucking—ankle!" she swore as she stomped the ghoul in the face over and over again. She held onto the tree root for dear life, but pulled her knee all the way up to her stomach to get the maximum amount of power into each kick. Apparently, Sabine was no shrinking violet in a fight —good to know.

The ghoul finally got a clue and released one hand to grab

Sabine's other ankle. She curled her rotten lips back with a snarl to reveal black and decayed teeth, rearing her head back to chomp down on Sabine's calf.

"No!" I yelled, tossing the flashbulb cantrip in her face from a few feet away. I shielded my eyes, but the flash still partially blinded me as well. Normally, I would have triggered it from behind cover, but dangerous circumstances often called for risky tactics. The ghoul screamed. I blinked to clear the spots from my eyes and heard it scurrying away.

"Sabine, are you okay?" I asked as I felt my way forward, vision slowly returning as I grabbed a tombstone to steady myself.

"Still here, and still not a ghoul snack," she replied with a slight quiver in her voice. "I take back what I said about your job —totally not boring. But I'm still freezing my ass off."

I reached down to help her up. She grabbed my hand and I pulled her up with a little too much effort, sending her stumbling into me. We collided and I grabbed her, instinctively hugging her close as her hands and face met my chest. My heart was pounding, more from adrenaline than anything. For a moment I flashed back to the cave, the night I'd lost Jesse.

"You scared the shit out of me!" I exclaimed.

Sabine stiffened in my arms, then relaxed slightly. She mumbled something unintelligible. I released her and gently put her at arm's length.

"Are you sure you're okay?"

She looked down at the ground, avoiding my gaze. I realized her scent was on me, a combination of lilacs, spring rain, and another smell that I couldn't identify but that made my heart race. *Fae pheromones? Faeromones?* I let go of her, and my arms drifted to my sides.

"Well, that was—new," she stated awkwardly.

I'd never really displayed that sort of emotion toward Sabine before. She was my friend, and I might have given her a friendly hug every now and again in greeting, but such displays of affection were always brief and passionless. I guess I just hadn't realized how much I cared for her.

I decided to clear the air. "Okay, so this is awkward. Sorry for the groping bear hug. I got a little emotional after seeing that ghoul try to eat you."

"A little? If you say so. Makes me wonder what you're like when you really get worked up."

The corners of her mouth turned up slightly, and her eyes crinkled at the corners. Dawn was just beginning to peek over the trees to the east, and the look on her face said she wasn't entirely displeased by how I'd reacted.

Damn it. I really wasn't interested in Sabine that way. At least, I didn't think I was—and the last thing I wanted was to give her that impression. I liked things the way they were, with zero complications. I had no idea how to deal with the fact that she might actually be interested in being more than just friends.

So, I did what any guy in that situation might do. I ran away.

"Look, I have to get after that ghoul while the trail is fresh. Sun's coming up, so it'll be safe to head back to your car."

I starting jogging after the ghoul, nearly tripping again over a grave marker as Sabine watched me go.

"I'll text you later!" I yelled as I took off at a run.

Smooth, Colin. Real smooth.

I tracked the second ghoul by scent through the cemetery, waving at a grumpy-looking caretaker as I neared the exit. The old man merely scowled and stared at me, keeping both hands on his rake and looking like my very presence was a personal affront.

"Running around in the dark'll be the end of you, young man."

His grumpiness made me smile. "I'll do my best to stay in one piece," I replied.

The old man harrumphed with a "get off my lawn" stare as I passed. *Old people, I'll never figure them out.* I headed through the gates and into the residential and commercial district beyond the cemetery grounds.

This area of Austin was in a state of transition, slowly being gentrified. The black and Hispanic community that had lived there for decades was being pushed out by ever-increasing property taxes and the promise of a disproportionately large payout on what once had been considered junk real estate. It wasn't uncommon to see a fifty by one hundred fifty-foot lot in this area with a rundown, one-bedroom shotgun house selling for a quarter-million dollars.

When you were someone who subsisted below the poverty level, and your yearly taxes jumped from a few hundred a year to more than you'd pay for a year's rent on an apartment in the suburbs, cashing in and pulling up stakes looked pretty good. Unfortunately, the inevitable, crushing advance of what the city council called "progress and revitalization" meant that ethnic communities in Austin—who had roots going back a hundred years or more—were now being broken up and cast to the four winds. It was both saddening and maddening, a reminder that political animals of every type and species all fed at the same trough: that of the almighty dollar.

I told myself I'd be doing my small part to save East Austin by making sure this ghoul wasn't around to terrorize the area any longer. Although, when I thought about the prospect of the ghoul chewing the faces off a few yuppies and hipsters, slowing the gentrification of the area just a bit, I was slightly tempted to just let it go for a day or two. Just slightly, mind you—I might have longed for social justice, but not at the cost of innocent lives.

Still, one could dream.

My chase led me several blocks out of the cemetery, through an alley and well past Chicon into a residential area. It was a mix of older homes and lots that had been cleared to make way for modern homes that looked so out of place they'd have given Frank Lloyd Wright nightmares. Most were wedged into tiny lots that forced architects to design multi-story monstrosities that stuck out like a mosh pit at a Taylor Swift concert. The scent trail led not to one of the more modern homes, but to a small abandoned shack of a house that had been marked for demolition.

The small, dilapidated one-story house sat close to the front of the lot, with a threadbare lawn and a rusted chainlink fence—the only features that separated it from the cracked and tilted sidewalk and freshly surfaced street. Light blue paint peeled away from the clapboard siding, and the smell of fresh tortillas being made at the factory down the street mingled with the crisp fall air and the scent of decay and death coming from inside the home. I chose to circle around the block and come at it from the alley behind the house, vaulting the chicken wire fence in the back and cutting through a weed-strewn yard to reach the ramshackle rear porch and entry. The wooden stairs leading up to the porch tilted at an odd angle, and the roof over the porch itself looked rotten and on the verge of collapsing. I stepped lightly on the stairs and porch, both to mask the sounds of my approach and out of fear of falling through the deck.

The back door had been boarded shut, along with all the windows. I located a window where the plywood covering had been pulled free on three sides, allowing me to pull the board up like it was hinged at the top. Muddy footprints, fresh dirt on the sill, and the stench of decay told me this was where the ghouls had been hiding out during the day. I pulled my short sword from inside my Craneskin Bag, where I'd stashed it before chasing the ghoul out of the cemetery. I triggered a cantrip to enhance my vision slightly and entered the premises.

Inside, it was pretty much what you'd expect from a recently abandoned home in this area; the family who had once lived here had cleared out most of their belongings, but some signs of their presence still remained. A TV stand that had been deemed too worthless to move or sell sat against one wall, along with some random photos that had been discarded along with the family's connections to the old neighborhood. I imagined someone's kids had sold this place after their parents had passed away, and pitied them for not valuing their family's history. Or, maybe those were photos of people and places they'd as soon forget. I knew how that felt, and reminded myself that I had no right judging others for wanting to leave the past where it belonged.

The rustling sounds of movement came from down a hall to my right, and I advanced through the home toward my prey. I suspected the ghoul would be bedding down for the day, hiding out and waiting for the opportunity to seek out food after dark. The danger with ghouls was not so much that they'd dig up graves to eat the dead, but the inevitable event that they'd develop a taste for fresher fare. At that point they'd kill, potentially spreading the disease they carried in their saliva to new hosts. These ghouls must have been freshly made, but what wasn't clear was how this one had advanced to such a pitiful state of decay.

I crept down the hall to an open door at the very end. Mold and stale air mingled with the now overpowering scent of the ghoul. It almost made me wish there was troll-scent nearby to cover it up—almost. The rustling sounds settled in the room beyond, so I stepped forward to peek in. As I did I stepped on broken glass, snapping it with a sound that may as well have been a gunshot in the early morning quiet.

The ghoul began to growl and sniff. I decided the time for stealth was over, and came around the corner swinging. She was partially covered under a pile of discarded clothing, newspaper, stuffed animals, and leaves. For a split second I marveled at how these creatures reverted to primal behavior in a bid for extending their second lives as long as possible, sheltering during the day and hunting at night like any nocturnal predator.

She spotted me and lunged out from under the detritus of her nest. I swung as she leapt, catching her just under the nose with the edge of my sword, cleaving her head cleanly and severing her brain stem. To my detriment, however, the fact that she was no longer animate didn't make a damned bit of difference to her momentum. Her corpse crashed into me with sufficient force to knock me over, and I landed in a pile of trash with three hundred pounds of rotting flesh on top of me.

I grunted and rolled her off, thanking my lucky stars that I hadn't stabbed myself during the fall. The stench was too much to bear. I turned over on my hands and knees, retching up bile and coffee all over the floor and trash beneath me. I crawled out in the hall where the smell wasn't as bad, sitting with my back to the wall until the dry heaves subsided. Then I wiped my mouth and thought about how I was going to get rid of the bodies. I could bury the other ghoul in the grave they'd dug up, but based on the size of this one, it was staying put.

I decided I'd either have to bury her under the house, or incinerate her so thoroughly with magic that not even her bones would remain. Since I lacked a spell for disposing corpses, it looked like digging was my only option. The corpse at the cemetery was my first priority, since it was exposed and likely to be discovered soon. Before heading back to the cemetery, I reluctantly took a quick look around, just to make sure there weren't any other ghouls holed up in the house.

As I opened the door to the other bedroom, my reticence turned to shock. The room had been cleared of all trash, furniture, and debris. The walls, floor, and ceiling were covered in arcane symbols. An iron tang hung in the air, and I realized with dread that the symbols had been painted in blood. A summoning circle had been drawn in the center of the floor, containing three eviscerated cats. Their guts had been arranged into more glyphs and symbols, obviously as part of the forbidden rituals that had been done here.

It seemed I was no longer looking for a rogue vampire. Instead, I was on the trail of a necromancer.

6

"Are you out of your freaking mind?"

I had Belladonna on the phone, and had just asked if she could get the Circle's research department to run a search on known necromancers. Apparently, that'd been a bad idea.

"Colin, do you know what kind of shit storm I ended up in after that mess you made at Crowley's place? Besides, it's not like I can just go to Research and say, 'Hey, I need you guys to drop everything and spend a couple of days looking into a few thousand random people—oh, and by the way, you'll need to suss that list out yourselves. Thanks!' I mean, you're cute and all, but that's not going to go very far with the eggheads in Research."

"Um—I guess I didn't think about that. Sorry I asked."

"Oh, it's not a problem, loverboy. If I had my way, I'd order all those geeks to get on your problem yesterday and have an answer for me by tonight. But I don't have that kind of juice in the Circle. Not yet, anyway. And especially not since Gunnarson put me on his shit-list after Crowley went off the deep end. He thinks I'm covering for either you or Crowley. My only saving grace so far has been that he can't figure out which one of you I'm involved with."

"You're not involved with either of us, Bells. Seems like you could just tell him that and get him off your case."

She snickered. "You just keep telling yourself that. I'll see you later tonight at Luther's, if I can get away from the crap detail Gunnarson has me on. I'll text you if I get free."

Just as I was about to hang up, I realized something she said had triggered my oh-shit-o-meter.

"Wait—what do you mean when you say 'just keep telling yourself that'?"

She giggled softly, then whispered just loud enough for me to hear. "Ciao, loverboy. We'll sort this out later."

"Bells, don't hang up—"

She made a smooching sound into the phone, which would have been corny if anyone else had done it. But with Bells, it just seemed normal. Then she hung up on me. *Damn it.*

The good news was that I'd already taken care of the ghoul and grave back at the cemetery. With any luck, no one would notice the buried ghoul until some development company turned the plot and cemetery into a concert center or condominium high-rise a hundred years from now.

I would have liked to have left him somewhere the cops could have found him, if only to give his family closure. But leaving a ghoul's corpse around would only create more questions than it would answer. An autopsy might reveal changes in the ghoul's physiology that just could not be explained—and besides, there was always the odd chance I might leave DNA on or around the body.

Plus, they'd want to know why he had human remains in his stomach, and the time of death would be all screwed up compared to the physical evidence. All of that amounted to a whole lot of nope on leading the cops to the corpse, and a whole lot of unanswered questions for his family and loved ones.

Sometimes, I really hated my job.

As for the other ghoul, I'd left her under some garbage at the abandoned house. A notice on the back door said it was marked for demolition next week. That meant I could leave her there a little while longer, just as long as I made sure no one stumbled over her before I got back. With that in mind, I'd put a see-me-not spell on her, along with a cantrip to hide the smell. That would keep her hidden until I could get someone over there who knew more about necromancers than me—namely, Finn. He'd been staying sober lately, and he'd know what to do. But first, I needed to clean up so I could get back to Luther with the news.

I was covered in mud and various body fluids of questionable provenance and odor, which made me glad I drove a Vespa —no seats or carpet to clean, and plenty of ventilation. Unfortunately, it was almost noon on a Saturday, so the junkyard would be hopping. Thankfully, folks who bought car parts from junkyards weren't usually the nosy, judgmental type. Once home, I managed to clean up and grab some fresh clothes without getting too many looks from customers and coworkers. Presentable again, I headed out to the yard to find Finn.

He had his head under the hood of a nicely kept AMC Gremlin. The Gremlin was considered to be either one of the ugliest or coolest production cars ever made in the US, depending on who you spoke to and how they felt about mid-seventies domestic hatchbacks. As I walked up, he noticed me coming and dropped the hood, wiping his hands on a mechanic's cloth before shoving it into the pocket of his coveralls. It was weird seeing him like this, with his white hair pulled back into a ponytail and his beard grown long and untrimmed. He looked like an outlaw biker or a Grateful Dead roadie. It was a far cry from the Finn I remembered from just a few years back, the guy who wore bespoke leather shoes and suit vests, who spoke and acted like a college professor.

This Finn smoked roll-your-own cigarettes, cursed like a sailor, and was as bawdy as a pirate on Viagra. I honestly couldn't decide which version of him I liked better. Or hated more, depending on the day and my mood. At least this Finn shot me straight, and I had to admit that since he'd sobered up he was a lot more fun than the old one. In spite of his efforts to atone and make amends, I still had a hard time being nice to him. For the most part I did my best to be civil, even on days when Jesse's memory had my heart aching like a fresh bruise.

I sauntered up to the beast he was working on. "A Gremlin, huh? Horsepower and ugly, all in one package. Ed have a buyer for this, or are you just pulling parts?"

He shook his head and pulled out a worn leather tobacco pouch and some rolling papers, proceeding to roll a cigarette with surprisingly steady hands. A month prior he would never have been able to manage it, not the way his hands used to shake. It was yet another sign of his recovery. I had to credit him that, at least.

"Naw, just a personal project. Something I've been messing with to pass the time." He lit his cigarette and took a long drag, pointing it at me as he licked a fleck of tobacco from his lip and spat it out. "You look like someone looking for advice."

He was baiting me and he knew that I knew it. I hadn't wanted or needed to come to Finn for anything since Jesse died, because I still blamed him for her death. He blamed himself as well, but no amount of self-castigation on his part was enough to make me forgive him. The request I was about to make sat like a lump in my throat, a bone stuck in my craw that I couldn't spit out and couldn't swallow.

I took a deep breath and steeled myself. "I need your help."

Rather than rubbing it in, he simply nodded and puffed

once on his cigarette, latching the Gremlin's hood and tossing his rag into the front seat after wiping his hands one final time. "Give me a minute," he said, and walked off toward the old van he stayed in at the back of the yard.

I sat on a stack of used tires and rims to wait, and Rufus showed up and laid his head on my lap. I scratched him behind his ears and was thankful for the company. Dogs had always understood me—or at least I felt like they did, which I suppose was just as comforting. I reached into my Craneskin Bag and pulled out a liver treat for him.

No sooner than Rufus had gobbled it up, Roscoe came trotting out from behind the rusted frame of a Ford pickup, tongue lolling and tail wagging. I tossed him a treat as well, and then treated them to a short game of fetch until Finn returned. Both dogs lost interest in me when the old man arrived, falling in behind him like a presidential detail. The old druid still had a way with nature's creatures, that was certain. He was wearing jeans that were almost clean, leather work boots, and a white tee under a long-sleeve retro western shirt. He almost looked presentable.

"How'd you know I needed you to come with me?"

His eyes narrowed and he looked away. "You'd hold it against me if I said."

He spat and began walking toward the office, waving at me over his shoulder.

"C'mon, we haven't got all day. I got the keys to the yard truck. Take me to see what has you so bent out of shape."

I filled Finn in on the way over, and on our arrival I parked around the corner from the abandoned house to avoid notice. We snuck in through the alley as I had done earlier. Normally

Finn would cast a see-me-not spell to hide us both, but his magic was still weak and unreliable. A few years of heavy-duty heroin use would do that to you, apparently. He didn't have much to say about it—except that it would come back, eventually. And since I didn't have enough juice to hide us both, we snuck in the old-fashioned way.

Probably wouldn't matter much if anyone saw us anyway—they'd just assume we were using the house to smoke meth or crack. We both looked just shy of respectable, which meant that we blended in fine with the neighborhood regulars. We snuck into the house without a hitch. No sooner had we entered the building than Finn was waving a hand in front of his face.

"Son of a bitch, but that smells bad. You can never get used to the smell of decomposition. I don't care how much time you spend around dead bodies." He sniffed again, moving his head back and forth until he homed in on the bedroom that contained the necromantic evidence I'd found.

"Hmmm. Whoever this person is, they sure aren't subtle about their craft."

Finn walked down the hall and gently pushed on the door. As the door cracked open, he staggered back and leaned against the wall to steady himself.

"Are you alright?" I asked.

"Sorry," he muttered. "It's just affecting me—the magic."

He glanced at me and his brow furrowed. "That isn't bothering you at all? You're not affected by that," he gestured toward the room, "in any way whatsoever?"

I shrugged. "No, not at all. Does that mean something?"

He shook his head slightly. "Must have something to do with the curse. Refresh my memory—how many cases did you and Jesse work that involved necromancy?"

His voice only caught slightly at the mention of her name. I decided that I wouldn't give him the satisfaction of noticing.

"Just the one: that goth kid who found those spells in his grandmother's attic. Remember that case? He was killing all his neighbor's pets, then raising them back from the dead. Kind of an exercise in magical masturbation, to be honest. We tracked down all the animals, burned them to a crisp, and then destroyed the spell book he was using just to be sure. You hired a witch to mind wipe him, and that was the last we heard of it."

I'd hated that case. The whole time we'd worked it, something had felt off in the pit of my stomach. The closer we'd gotten to where he performed the rituals, the worse it got. The nausea and sensation of wrongness had remained until we'd destroyed every last bit of evidence.

I felt none of that sensation now. *Not cool.*

"So, what you're saying is that I should be feeling those same sensations of discomfort that I felt during that case?"

Finn rolled a smoke, licking the paper and smoothing the seam down before putting it to his lips. He lit it with a cheap pocket lighter and leaned against the wall as he took a drag.

"Worse, actually. What that kid did was child's play compared to the rituals done here. This necromancer has been honing their craft for a long, long time."

The old man pushed off the wall with an effort and entered the room, shivering as he crossed through the doorway. He stopped dead in his tracks when he saw the runes on the walls and floor.

"Have you seen any of this magic before?" I asked.

He shook his head, but his eyes said otherwise. I decided to let it be, for now. Finn knelt in front of the summoning circle and extended a hand toward it, stopping at some imaginary boundary that I hadn't noticed.

"Do me a favor and reach over this circle."

I did, and felt nothing. "Am I supposed to be affected by it?"

He squinted and pursed his lips. "Normally, yes. A druid's

magic relies on the natural order of things—life, and the conti-
nuity thereof. Necromancy is the exact opposite of what we do.
We use life and the energy around us to perform magic—gathering it, focusing it, and magnifying it. Necromancy, on the other
hand, interrupts and diverts it. In other words, druidry is
harmony with nature, while necromancy is a distortion or
destruction of the natural order."

I rolled my eyes. "I remember my basic magic classes, Finn.
The question is, why is it affecting you and not me?"

He puffed on his cigarette and blew smoke around the room.
Wispy tendrils probed the circle and withdrew, while others
conformed to the shape of the runes on the walls and ceiling. As
smoke surrounded each symbol, it took on a pale silver luminescence. With each rune that was altered, I noticed Finn stand just
a bit straighter. The tight lines in his face relaxed.

"I don't care to speculate just yet. Give me some time to look
into this, and I'll share what I find once I have more
information."

He waved his cigarette at the circle on the floor, which had
not been surrounded by his magic.

"Since you're not currently affected by this filth, we can use
that to our advantage. Break the circle and symbols on the floor,
and while you're doing that I'll take a look at this ghoul you
killed and dispose of it as well."

I snapped some pictures with my phone, thinking they
might come in handy later. Then I did as he asked, smudging
out the runes and glyphs inside the circle one by one. As I broke
each rune, the smoke and luminescence around a corre-
sponding rune on the wall or ceiling dissipated.

After I scuffed out the last symbol in the circle, I pulled a can
of spray paint from my Craneskin Bag and marked out all the
remaining runes. Now no one who stumbled across this mess
would be able to copy it. The last thing we needed was some

teen stumbling across this place and reproducing it elsewhere. Accidental magic was more dangerous than intentional magic, and preventing it from happening was always a top priority on jobs like this one.

Finn walked back in just as I finished. "I took care of fatso for you. She'll be completely decomposed by this evening."

"Just because she's a ghoul doesn't mean you have the right to body shame her. She was human once, you know."

He scowled. "Would you prefer that I created a safe space for her instead?"

I shook my head. "Never mind. How'd you manage to get rid of her?"

"It's a simple cantrip—I could show you, if you have time."

"Maybe later. Just tell me how to track this necromancer down so I can deal with him."

Finn looked away, dropping his cigarette butt to the floor and crushing it under his heel.

"You can't, at least not until he shows up again and raises more dead. But this person is bad news, Colin, and I don't suggest that you take him on alone. My advice is that you go talk to Maeve and see if she can't provide you with some assistance—both in tracking this fucker and in disposing of him once you find him."

I sighed. "Just what I need, to become further indebted to Maeve."

He scowled. "She only has as much power over you as you allow. Besides, she needs you as much as you need her. Once you accept that, her hold over you will be broken. But enough talk—I'm starving. Let's go get some tacos." He pulled the keys out and jingled them in front of my face.

"I'm driving, so I guess that means you're buying."

Too tired to argue, I nodded in agreement and followed him out of the house, reflecting on how his rolling gait and clothes made him look like a washed up rodeo cowboy, not a two-thou-sand-year-old sage and druid. Something told me I was out of my depth with this case, and I suspected I'd need his help again before this thing was done.

Hard as it would be to ask, I figured he owed me that much.

7

I tried calling Luther on the way back to the yard. No joy. He was old school, like old-old school, and rarely answered the phones at the cafe when he served customers.

"I don't do take out, so I can't understand why someone would call," he'd say. "Can't they just come in and speak in person? I swear, technology has spoiled people on manners and common sense."

He reminded me a lot of my mother when he got on his soap box about it.

Anyway, as expected I didn't get an answer, so I wasted no time in getting over there after I drove Finn and his tacos back to the junkyard. The place was busy with a lunchtime crowd when I arrived, so I waved at Luther from behind the line and pointed at the back room. He must have recognized the concern on my face, because he frowned slightly as he nodded.

He handed things off to one of his part-time baristas and tapped me on the shoulder as he walked by. I followed him to the rest room area, where he unlocked a door marked "MAN-AGEMENT" and waved me inside. Beyond sat a cramped office space that he rarely used. He rolled back a bookcase that sat in the corner behind his desk, revealing a set of stairs that led up to his second-floor apartment.

"I figure it's serious business, by the look on your face when you walked in. Lock the office door behind you, kid."

I obeyed and marched up the stairs after him. I'd been in his apartment before, but it had changed somewhat since the holiday party I'd attended the previous year. His place had been brightly decorated back then, but now it seemed more drab and less inviting. I imagined that was because his ex, Victor, had moved out. Luther had never explained why, and I didn't ask about it.

I assumed it might have had something to do with immortality and Victor's lack thereof, which was a common theme among vampire-human relations. Once a human was clued in to the world beneath and they found out their lover could grant them immortality, it was bound to cause problems at some point. I mean, who wants to grow old while their lover never shows so much as a wrinkle as the years progress? But as far as I knew, Luther had never made another vampire; I'd never met any of his progeny, and he'd never mentioned any, either. He was also a closed book in regard to his personal life, and I made it a point to respect his privacy.

He sat ramrod straight on the edge of a Victorian-style pearl leather sofa, and looked me in the eye. Taking the cue, I sat across from him on a very uncomfortable matching leather chair. That was one thing about the older undead; they forgot all about how important comfort was to humans. Walk into any ancient vampire's home, and you were bound to find it furnished with couches and chairs that would make school cafeteria benches seem lush.

"So, what is it? Is it one of mine?" The way he was sitting stock still creeped me out. I supposed he was expecting the worst—was this how Luther acted when he was nervous?

"No, nothing like that. But, it's bad. It looks like we have a necromancer on our hands."

Luther fixed me with an unblinking stare for what seemed like an hour, but it must have only been thirty seconds or so. If I didn't know any better, I might have said that his skin grew ashen, but it was probably just a trick of the light. Most vamps used make-up to appear more lifelike, and combined with practiced gestures and forced patterns of breathing, it allowed them to pass for human. Luther always had a slight blush on his cheeks and a natural way of moving, especially around humans; he'd had centuries to practice, after all. I'd never seen his carefully polished facade falter, and to anyone but the most practiced eye, he appeared human in every last detail.

He looked away, finally, noticing my discomfort. "Can you dispose of this—this abomination? Before it gets out of hand?"

"I'm not sure. Finn says this necromancer is powerful. I'll likely need to bring in some help, but I'll do my best."

His chin dipped slightly. "Good. That's good. Thank you. I'll make sure you have everything you need."

For the first time since I'd known him, Luther appeared out of sorts. And he was freaking me out.

"Please, keep me posted. In the meantime, I'll call someone reliable to ward the cafe, and instruct my people to have their homes warded and to stay inside as much as possible. The last thing we need is an incident."

"I'd do it for you, but I don't know all that much about necromancy. Sorry, Luther."

He smiled, but the way he was acting gave me chills rather than putting me at ease.

"That's fine, Colin. Just focus on finding him. I don't need to tell you that if one of my people were to fall under the control of someone so evil—well, it would be a catastrophe."

"Understood. I'll do my best."

As I stood to go he remained seated, not moving or breathing at all. I suppressed a shiver. Then his head snapped toward me, unnaturally quick, and his eyes fixed me with an almost predatory look.

"You'll understand if I don't show you out? I have some people to contact, and much to do."

My voice faltered a little as I replied. "Sure, *ahem*—no problem. I'll call when I find something out, alright? Just make sure to answer your phone. Or get a cell phone, and call me so I have your number."

I stalled at the door to the stairs. "Luther?"

His head turned slowly to acknowledge me.

"I'll make this right." He nodded once more, and I headed out the door to find this monster who gave other monsters pause.

On leaving Luther's, I stopped to check my voicemail. Hemi had left me a frantic message, saying he was at central booking and being held for questioning in a murder case. Since I was the only real friend he had in town, he needed me to find him a lawyer to get him released and cleared. *Great, one more favor I'll have to ask of Maeve.* He was a stand-up guy, so no way was I going to leave him hanging.

I hopped on my scooter and headed for the queen's mini-mansion, racking my brains for a way around asking Maeve for assistance. I pulled up to her place about twenty minutes later, dreading what I was about to do. The problem was, Hemi was a supernatural, and therefore had probably gotten mixed up in the case under supernatural circumstances. Such situations required a lawyer who was clued in to the world beneath. Since I didn't know any supernatural attorneys, and since

Maeve was beyond wealthy and the most well-connected individual I knew, I was pretty much stuck with asking her for a
referral.

The last thing I wanted was to get further into debt with
Maeve. Finn could jabber all he wanted about how she only had
as much power over me as I allowed, but the truth of it was she
had me over a barrel. Maeve had recently revealed she was
nearly the sole benefactor and financier behind my mother's
career as an artist, and she'd amassed a tremendous collection
of her work over the years. If she wanted, she could ruin my
mother's career at any moment by flooding the market with her
pieces. I couldn't allow that to happen, so for now I was Maeve's
errand boy.

I headed up her front walk, her new security staff eyeing me
the entire way. After I'd killed her previous security guard,
Ookla's son, she'd opted for a pair of gargoyles to guard her
entrance. Strange choice, but smart. They were loyal, tough, and
would be on guard 24/7. I wondered if I could take them. The
trolls hadn't put up much of a fight; perhaps the stone guardians
would present more of a challenge. No need to find out today,
though.

I never had figured out how Ookla's son and Crowley had
been connected. They'd been trying to start a war between the
fae and the local wolf pack, as a distraction to throw Maeve off
Crowley's trail. There had been other players involved, and I
suspected one of them was Maeve's granddaughter many generations removed, Siobhan. That was the only way to explain the
connection between the mage and the troll. Unfortunately, my
"investigation" had turned up nothing in the way of concrete
evidence against Siobhan.

Pity, that.

The door opened just as I was about to knock. Speak of
the devil.

"Well, if it isn't our resident druid and expert on junk automobiles."

Siobhan wore a little black dress that would seem out of place on anyone else this time of day, a saucy silk number with a hemline that hit at mid-thigh. She somehow pulled it off without looking trashy—the simple but elegant look of a bored, moneyed strumpet. She'd let down her long blonde hair, wearing it straight so it fell across her shoulders and framed her fine, pert features. Her bright green eyes looked me up and down, and she sniffed contemptuously.

"You smell of troll musk and dead things," she stated simply, before walking off into the house.

Since she'd left the door open, I took it as my cue to follow. I shut the door behind me and hurried after her, never losing sight of my guide. I didn't want to get lost in Maeve's home—that would be inviting disaster. So, I stuck close to Siobhan out of self-preservation. And if I noticed the strappy black heels she wore, and the tone of her long, slender legs, it was only because I didn't want to get lost in Maeve's great big interdimensional doorway of a house. Or so I told myself.

"Maeve has been waiting for you to show. It appears you serve some purpose in her grand scheme." She tossed her hair back and glanced at me over her shoulder. "I, however, remain unimpressed."

I tsked. "Maeve might not appreciate you sharing her secrets, Siobhan."

She paused in mid-stride. "Oh, it's hardly a secret how Maeve has you tangled in her web. Still, consider this a friendly warning to watch yourself as you go about her business. One never knows what they might step into, doing the dirty work of the fae."

She sniffed again. Her expression soured slightly, then she

resumed her steady march through as yet undiscovered parts of Maeve's ever-shifting manse.

Our path led into the same study I'd found Maeve in the last time I visited, just after my battle with the fachen and Crowley. However, the route we'd taken was completely unfamiliar. I doubted I could find my way back to the front door if my life depended on it. Fae homes were tricky, and rooms in Maeve's house seemed to shift places constantly; in the times I'd been here, I'd never walked through her home the same way twice.

Siobhan curtsied as she approached her queen, a reminder that I was in the presence of fae royalty—albeit royalty who looked like nothing more than an attractive, well-heeled soccer mom. That guise was pure deception; Maeve put on a great show about being a harmless society hostess, but in fact she was queen of the Austin fae, as dangerous as a hat full of rattlesnakes on a hot summer day. The last time I had entered this room, she'd been studying some arcane tome that had given me a headache when I stared at it. Today, she was reading an ancient-looking illuminated Bible. Revelation, if I had to guess.

"That'll be all, Siobhan. Thank you."

Maeve dismissed her great-granddaughter with a wave of her hand. Siobhan curtsied again and left the room, giving me a brief warning look as she departed. I didn't know what she was playing at, but based on my previous if limited experiences with Siobhan, her "friendly warning" had been anything but.

I turned my attention to the fae queen and her current studies. "The Bible, Maeve? Really? I wouldn't have pegged you as the type."

She arched an eyebrow and pursed her lips slightly. "'Devils also believe, and tremble,'" she stated simply, closing the huge, leather-bound book and setting it aside. "You're no stranger to it, from what I gather."

That was true, but I stood as far from mainstream faith as

you could get. My mom had raised me Protestant, but after my first glimpse into the world beneath, you could say I'd had a crisis of faith. However, my therapist Dr. Larsen had insisted I needed a spiritual community for support and encouragement during my recovery. Instead of returning to those saccharine sweet rock concert churches my mom seemed to favor, I'd ended up at the Eastern Orthodox Church downtown, the polar opposite of the evangelical churches of my youth.

Many of the parishioners there were either refugees from religious persecution overseas, or they had relatives suffering the same. I felt more at home around folks who prayed their relatives wouldn't starve to death, or that they'd be spared execution just one more day, than I did around people who prayed for things like a better job or that Johnny would pop the question. It was petty and judgmental of me, without a doubt, but the best I could manage most days.

I cleared my throat. "I came to you today because Finn suggested I might need your—advice—on a certain matter I'm dealing with."

She smiled briefly, as if she'd gained some minor victory. Whether it was due to my discomfort regarding the topic of my faith, or being forced to ask for her assistance, I wasn't sure. I assumed both. With Maeve, a razor's edge was all she needed to turn things in her favor.

"You've come across the work of a necromancer. And you need my advice on how to stop this person, before they cause Luther any serious trouble."

"Have you been spying on me, Maeve?"

She chuckled. "Of course, my boy. Of course I have. But I smelled it on you when you walked in—I mean, you absolutely reek of necromancy. If I didn't know any better, I might say you had been participating in a ritual yourself."

I resisted the urge to sniff my pits, and decided I'd take her word for it. As had happened with Finn back at the condemned house, I was somehow inured to the scent and effects of the necromancer's magic. I hoped that wouldn't cause me any trouble in tracking this person down, and decided I should focus my query on that very topic.

"Well, it's good to know you care. Now, are you aware of any means I might use to track this individual down? So far I've killed two ghouls, and I suspect there will be more showing up soon. Imagine if one got loose in Zilker with the music festival in full tilt. One ghoul among 100,000 people could do a lot of damage."

She sat back and clasped her hands in her lap, careful not to wrinkle her white linen pants. It might have been after Labor Day, but this was the South, and ladies wore white all the way until Thanksgiving. Maeve, being the epitome of understated fashion she was, wore it with aplomb.

"Impossible for that to happen. We long ago warded the park to keep the undead out, for fear they'd hunt humans after dark. This was before your time, and well before the Circle and Luther's kin had hammered out their truce."

"You decided to keep those wards in place, even after the city had achieved a relatively stable peace?"

She arched one eyebrow and slightly closed her eyes.

"We fae aren't eternal, but we come close. After you've seen factions come and go over the millennia, and witnessed wars between those factions and the relatively short-lived times of peace that always follow, you learn to be skeptical about such matters."

Maeve straightened her pant leg and her expression darkened.

"War will return to this city. When it does, the fae will be ready." She leaned forward and crossed her legs, resting her hands on one knee. "Now, as for your immediate situation, I would advise you to seek the knowledge of someone who is familiar with the act of reanimating the dead. And, in doing so, perhaps you might even find your necromancer, hmm?"

"Sounds reasonable. Who would you suggest?"

She reached into the top drawer of her desk and pulled out a business card. Maeve always seemed to have someone's business card handy, like some supernatural majordomo who specialized in making connections between wizards, witches, and things that went bump in the night. She handed a cheap, multicolored card to me.

"Here. This is the person you need to speak with."

"Madame Rousseau's palm and tarot readings?" I sighed and slipped the card in my pocket. "If you say so. But I fail to see how some third-rate shyster is going to help me find a necromancer."

"Madame Rousseau—not her real name, obviously—is a vodoun priestess, and perhaps the area's chief expert on magical zombism. If anyone should know how to track down a necromancer, she will."

I nodded. "And you think she might be connected in some way?"

Maeve tilted her head. "Unless you wish to have another curse placed on you, I suggest you don't insinuate anything of the kind when meeting her. But yes, there's a possibility—necromancy is a very small world. Now, if you'll excuse me, I have other matters to which I must attend."

She favored me with a glance, then turned her attention to the ancient tome once more.

"Um, there is one more thing." I cringed as I said it.

"Yes?" She looked smug as she waited for me to elaborate.

"I have this friend who needs an attorney—someone who can be discreet regarding supernatural affairs."

"I know just the person." She reached into her magical business card drawer and pulled out another, this one printed on thick white linen paper.

I read the card. "'Borovitz and Feldstein, Attorneys at Law.' Can I trust them to be discreet?"

"In all matters, mundane and supernatural. If your friend is having legal troubles that are due to magical complications, well —they'll be in good hands."

I tucked the card safely away. "You've been a great help." I turned to leave, but paused. My eyes narrowed. "Alright, what's the catch?"

"The catch? You mean in exchange for my advice, or for the Maori's legal fees?"

I tried not to let my surprise show. Damn it, but she knew everything.

"Both, I suppose."

"I'm sure I'll think of something. No need to worry about it this very moment, however. You do have a necromancer to catch, do you not?"

At that, she waved me off like she had with Siobhan, returning to her reading without so much as a goodbye. The moment she dismissed me, Siobhan appeared in the doorway. I followed her out of the study and into yet another unfamiliar passage, one completely different from our earlier route.

"I trust your conversation with Maeve was enlightening?"

She spoke without bothering to look at me, as we strolled into a room I'd never seen on any of my previous visits. This one was some sort of trophy room, with antique firearms in glass cases, suits of armor on display, and weaponry on the walls. I wondered where they'd come from, since fae weren't known to use iron weapons. Then I realized they were actual trophies. Maeve would never be so gauche as to hang a human's head on the parlor wall.

"It was helpful, I think. At least now I have something to go on."

Abruptly, we arrived at the front entrance. Our journey out had taken much less time than our journey in; I decided not to dwell on how we'd done it. Siobhan opened the door for me, leaning on it languidly as I exited.

"Just remember what I said, druid. False steps are easy to come by when you're dealing with the fae."

I paused on the doorstep and tipped an imaginary hat to her. "I'll keep that in mind."

"You do that." She smiled, not in a friendly way, and shut the door in my face. I swore the gargoyles laughed at me as I walked off.

8

Things were about to get serious, so I decided to get my shit in order before I really stepped in it. My priorities were first, to get Hemi released, and second, to follow up on this vodoun priestess Maeve wanted me to see. But before that, I needed to make sure I was ready for things to get ugly.

I kept most of my gear and weapons in my Craneskin Bag, a magical artifact of no small importance handed down through the MacCumhaill family since the days of Fionn himself. The bag had some very peculiar properties, and I suspected its magic had grown over the centuries. For one, it acted as a portal of sorts to a pocket dimension, one accessible only to me. As far as I could tell, it was capable of holding an infinite number of items, so long as they fit through the bag's opening. This meant I could store any manner of handheld tool or weapon inside. Since items inside the bag resided elsewhere in time and space, the bag never increased in size or mass—no matter how much I put in it.

An important characteristic of the bag was how it worked, which also limited its utility quite a bit. When you stored something inside, somehow the bag would mark its "place" so you'd know where to find it again when you needed it. Unfortunately, the bag worked a lot like a computer, having only so much short-term "memory" available for immediate access, while storing the remainder of its contents in long-term storage. Meaning, I could only place so many items in quick access inside the bag. Seven, to be exact. This forced me to be very judicious with my gear selection and how I arranged everything.

It wasn't that I couldn't access the other items inside; it just took a great deal of concentration and rummaging to do so. Not to mention that it was generally unpleasant, as I had to communicate with the bag's intelligence to locate what I wanted. I found the sentience it possessed to be altogether creepy and alien, so I avoided digging around inside the bag whenever possible. I was pretty sure its sentience was Lugh's doing. No one, not even Finn, had ever been able to confirm or deny my suspicions.

This was also the primary reason I kept the bag within arm's reach at all times. Like all powerful magic items, it was both a blessing and a curse, because the thing was ornery as hell. One of its favorite "tricks" was letting semi-sentient objects loose from within its depths, which I supposed it did just to see what would happen. That was another mystery of the bag; no one really knew everything it held. Considering that some seventy generations of MacCumhaills had carried this bag, and knowing all the trouble they'd seen, it was a foregone conclusion that the bag held things better left alone. More than once when I'd neglected the bag for an extended period, it had released magical items that caused no small amount of grief.

Like I said, it was a blessing and burden both.

Whatever eldritch magics had been used by the Tuatha Dé Danann to create it, the actual mechanics of how it worked were a mystery. Knowing the fae, I wouldn't have been surprised if there was an entire world on the other side of the bag, with little alien people running around dusting my belongings and handing them to me when needed. I'd never worked up enough courage to stick my head inside the bag to find out, fearing I'd see the vast emptiness of the Nameless Depths and lose my sanity, or have my head bitten off by some Elder Thing. Certain mysteries were better left unanswered, and even a fool like me knew when to leave well enough alone.

Despite how I dreaded digging around inside the bag, I needed to make sure I was prepared for any emergency. I reluctantly spent a few minutes rummaging around inside, with that alien intelligence plucking information from my mind all the while. Often, the bag would show me an image of what I wanted before the thought had fully formed.

Damned creepy, that.

I tried to be as quick as possible, grabbing useful items and placing them within easy reach. Med kit? Check. Short sword? Check. Possibles bag full of various useful spells I'd prepared? Check, even though the concept of a magic bag inside a magic bag seemed a bit ridiculous. Spare change of clothes? Never left home without them. That left three slots.

Since I'd shredded my urban hunting uniform when my ríastrad had taken over during my fight with the fachen, I definitely needed some protective gear. That meant pulling out an old set of armor from my days with Jesse, and dragging out old memories as well. But it couldn't be helped; it'd take too long to ward a new outfit, and I simply didn't have the time to spare. So, I snagged a set of my old motorcycle leathers from long-term storage, placing them within easy reach.

Two slots left. Time to pick an equalizer or two.

My first selection was an easy choice, a silenced Glock with a thirty-round magazine. Sure, I was druid-trained, but I'd also been taught to use modern technology when it suited the job better than magic. And few magic spells were as quick and sure as a 9mm hollow-point round to the head, especially where the undead were concerned. I made a note to load it with silver-tipped ammo when I had time, just in case. It paid to be careful in this line of work.

Finally, I'd need something for hand-to-hand combat with a little more oomph than a mundane short sword. Good old cold iron was fine for most creatures, but it never hurt to have something with extra juice as back-up. At first I reached for my enchanted, always-returning spear, but then I decided against it. It was too long for working in close quarters, and I was most certainly going to be doing some of that before this job was through. Instead, I hesitantly reached for an old standby, the perfect tool for the job even though I had reservations about using it.

All set. It was time to recruit some backup.

I called Belladonna and told her what I intended, and despite her protests she agreed to set the meeting up with Gunnarson for me. I sipped a cup of cold brew in a secluded corner of Luther's coffee shop, waiting for her to show up and wondering whether this was a good idea. For a moment I considered calling the meeting off, then I heard the barista greet Bells by name. *Too late to change your mind now, McCool.*

I stood and extended my hand as they entered, attempting to be as cordial as possible. "Commander Gunnarson, thanks for coming."

He regarded my hand as if I carried leprosy, and his Sam Elliott mustache twitched as he sneered.

"I'm not here to make friends with you, McCool. Becerra already filled me in on this potential ghoul infestation. Why don't you just give me your pitch, I'll hear you out, and then we can both agree not to see each other until I attend your funeral. Deal?"

I held my tongue and nodded, then took a seat. Bells stood loosely at parade rest behind her commander. Gunnarson sat opposite of me, arms crossed while he fixed me with a steely gaze. This was going to be a tough sell.

"Commander, Becerra told you the truth. I was with a group of trolls who killed three ghouls near Rendon Park, just a few nights ago. I saw the bodies myself, and helped take one out. Earlier today I found and killed two more—one at City Cemetery, and the other after it fled to an abandoned house where I found this."

I pushed the photos I'd taken across the table. The commander looked through them and growled with irritation.

"How long ago were these taken?"

"Just this morning. I destroyed the runes and summoning circle after taking them."

He sighed heavily. "Necromancy. Damn it, just what I need. Bad enough I have your cursed ass raising hell all over my city, and that I have to put up with vamps running around right under our noses. But a necromancer? I need a fucking vacation."

He rifled through the photos and grimaced. "Can I keep these?"

"They're yours."

Now that I had his attention, I took a deep breath and prepared to plow ahead. In for a penny, in for a pound.

"Look, I'm sure you know I've been—*freelancing*—for various factions around town. Luther has employed me to look into the matter, and Maeve has strongly encouraged me to pursue it as well. I'd like the Circle's help in tracking this necromancer down and taking him out."

Gunnarson let out a short, mean laugh. "Yes, McCool, I know you work for the bitch queen, and that you're on friendly terms with the vamps. Hell, if it wasn't for Maeve, I'd have punched your ticket the moment you stepped foot in my city."

He measured my reaction and smiled broadly at what he saw. "Oh, you didn't know she was protecting you? Ah, you thought it was Luther's doing. Well, there's a lot you don't know about her. Might be something to look into, being as you're her butt boy now and all. Oh, it's common knowledge—hell, everyone knows about Maeve's 'Junkyard Druid,' especially after you took out one of my best wizards, and a fachen as well."

He leaned in and placed both palms on the table.

"Don't try to deny it, McCool—we don't have any proof, but I know you did it. Maybe Crowley decided to take you out, or maybe you two got into a fight over Becerra here." He nodded over his shoulder at Belladonna. "But as far as I'm concerned, he was doing everyone a favor by trying to kill you. Unfortunately, it didn't work out for him. Instead, I lost a good wizard, and you're to blame. You and I both know the only way you could have killed that fachen was by doing what you did to those poor souls in Kingsland."

I bit my lip, hard enough to draw blood. I didn't need this asshole to remind me of what I'd done. But I did need his help, and that was why I mustered every ounce of self-control and restraint I had in an attempt to keep the conversation on track.

I took a deep breath, and let it out slowly.

"Let's just concentrate on the task at hand, Commander. This city has a problem, I've been asked to solve it, and I need your help to do it. Let's set our differences aside and work together on this."

He looked around the cafe, then leaned back and clasped his hands behind his head. "I see someone's conspicuously absent today. That riled up about this, is he? Staying out of sight, keeping his people off the streets. Seems like this is working to our advantage if it keeps the vamps out of our hair. So what makes you think I'd be inclined to help you?"

I shrugged. "Doesn't matter if you do or if you don't, because eventually you're going to be pulled into it anyway. The Circle has the self-appointed responsibility to protect the human mundanes from supernatural threats, just like the druids always have. I'm merely suggesting that instead of stepping all over each other here, we can work together to resolve this matter as quickly and neatly as possible."

His expression soured, even though his smug grin never left his face.

"Personally, McCool, I'd love to sit back and watch you trip all over your dick, and then step in to take you out when you go nuclear." He leaned in and stabbed the air with an index finger. "But, the Circle does have a responsibility to preserve human life in the face of supernatural threats. You're right about that."

Translation? If he ignored my plea and something really bad happened, he'd look like an asshole and his superiors would have his ass in a sling. I'd known that before I'd asked for this meeting; Finn had filled me in on the Circle's political machinations. Most of the people in command positions in the Circle were nothing if not political animals. Gunnarson didn't give a shit about protecting innocents. All he really cared about was getting a seat on the Circle's ruling council. That brought influence, prestige, and access to powerful magical resources.

Influence, power, and wealth. That's what it always boiled down to for these assholes. To hell with the little people.

He rubbed his chin and nodded. "I'm not saying I'll commit major resources, but tell me what you need."

"First, I want you to assign Becerra to work with me on this case."

He chuckled. "She's been a pain in my ass since she graduated from field training. Too damned good at her job—and too connected, I might add—to dismiss. But also, too much of a gods-damned cowboy to contribute meaningfully to a team. I thought when she and Crowley entered into a relationship, it might cement their partnership—"

He paused and ran a hand over his salt and pepper flat top. "Anyway, I'll be more than happy for you to embroil her in whatever fuck-ups you manage to stumble into moving forward. Done. What else?"

"I'll need to have access to your research department and archives—through Hunter Becerra, of course."

"I have no issues with that, but it will be limited access. No classified files. Anything else?"

"I'll need your assurance that when it comes time to take this necromancer down, you'll provide us with extra manpower to do so."

He cleared his throat. "I doubt you'll get that far, but okay. Now, tell me: what I get out of this?"

I placed my elbows on the table and locked eyes with him. "It's simple. If Becerra and I collar this asshole and take care of the ghoul problem, you get full credit by way of assigning Becerra to this case. I step back and let you bask in the glory, and you look like a hero to the ruling council."

I clasped my hands and did my damnedest not to blink, hoping he wouldn't notice how much my hands were sweating.

"And, of course, Becerra gets a promotion in recognition of her small part in securing a victory for the Circle."

He tongued his cheek and narrowed his eyes. "And when you two fuck this up? Not if, but when?"

I glanced at Belladonna, who looked like she was ready to bust a gasket. Whether it was from excitement or anger, I couldn't tell.

"Then you get to dismiss Hunter Becerra from your ranks, or dispense of her as you see fit. Reassign her to a desk job, or send her away to a duty assignment in BFE. And, I'll leave the city and never come back again."

The commander shook his head in wonder and gave me the shit-eating grin to end all shit-eating grins.

"By Sleipnir's sixteen tits, McCool—you mean I get to write-off two of my worst headaches at once? Where the hell do I sign up? Sure, take Becerra and my whole fucking research department if you need to."

He slapped his hands on the table and stood up, looking like a man who just won the lottery while getting laid.

"Thanks for making my day, McCool. Becerra's all yours."

Belladonna came to attention as he walked out, but he never even spared her a second glance. Once Gunnarson was gone she plopped down in the chair he'd just occupied, looking at me with her mouth agape.

"Colin, I don't know whether to thank you or slap the shit out of you right now."

"I suggest you delay that decision until after we find this necromancer." I squeezed one eye shut and chewed my thumbnail. "And, by the way, horses only have two teats. So, by my count, Sleipnir should only have four nipples."

She rolled her eyes and looked up at the ceiling. "Oh mother of mercy, what have I gotten myself into?"

9

I called the number on the card Maeve had given me, and was told that Borovitz was on the case. Eager to see Hemi released, I headed to the county lock-up downtown. When I arrived, numerous bystanders, news crews, and police cars blocked the street along the north side of the building. I zipped between the crowds and news vans until I located a place to park. Times like these made me glad I drove a scooter.

Crime scene tape marked off the park across the street. Numerous cops were on scene, interviewing bystanders and running crowd control. With the county medical examiner's van and a crime scene van parked nearby, I assumed a murder had occurred—a rarity in Austin. It was too coincidental; my gut told me it had to have something to do with our necromancer. But I wasn't about to push my luck with the fae queen by making her attorney wait while he was on the clock. First, I'd make sure Hemi had been released, then I'd check out the crime scene.

Just as I hit the courthouse steps, Hemi exited the building alongside a thin, bald-headed man in an expensive pinstripe suit. The man was average in height and appearance, clean-shaven, and unassuming in every single way but how he dressed. He wore wire-framed glasses that were obviously for show, and picked me out of the crowd of people entering and exiting the courthouse long before Hemi spotted me. I met them at the bottom step, happy to see a relieved grin on my friend's face.

"Colin!" the big man boomed. "I knew I could count on you."

"Mr. McCool, I presume?" The attorney was all business as he handed me his card, identical to the one Maeve had given me earlier. "I'm Mr. Borovitz, and I'll be handling Mr. Waara's case."

"Thanks for agreeing to help, Mr. Borovitz." He gave me a look that said he wasn't here out of the kindness of his heart. I glanced at Hemi. "What exactly happened?"

Borovitz answered for him, which earned him an annoyed look from the big Maori. "It appears Mr. Waara was held for questioning based on an eyewitness account that placed him at the scene of a murder. The police didn't have enough to hold him, and I'm certain he will be fully exonerated once we get a copy of the video feed from the nightclub where he works. Until then, I've advised Mr. Waara against discussing the details of the night in question with anyone."

Hemi, being Hemi, ignored Borovitz's advice completely. The big Maori smirked and arched one eyebrow at the attorney. Then he began telling his story, eliciting a slight frown from Borovitz.

"I've been working security at Chugger's to pick up some extra money. Last night, I have to get a little rough as I kick out this Charlie who's completely wasted. No big deal, eh? Later, someone finds him dead in the alley behind the club, and when the cops show up this detective decides to arrest me. But me? I've seen every episode of Law and Order—they weren't going to trick old Hemi into admitting a thing."

The big man crossed his arms across his massive chest, looking smug. At least he hadn't talked to the police—that was something. People always thought that cooperating with the cops was the right thing to do. It wasn't. The best thing a person could do when questioned by police was to tell them you'd be happy to cooperate... just as soon as you spoke with your attorney.

I leaned in and whispered to Borovitz. "Maeve says you're clued in."

He gave a tight-lipped smile. "I'm aware that—peculiarities —exist among certain special populations in our city. I am also aware that Mr. Waara here counts himself among those special populations. Our firm has represented Maeve's interests for many years, and we've also represented Mr. Cantrell's associates on a number of occasions. Rest assured, anything you or Mr. Waara discuss with me is subject to attorney-client privilege. Your secrets are safe with me."

"Mr. Cantrell" was Luther. Not many people knew him by his last name. I was pretty sure he preferred to keep it that way.

"Good to know. Please forward Hemi's bills to Maeve, but keep the account in my name. I am making arrangements with Maeve regarding your fees."

He smiled ever so slightly and nodded. "Certainly. Might I make a suggestion, then? I could bill you—or Maeve—by the hour to send a legal assistant to retrieve a copy of that video feed. Or, you could save hundreds of dollars in unnecessary legal fees by retrieving it for me."

"We can do that," I said.

"Excellent. Drop it by my office and I'll make sure it gets in the hands of the investigator assigned to this case."

I frowned. "Shouldn't they have already gotten it themselves?"

"They'll have to get a judge to subpoena the evidence, which will take time. We can speed things up by getting our own copy, and by having Mr. Waara here convince his employer to voluntarily provide the police with a copy. I'm certain that once we have that evidence in hand, he'll be dropped from the list of suspects.

"Oh, and one last thing, Mr. McCool. Don't lose that card. If you should ever find yourself on the wrong side of the law, tear the card in two and keep it on your person. Do so and I or one of my associates will be along in short order."

He nodded and straightened his tie. "Good day, gentlemen."

Borovitz bustled away, looking like the world's best-dressed power walker. Hemi and I exchanged a glance.

He shrugged. "Seems like a nice enough fella."

"Don't let him fool you, Hemi. Here in the States, you can never trust attorneys, politicians, or used car salesmen."

The smile he constantly wore left his face. "I owe you one, Colin. And I pay my debts."

I slapped him on the shoulder. "Something tells me you'll get a chance to repay me soon. Don't sweat it."

"Anything you need, Colin. Anything."

I glanced across the street, worried that my window for finding a lead was closing fast.

"You mind giving me a minute? I need to see what happened over there, and it's probably best right now if you're not spotted hanging out at the scene of a crime."

Hemi glanced across the street. "Good thinking, eh? Anyhow, I see one of the detectives who brought me in— unpleasant fellow, don't care to run into him again. I'll just wait by your car."

"Well—I rode my scooter over here."

He scratched his head. "I'm bloody well not riding on the back of that thing with you, that's for sure. Tell you what: meet me at the club in an hour. I need to get my car anyway."

"Alright. I'll be there as soon as I check things out. Stay out of trouble until I get there."

"Right! Then we'll find some trouble together. Excellent plan."

I sighed and headed across the street.

I slipped into the crowd as I scanned the scene. Several local TV crews were out here, as well as a slew of cops and two ambulances. Some of the cops were questioning eyewitnesses, while others were handling crowd control or marking and bagging evidence.

A large male detective stood out, and I wondered if he was the guy who had arrested Hemi. He had a bulging gut and was wearing khakis, a red button-down shirt with the sleeves rolled up, and a gray tie, chewing gum like it was going out of style. In the time it took me to take in the scene, he'd already spat one piece out and popped in another. Dimes to doughnuts, he was a recovering smoker.

The detective was questioning one of the homeless who hung out in the park, although "harassing" might have been a better word for it. He kept raising his voice and threatening to arrest the homeless guy if he didn't cooperate. What an asshole. I made a mental note to steer clear of him, just in case I got made.

Time to find out what happened. I looked around and spotted a likely candidate: a youngish guy with dirty blonde dreadlocks, dressed in a ratty t-shirt, filthy jeans, flip flops, and a drug rug hoodie. Definitely homeless. I tapped him on the shoulder to get his attention.

"Any idea what happened here?"

"Nope. I just walked up a minute ago."

"But surely you must have been around when this happened?"

"Naw, man, I'm not from around here. I'm just in town to meet with potential investors for my software start up. Maybe one of these homeless dudes around here knows what happened.

"But hey, if you know anyone who might be interested in investing in a technology company that's perfectly positioned to leverage rapid market growth in the medical marijuana industry—"

He handed me a card, then turned his attention back to the activity on the other side of the crime scene tape. *Only in Austin*, I thought. It was obvious that I wasn't going to find out much by standing on this side of the yellow tape. I decided it was time to get a firsthand look at what had happened. I triggered a weak see-me-not cantrip and made my way to the edge of the cordoned area.

A quick survey revealed a body being loaded in the coroner's van, a section of sidewalk and grass spattered in blood, and a paramedic treating a homeless woman on the other side of the scene, far away from the crowd. I slipped under the tape and past the cops and techs gathering evidence, skirting the bulk of activity as I headed to the ambulance.

After a short wait, the paramedics finished bandaging the woman up and she left the vehicle, shuffling off toward the far side of the park, away from the cameras and police. I followed her at a distance, watching as she sat down under a tree amidst a sea of trash and debris. She pulled a half-full bottle of water from her backpack and took a swig.

"I know you're there," she said without looking at me. "Heard you following me from the ambulance. You may as well come on over."

I looked around, on the odd chance that she might be speaking to someone else, and then did as she suggested. As I got closer, I realized she was blind. Her eyes looked normal, but they were unfocused and never made eye contact. I noted she was relatively clean and well-groomed, and surmised that she wasn't a junkie—merely down on her luck. I squatted a few feet from her, close enough to talk, but not close enough to be a threat.

"I'm Colin."

"Nelly. You wanting to know what happened to that poor guy?"

I nodded, feeling foolish. "Yes, Nelly, I do."

She tilted her head and looked just past my shoulder. "You a reporter? I don't want to be on no five o'clock news. S'good way to become a joke on the Internet. You remember that 'got no time for that' woman? Laughing stock, people made tons of money, and she never got a dime. Got any food on you?"

"Nope on both counts. But I do have a few bucks I can spare. Would that help?"

"It would. I promise I won't spend it on drugs or cheap booze. I don't do that. Not all of us are waste cases, you know."

"I didn't assume you were," I lied, feeling like an asshole for jumping to conclusions earlier. I reached into my Craneskin Bag for some cash I kept for emergencies.

"Whoa!" She scooted back against the tree. "What did you just do? It felt like a door opened up into nothing." She got up to leave. "I been around enough weird stuff today, mister. Don't need to be involved in any more."

I pulled the cash out and shut my bag. "Please, don't go—it's harmless, I promise." My second lie to her in under a minute; I was on a roll. Something in my voice must have convinced her to stay, because she harrumphed and then settled down under the tree again.

I handed her a twenty and a five. Nelly rubbed them between her fingers and shook her head. "This is too much." She handed the twenty back to me.

"Keep it. Just tell me what happened here. I promise you, the information is worth it to me."

Nelly nodded and tucked the money away like a magician palming a coin; one second it was there, and next it had vanished. She swigged some water, arranged herself comfortably, and took a deep, shaky breath. I realized for the first time that she was rattled. She hid it well.

"Well, about an hour ago I was sitting here under my tree when Douglas started shouting for help. We've had some attacks down here, you know. Mostly against women and mostly at night, but not always. Sometimes kids come by just to beat a loner up for fun, and sometimes people come from other camps to cause trouble. So, we stick together to protect ourselves."

She pulled the cheap windbreaker she wore tighter around her body, even though it wasn't that cold out. "I went over there, knowing I couldn't help much but thinking the more people, the more likely to scare someone off. When I got over where Douglas sleeps, some guy was eating his face off. Least that's what they said happened."

She said it matter-of-factly, as if eating someone's face off was the most natural thing in the world. "Probably took him away by now—he was dead by the time the ambulance arrived. Poor Douglas."

"I'm sorry about your friend."

She shrugged. "He wasn't no friend. But he wasn't an enemy, either. A lot of people die out here. Doesn't mean it don't matter."

"Nelly, do you have any idea what happened to his attacker?"

"Cops shot him, least a dozen times that I could count. Finally killed him. Think they took that guy away, too."

Crap, that meant two potential ghouls at the morgue, if Douglas had turned. Not cool. I'd have to sneak in and make sure they stayed dead before someone at the medical examiner's office got a nasty surprise.

I was starting to wish I hadn't taken this case. Luther had connections, and could have hired anybody to handle it for him. He had only given it to me because he knew I could use the money. It looked like I was going to earn it and then some.

A glance at Nelly brought me back to my senses. I resolved not to complain about having gainful employment.

"Anyone else get a good look at Douglas' attacker?"

"Petey did, but he split before the cops got here. You might look for him at the library—he hangs out there sometimes to get online and send emails and stuff. They call him Petey because he always has a black eye—least, that's what they tell me. Shouldn't be hard to spot. Just head to the computers, and you'll probably find him there."

"You've been a big help to me, Nelly. Anything I can do for you before I go?"

"Nah, but thanks. I'll take the bus down to the women's outreach later, get a hot meal. Good luck tracking down Petey."

I lingered for a moment, then realized there wasn't much I could do to ease her situation. Eager to do something to help her out, I went to the courthouse to buy some snacks and a soda from the vending machines. She was gone by the time I returned, so I left my purchases under the tree, hoping she'd come back and find them there. Then I headed to the library to find Petey.

10

Petey didn't have too much to offer, other than saying the guy who'd killed Douglas was big, fast, and wearing a dark blue Dallas Cowboy's hoodie. Petey was a tweaker, and after I slipped him a ten he was only interested in getting a fix. Guess I should've waited until after to give him the cash. Live and learn.

The morgue was close to the bar where Luther worked, so I headed there first to ensure neither the victim nor the perpetrator would get up and start munching corpses—or the medical examiner, for that matter. The general policy among the supernatural community was the fewer people in government and law enforcement who knew about us, the better.

Confirmation bias and fae magic helped keep the world beneath a secret to 99.99 percent of people out there. But folks who were hyper-inquisitive or who had an innate sensitivity to the supernatural were apt to stick their noses where they didn't belong. Police detectives and coroners were the worst, because cops tended to have instincts for digging up weird shit, and coroners were trained to look for the unusual. And never mind that advances in medical science had made it harder than ever for those of us in the know to keep a lid on things.

For that reason, Maeve, the Circle, Luther, and our local alpha Samson all had their own agents working inside law enforcement and government. Each faction had their own agenda, but they all agreed that keeping mundanes from discovering the inexplicable was their top priority. The good news was Luther and Maeve both had moles in the medical examiner's office; unfortunately, I didn't know either of them because I'd been out of the game too long. Besides, Luther's guy wouldn't be coming on shift until after dark, and for all I knew Maeve's inside person was at a crime scene or hauling a corpse back to the lab. So, for the moment I was on my own.

I parked a block away and triggered my see-me-not cantrip again, hoping I didn't run into another blind person while I poked around. My experience with Nelly earlier had been a reminder that magic didn't offer perfect concealment, and the last thing I needed was to be caught mutilating and desecrating corpses in the county morgue. I resolved to be extra careful to avoid getting caught.

I walked around the building to the loading dock in back, which was on the lowest level of the morgue. Based on past experience, I knew they often left the bay doors open, and that the main autopsy room and walk-in cooler both sat just on the other side of those doors. Lucky for me, the roll-up door had been left open to air the place out, and a quick look under it told me no one was inside. I strolled up and rolled through the opening, coming up in a crouch just in case I'd made a mistake and someone was in the vicinity.

As soon as I hit the other side, the stench hit me like a ton of bricks. People who have only ever seen autopsy rooms on television have no idea what a real morgue is like. Travis County's morgue was more reminiscent of a scene from *Saw* or *American Horror Story* than something from *CSI*. Once you got past the stainless steel autopsy table and surgical lights in the middle of the room, that's where all similarities to TV autopsy suites ended.

The room itself was dark and dingy, and the air was thick with the fetid odor of rotting corpses. A quick glance at the rough concrete floor beneath my feet revealed an autopsy had recently taken place. Blood and unidentified body fluids still swirled in water that had pooled in a depression next to the drain. An industrial water hose sat on the floor, the nozzle leaking water that collected and ran in a tiny stream to the drain. Rubber butcher's aprons hung on hooks along a nearby wall, and a radio played pop music from a local station in tinny, static-filled tones.

There were a few empty body bags on the floor. One of them still contained a yellow viscous fluid inside, indicating it had held a badly decomposed corpse. I surmised that most of the stench was coming from that bag, and tiptoed over to zip it before donning an apron, surgical mask, and thick pair of rubber gloves. The mask and apron would make it easier for my see-me-not spell to work, and if I got caught they'd make it harder for me to be identified. The gloves I put on to avoid leaving prints—and to keep dead guy gunk off me.

I hopped over to the walk-in cooler door where they kept most of the bodies, pausing as I grabbed the handle. What if there was a live ghoul on the other side? I didn't have any weapons handy, because a guy holding a sword or a spear in a morgue was just too damned incongruous; it'd burst my see-me-not glamour like a balloon in a mesquite tree. After a quick search, I grabbed a wicked-looking stainless steel hammer with a hooked handle from a nearby table, then yanked the door open and stepped back.

The single bare light bulb just inside the doorway flickered slightly, but it illuminated the space inside well enough to reveal what had happened. Several body bags had been ripped open, corpse parts and pieces were strewn all over the cooler, and gastric contents and fecal matter had been smeared about as the ghoul had fed. My worst fears were confirmed; the ghoul the cops had shot had only been partially incapacitated, and it had recovered after arriving at the morgue.

I held my breath as I hastily checked the tags on the other body bags, gagging at the rich, cloying stench of corpses in various states of decay. I finally located the victim from the park, who was in so many pieces that it was highly unlikely he'd be coming back to life. Just to be sure, I flipped him over and bashed the back of his head in with the autopsy hammer, mouthing a weak apology. The deed done, I turned him face-side up again and zipped his body bag closed, despite the fact that it was shredded beyond repair.

The question now was, which way had the ghoul gone? He could have still been in the building, or he might have slipped out the way I'd come in. I exited the cooler and shut the door behind me, leaning on it and taking deep breaths of the comparatively fresher air beyond that had repulsed me just moments before. I hunched over with my hands on my knees, smearing blood and brain matter from the autopsy hammer on the front of the apron. After a few breaths, I recovered my composure and scanned the room for signs of where the ghoul had gone. There were no blood marks or prints on or around the bay door, so I had to assume he was still in the building. I swept my eyes across the room and spotted a gory streak on the wall near the stairs, leading to the offices above.

It was after five in the evening, so I assumed the only people still working would be a janitorial crew and whoever had been cleaning up after the last autopsy. Tactically speaking, the time for stealth was over. I set the hammer aside, pulled the apron off and hung it back on a hook, and discarded the gloves in the trash. Then I pulled out my short sword and vaulted up the stairs two at a time. If I was lucky, I'd get to the thing before it got to anyone else... but luck hadn't been on my side thus far.

I adjusted the strap on my Craneskin Bag before opening the door to the offices upstairs, making sure I could reach it in a hurry if needed. I wanted that spell bag within easy reach, just in case. I eased the door open, peeking around and listening for any sign that the ghoul might be waiting in ambush.

Ghouls weren't the brightest of the undead, but they could be crafty when necessary for their survival. More than a few hunters had regretted underestimating a ghoul's canny and unpredictable ways. A quick scan of the hall outside revealed nothing to arouse my suspicions, so I moved into the office space, following the hallway to the offices proper. Doors lined the hall at regular intervals, with name plaques indicating who or what occupied them. The lights were off in the offices, and except for the hall lights, all was dark and nothing stirred within. I passed a junior medical examiner's office, an investiga-tor's office, and a storage space, finally ending up at the recep-tion desk. There was no sign of the ghoul at all, and I started to wonder if I'd missed him while I'd been searching the basement level.

Then a loud scream pierced through the quiet. A second scream came from the stairway I'd exited a moment before. Had I missed the ghoul downstairs? I ran back down the hall, burst into the stairwell, and immediately saw my mistake. In my haste to get into the building, I'd failed to see there were more stairs leading up. I'd also missed the bloody streaks on the walls leading to the second floor.

Another scream came from above, so I sped up the steps two and three at a time, hoping I wasn't too late. The man sounded desperate—or at least desperately scared. I exited the stairs to the second floor and entered another hall, following the screams and sounds of struggle until I came to a conference room. A peek through the window revealed the ghoul, a victim pinned under it on a conference table. It gripped the man by the shoulders, inching its mouth closer to the man's face. The ghoul's intended victim strained to push the ghoul away, his hands white-knuckled and latched onto the ghoul's neck. It was a losing battle. With every second, the ghoul's superior strength and inability to tire brought the man closer to death.

I tried the door. *Locked.* I busted the small window with the pommel of my sword and reached inside. After fumbling a few moments for the latch, I finally unlocked it, slamming the door open with my shoulder. Leaping across the room, I struck the ghoul with the sword's pommel instead of chopping its head off, fearful I might cut the man if I used the blade.

You never knew what kind of condition one of the undead was in until you hit them—sometimes they were crunchy, sometimes squishy, and sometimes they were hard as granite. Ghouls were even trickier, because the longer they were undead, the thicker their bones became. Unlike zombies, they were able to slowly regenerate and heal minor wounds—so long as they had fresh meat to feed upon.

Sadly, striking it over the head only seemed to piss it off. In response, it backhanded me into the wall, where my upper body and head left a depression. That pissed me off, and worried me. The beast inside me, my "Hyde-side," had been nice and quiet since the events at Crowley's farm. That part of me was a result of my curse, an ultra-violent alter-ego that showed up only when I was under extreme duress. Unfortunately, I could neither control nor contain the beast. I preferred to keep it hidden away, for obvious reasons. So, I tossed the sword into my bag and reached for the heavy artillery, my battle club.

I had used the weapon often in my early days of training under Finn, until I'd discovered it was semi-sentient. In my experience, semi-sentient weapons and artifacts were pains in the ass. They'd get lost at odd times, or leapt from your hands and attacked people just to start fights, and generally acted like they had a mind of their own... because in essence, they did.

By all appearances, this weapon was nothing more than a worn ash wood bat. But underneath the glamour, it was a fearsome weapon. Iron shod and fire-hardened, it had been passed down to me from my father, and the rumor was it had been made by old Lugh himself. In the past it had proven effective on all manner of fae, as well as an undead dwarf. Time to see how it fared against other undead creatures.

I pulled it from my Craneskin Bag like a samurai drawing a katana, using the draw stroke to backhand the ghoul under the jaw. As the weapon struck the creature's face, it sounded like a gong. That was another reason I didn't like using the thing; the magical sound effects it came with were noisy as all hell. The good news was that it worked just fine on ghouls, and the blow knocked the thing off the poor guy it had been attacking. The intended victim scrambled away and cringed in the corner of the room behind me. *Good.* Now I didn't have to worry about hurting him as I kicked this ghoul's ass.

The ghoul quickly shook off the effects of my initial attack. It sprang to its feet and roared at me, revealing a row of crooked yellow teeth stained with blood and gore. Its skin was split in several places and stitched back up, and it had a grey pallor to it that was more common among nosferatu than ghouls. And shit, that thing was big. It had to have been a bodybuilder or football player or something similar in a previous life, because it was damned near Hemi-sized and might have carried more muscle. It had a Dallas Cowboys hoodie on under a grimy black jacket, carpenter pants, and work boots. Not the sort of thing you saw someone buried in, that was for sure. It made me wonder where the necromancer was getting bodies to raise from the dead. *Better get back on task, Colin.* I could ponder the mysteries of necromantic body snatching later; right now I had a ghoul to kill. I waited for it to pounce, winding up for a swing by rolling the tip of the club around in circles over my shoulder like a batter at home plate. *C'mon, you ugly sack of shit, attack*, I thought, picturing its head coming clean off.

"What are you waiting for? Kill that damn thing!" the guy behind me shouted.

I didn't bother looking at him as I replied, preferring instead to keep my eyes on the ghoul. "Oh, I will. Just as soon as he—"

The thing leapt faster than I anticipated, catching me off guard despite my readiness. That threw my aim off, and I caught it in the chest instead of the head. There was a thunderous impact, and I felt rather than heard ribs crack via tactile feedback from the club. As I followed through, the ghoul flew over the conference table and out a plate glass window that overlooked Sabine Street below. I vaulted the table and swept shards of glass off the sill so I could lean out and see where it had fallen. By the time my eyes adjusted, I caught just a glimpse of a dark figure limping off into the night.

"Shit!" I slammed the bat on the conference table, breaking it in two. The guy in the corner looked at me like I was nuts, making me thankful I was still wearing the surgical mask. He stood, shakily, and stared at my handiwork.

"My boss is going to be so pissed about that table. It's brand new—we had to special order it from Canada."

I blew a fuse.

"Seriously? I risk my life to save your ass, and you're worried about the furniture? First off, why the hell would the local government spend my tax dollars on furniture made in another country, when they can buy perfectly good tables here in Texas? Second, I believe a thank you is in order."

I stared him down, resisting the urge to menace him with the club in my hand. *Temper, temper, Colin. Remember, he's not the bad guy. And it's not his fault you let the ghoul escape.*

"Um, thanks?" He brushed himself off, grooming being a common affectation brought on by emotional shock. "But someone needs to pay for the table and window. We're working on a very limited budget around here, you know."

I was a hair's breadth from throwing him out the window, when a mousy-looking guy with stringy blonde hair and a bad complexion walked in. He wore a dark blue Travis County Medical Examiner windbreaker, and the pale-skinned look of someone who had worked the night shift for—oh, the last few decades. He took in the scene, then looked at me and the man in the corner and sighed.

"You just had to let a mundane see, didn't you? Damn it, druid, I'll be here all night mind wiping him now."

The ghoul's intended victim looked relieved to see the new arrival. "Brandon, I'm so glad you're here. I was just attacked by a zombie. Holy shit, that just came out of my mouth. A freaking zombie tried to eat my face off."

He righted a nearby office chair and sat down, dazed. The adrenaline had finally washed out of his system; now he'd be easier to deal with. A cool breeze rattled the vertical blinds on either side of the window frame as the man stared out into the night.

Brandon walked over to him and snapped his fingers in front of his face, getting his attention.

"Sam. Sam. Sam!"

Finally, the shell-shocked man acknowledged him. Brandon squatted before Sam to get at eye level with him. He snapped his fingers a second time, then wove his hands in complex patterns while muttering under his breath.

"Sleep," he whispered. At that, Sam went out like a light.

"I take it you're Maeve's fixer."

He ignored me and performed a quick physical assessment of Sam. It made sense. The guy might have had internal injuries, and the death of a medical examiner's assistant would be much harder to cover up than a break in. Finally, he glanced my way, disapproval and irritation written all over his face. He crossed his arms and glowered at me.

"This is some mess you've left me. Bad enough I have to wear this disgusting glamour all the time, but cleaning up after someone else's fuck up takes the cake."

"Oh, so it's my fault that you guys brought a live ghoul into the medical examiner's office. If you'd have been on day shift, this never would have happened."

Brandon's eyebrows drew together as he clucked his tongue.

"Unfortunately for both of us, I'd agreed to cover for that dreadful vampire who works for Luther. Ugh, such manners he has. Can't say I blame him, though. None of them want to be out right now, what with..." he swept his hand around the room, "... this going on."

He took another look around, then waved his hands at me in a shooing motion.

"Well, scurry along now. I'll handle this. All you'll do is get in the way, and with this mess that weak little see-me-not spell you've cast on yourself isn't going to fool anyone. Go show yourself out. And do try to avoid being seen as you go, hmm?"

He abruptly turned away from me, resting his chin in the crook of his thumb and forefinger, examining the scene as if figuring out a particularly difficult puzzle. As far as Brandon was concerned, I no longer existed. Not that I cared what the fae thought of me, but it did sting a little to be dismissed so handily. *This is why I detest working with the fae,* I reflected.

I sighed and stuffed my club in my bag, leaving through the back way before the cops showed up.

11

Hemi was waiting for me at the club, hanging out at the bar drinking a beer when I walked in. The place was busy, which wasn't a shock considering how many people came into town this time of year. Most of them were at Zilker at the music festival, trampling grass and getting high, but quite a few always seemed to end up here on Sixth Street, braving the frat boys and serial muggers in order to get their party on.

I was surprised that the police would arrest Hemi on suspicion for a mugging that had just happened to occur behind his place of work. Sure, Austin had a very politically savvy chief of police, and he was known to pressure his detectives into closing cases quickly—especially when the risk of scaring tourists off was high. But the evidence seemed kind of thin. I figured it was just Hemi's bad luck to be in the wrong place at the wrong time. It seemed unfair, but once we had proof to clear his name we could be done with the matter.

He waved me over as I entered. I took a quick look around the place, and it failed to impress. The fading sunlight streaming through the front windows revealed the interior for what it was: a glorified juke joint, well past its prime. Scuffed wooden floor, scarred and battered tables and chairs, discarded swizzle sticks nestled in corners keeping dust bunnies company, and the smell of sexual desperation and misspent youth undergirding it all. I'd been inside a lot of night clubs during daytime hours while on investigations, and they were all the same. If people knew how nasty they really were, they'd probably choose to drink at home most nights. I found both options equally depressing.

The big Maori slugged down his beer and stood, towering over me. Most people had to hop or step down from a barstool, but with Hemi it looked almost like he was stepping up.

"Been waiting here a while. Did something turn up at the park?"

"Had to make a stop along the way to check something out—I'll tell you about it later. Right now, I just want to get a copy of this video to Borovitz so he can clear your name."

"Office is this way. C'mon."

I followed Hemi through a door at the end of the bar, into a storage room stacked with boxes of no name whiskey and cases of cheap beer. We exited into a short hall and hooked a right into an exceptionally tidy, cramped office. Hemi sat behind the desk, and the old wooden office chair creaked and groaned under his weight. He clicked something on the desktop and pulled up a live feed of the interior of the club and the alley out back. The screen was split in four sections, with two views of the lower level and one of the upper level. The final view showed the alley from a camera above the rear exit.

I looked at the feeds on the screen and felt a glimmer of hope. If we were lucky, we could track the victim's movements before his death, and possibly get a lead on the real killer while we were at it. Still, I found it surprising that the cops had arrested Hemi without pulling up this footage. The whole situation just wasn't making sense.

"Hemi, are you sure the cops didn't look at this footage before they hauled you in?"

"Said they'd pull the feed later. Why?"

"Something doesn't add up. Before you show me the footage from last night, run down the events of the evening."

He swiveled to face me and shrugged. "Not much to tell. I showed up for my shift around eight, hung out for a while on door duty until the place got busy. Then I switched out with one of the other doormen so I could go on roving duty. Some fella looked a bit suss—just the way he was looking around the club, all nervous like. So I kept an eye on him for a while, then a fight broke out among some others and I had to throw a few of them out. They were completely pissed, but nothing out of the ordinary. Pretty much a regular night here."

"What happened to the suspicious guy you were watching?"

"He was gone by the time I got back from kicking those fellas out. The detective who arrested me said one of the fighters was the guy that was killed. I remember him, because he looked like he had money, like he was used to getting his way. He gave me the hardest time of them all—took a swing at me, but I was never in any danger. Head of security called the cops, but it was a busy night and they were tied up elsewhere. So, I escorted him out and left him on the front walk."

I shook my head. None of this made any sense. "Play the footage for me. Start with the nervous guy, and work forward from there."

Hemi pulled up the recording from the night before, pointing at the screen. "There—that's the guy who was acting jumpy."

The angle was bad and the lighting wasn't great, but if I didn't know any better I'd have said it was my friend Elias from CIRCE. It was possible he'd just been down here to get drunk or hook up, but he didn't seem the type to me. Besides, he wasn't talking to anyone in the video; he was just leaning up against the wall and nursing a drink, looking around the place like he was up to no good.

"Fast-forward to the fight."

Hemi did as I asked, and the video quickly advanced until the brawl, if you could call it that. Two guys who looked like they'd be more at home on Martha's Vineyard than Sixth started a shoving match with a group of local frat boys wearing Longhorns gear. I imagined they'd probably mentioned our recent losing streak—a sore subject among fans these days. We watched Hemi and two other bouncers break the fight up and escort the two rich kids out of the club.

Hemi sighed and leaned back in the chair, interlocking his fingers behind his head. "And that was that. We walked them out, they yelled and cussed at us and told us they'd be back with friends. We ignored them, and they headed up the street, probably to find another club."

I pulled a sticky note off the desk and jotted down the time of the fight. "Huh. What time was his body found?"

"I dunno, maybe an hour after this happened? All I know is, the cops showed up at around midnight." The time stamp on the screen said 10:17 pm. That meant the guy had probably been killed not long after he'd gotten kicked out.

"Play the video."

My hunch was right. At 10:53, the camera in the alley showed one of the rich kids stumble into view. He stopped by a dumpster to take a piss, then he got hit by a blur that knocked him out of the camera's view. I checked the other camera views and spotted Hemi standing inside the club near the front door at the time of the attack. I copied down the time on screen and leaned over Hemi's shoulder.

"Rewind that and advance it frame by frame. Let's see if we can get a look at what attacked him."

As the footage advanced, the blur came into view from the left. For a single frame, the figure was illuminated in a circle of light at the center of the screen.

"Son of a bitch." I clapped Hemi on the shoulder. "Make me two copies of that footage, and make sure it includes the entire night."

Hemi nodded. "Will do. Does this mean I'm free and clear?"

"I'm pretty sure once we get this footage to Borovitz, he'll get the cops off your back and point them toward the real killer. The only problem is, I think the real killer is a ghoul."

I stared at the screen, where a very large man in a dark jacket and hoodie stood frozen in mid-stride. Was it the ghoul I'd just tangled with? If so, it was hunting the downtown area right in the middle of one of the biggest festival weekends of the year. That was bad, astronomically bad. I needed to track it down before more people died. Or before it caused an undead outbreak of epic proportions.

I went straight from the bar to Borovitz and Feldstein's offices, leaving the footage in their mail drop. I called their answering service to let Borovitz know it was there, then headed back to the junkyard to review the footage again. After watching it a half-dozen times, I was almost positive the attacker was my ghoul. I was also confident that Elias was in the footage from earlier in the evening. I should have been out combing the streets for the killer ghoul, but after running for a full 24 hours straight, I was dead on my feet. So instead I crashed out and vowed to start looking first thing in the morning.

I turned up exactly squat during my search the following day, and returned to the junkyard empty-handed. I spent the rest of the afternoon catching up on work Ed had left for me, then searched the yard for Finn to see what he thought about the whole thing. Finn was MIA, so I headed out again after dark to search for the ghoul, who I'd started to refer to as "super-ghoul" due to his size and strength. Again, I found absolutely nothing. Looked like it was time to take Maeve's advice and visit that vodoun priestess she'd mentioned.

Madame Rousseau operated out of a converted two-story home on the I-35 access road, just south of Highway 183. I pulled up to the place after a harrowing trip up I-35 on my scooter, vowing never to take the freeway again. Austin's infrastructure was amazingly inefficient, and unlike most large cities in Texas it lacked a loop to divert traffic around the city. That, combined with all the trucking traffic coming up from Mexico due to NAFTA—and a staggering population growth rate—made I-35 a death trap most days. I swore that next time I headed up this way I'd take Lamar, even though it'd take me three times as long. Some things just couldn't be rushed, and my death was tops on that list.

As I approached the front entrance to Rousseau's, I considered turning back. "PSYCHIC," "TAROT READINGS," "PALMISTRY," and "FORTUNE TELLING" prominently displayed in bright neon made her establishment impossible to miss. Such businesses, if you could call them that, were considered to be beneath the notice of truly accomplished practitioners of magic. For one, anybody with any real magical skill could find much better ways to earn a living than fleecing housewives and desperate business owners. The I-Ching, palmistry, and card reading were mostly guesswork, and about as useful as fortune cookies in foretelling a person's destiny. Just as time travel was beyond the reach of even the most powerful magicians, so was the art of seeing the future.

Thus, most wizards wouldn't be caught dead at a place like this, and personally I wasn't looking forward to meeting

"Madame Rousseau" at all—if that was even her real name. But if she was the local expert on voodoo and zombism, I'd need to keep an open mind during my visit. Also, the last thing I wanted to do was piss off a vodoun priestess. Like Maeve had said, curses were not something to be taken lightly. I was living proof of that.

I took a deep breath and headed up the steps, pausing briefly to check my protection wards before I opened the commercial glass door and stepped into the waiting area. A chime rang somewhere in the shop as I entered, presumably to let Madame Rousseau know she had a guest. Based on that alone, I decided she wasn't much of a psychic—and probably not much in the way of an expert on zombies, either.

"I'll be right there!" someone called from the back of the place.

I busied myself by taking in the interior of the building from where I stood. A table off to the side held brochures printed on glossy paper, offering upsells for Madame Rousseau's services and package deals for clients who wished to purchase readings in packs of ten or more. A glass counter to the right displayed all manner of crystals, incense, trinkets, and the like, and bookshelves lining the space sold titles on everything from alien visitations to finding your chakras to getting in touch with your spirit guides.

That last part made me shiver; people who tried to contact the other side often ended up inviting things in that were better left alone. More than a few deadly hauntings had started with nothing more than some kids messing around with a Ouija board at a party. People needed to leave well enough alone; the dangers simply weren't worth the thrills.

Out of curiosity, I used my second sight to scan the items in the case and the various occult decorations strewn around the room. With the exception of some fairly standard wards on the doors and windows, the contents of this place were completely magically inert. *Shocker*.

A petite, middle-aged Anglo woman with strawberry blonde hair bustled out of an adjacent room, parting the beaded curtains that blocked the door frame. She was simply dressed in jeans, sandals, and a Hello Kitty t-shirt, and wore her hair straight and parted down the middle. A crystal on a thin silver chain adorned her neck, and her arms sported various bangles and charms that were just as devoid of magic as the items in the case.

My face must've betrayed my surprise, because she smiled and winked at me. "Not what you were expecting, hmm? I can assure you, your reading will be both fast and accurate."

I held my hands up. "Oh, I'm not here for a reading. I was referred to you by Maeve."

I paused to gauge her reaction, and her eyes narrowed slightly at the name. She dropped all pretense of pleasantness and motioned for me to follow.

"I don't discuss such matters where they might be overheard. This way, please."

I followed her through the beaded curtains and down a hallway with several shut doors, except the first one, which revealed a table covered by a black velvet cloth with a crystal ball in the center. How predictable. But I supposed, like most things in life, Madame Rousseau's success depended on meeting consumer expectations.

We stopped at the end of the hall, in front of a door with an electronic keypad above the door handle. She typed in a code and opened the door, waving me into a small kitchen area. "Have a seat."

I complied and waited as she prepared some hot tea. I was growing impatient, but couldn't really bring myself to be rude. Besides, I'd never been the type to lean on people, throwing my weight around to get what I wanted. I saved that sort of treatment for fae and other nasties.

Momentarily, Madame Rousseau sat down and poured us each a cup of Earl Grey.

"Alright. Tell me what brings you here, mister—?"

"You can just call me Colin."

"I'm Janice, Colin. Pleased to meet you. So why did Maeve send you over? It wasn't for a palm reading."

"Oh?" I queried, leaving my response open to interpretation.

"Yes. I can tell that by the charms and spells you're carrying. And—never mind."

"'Never mind' what? Please, I'd like to hear what you have to say."

She blinked a few times and swallowed, then she met my gaze. "There's a shadow hanging over you, Mr. Colin. You've been cursed, and not by some hedge witch."

"So you do actually have some magical acumen."

She tilted her head to acknowledge my comment. "I do. Don't let the trappings fool you. The Circle employs me as a sort of disinformation outlet, to keep members of the public who are curious about supernatural affairs away from real magic."

"Ah—you're in psy ops. Clever."

"It is. The fewer mundanes who know about the world beneath, the better. So, if I can steer the bulk of them toward beliefs and practices that are mostly harmless, it saves the entire supernatural community a ton of headaches. And potentially may save some lives as well."

I sipped my tea; it was quite good, in fact. I stirred some honey in, taking my time as I considered her work. I didn't know how I felt about bilking the public out of their money while selling them false hope, but it beat fae death squads and Circle interrogations.

"Well, I'm not here to criticize the Circle's motives for setting up this operation. I'm really here to find out what you know about raising zombies."

She cleared her throat. "Real zombies, or vodoun zombies?"

"I'll bite—what's the difference?"

"Well, vodoun zombies aren't really undead, you see. In Haiti, vodoun priests and priestesses act sort of like tribal intermediaries for interpersonal disputes. They also enforce the law when the system fails to deliver justice, for whatever reason. The way they do that is to turn evil people—those who have committed serious crimes and escaped the law—into zombies.

"But these aren't real zombies—at least not the undead variety. Instead of killing the offending party, the priests and priestesses use a powder that contains pufferfish toxin and some other ingredients to put the intended target into a death-like state. Then, they allow that person to be buried alive. Hours later, they come for them at the graveyard in the dead of night, digging them up and keeping them in a drugged state. The victim believes they have died and been brought back as a zombie, and the vodoun priest keeps them in a zombie-like state from then on. Typically, these 'zombies' are placed into forced labor in the fields."

I shook my head. "That seems—drastic."

She shrugged. "We're talking about a third-world country where local government is often corrupt, where police and magistrates can be paid to look the other way. The vodoun priests and priestesses act as a sort of backup system, to ensure that people who are powerless are not taken advantage of by those in power. Because in Haiti, everyone fears the wrath of the Houngans and Mambos."

"Okay, fair enough. Maeve thought you might also know about the other kind of zombie, and how to raise them."

She nearly choked on her tea. "Wait a minute—you think I can raise the dead and make zombies?"

I'd obviously offended her. "Um, no? The truth is, I'm not sure what you can do. I simply need the advice of someone who knows more about necromancy than I do, because I think we have a necromancer on the loose here in Austin."

"Oh, I doubt that. See, in vodoun there do exist dark priests and priestesses who practice necromancy, but it is forbidden. We Mambos and Houngans are taught to recognize it, and we kill them on sight. I haven't heard of a true necromancer being active in all the time I've been a priestess."

"Okay, but for the sake of this discussion, humor me for a moment. If there were a necromancer on the loose, and they were raising zombies and ghouls, how would I go about stopping them?"

She rubbed her chin and considered my question. "According to what I was taught, like most magic users, necromancers need a focus for their power. Typically, that's where they store the energies they take from animals or people they sacrifice in their dark rituals, along with power they get from evil loas. That energy is then used to animate corpses to create true zombies."

"That sounds sinister. Would a necromancer carry this focus or phylactery on their person?"

"Maybe. I would think they would need it close by to perform magic. However, because of the unique signature that necromantic energy leaves, I doubt they'd want to have it on them all the time. That would give them away to any non-evil magic user, and they'd be hunted and destroyed immediately. No—I'd say they'd have it near, but not necessarily on them at all times."

I downed the rest of my tea and stood. "Janice, you've been very helpful. Thank you."

She stood and extended her hand. "My pleasure. Besides, I

owe Maeve a favor—one that she won't ever let me forget, it seems."

I smirked. "You too, huh? She must have her claws in everyone in this city."

Janice sighed. "My advice to you is to get out from under her thumb as soon as you can. You give the fae an inch, and they'll take a mile. At least, that's what I've found."

I laughed humorlessly. "Way ahead of you on that point. Way, way ahead of you."

12

Lacking any truly pertinent leads to follow up on, I took a long shot and headed back to the abandoned house near the cemetery. Figured there might be a bit of evidence I'd over-looked, or perhaps a neighbor who might have seen something. I was grasping at straws, but the house was all I could come up with. For now, it'd have to do.

Fortunately, we now had Gunnarson's blessing, which put the Circle's intelligence resources at our disposal. At the moment Belladonna was looking up known necromancers in the Circle database. But unfortunately, there weren't as many necromancers as we might have thought—at least, not in the records. Janice the vodoun priestess had been on the money when she'd said it was a very small community, if you could even call it that. Apparently necromancers kept to themselves, what with the fear of being killed on sight and all.

Necromancers were universally despised by anyone who gave a shit about that sort of thing, which was pretty much everyone in the supernatural community. Nobody wanted ghouls and zombies showing up in their backyard; it was bad for business, bad for keeping a low profile, and generally bad for everything. So, necromancers always operated on the sly. Except this one. Damned if I couldn't figure out why this person was causing such a stir.

I parked my scooter in front of the house and pulled a clipboard and pen from my bag. Years ago, I'd learned that carrying a clipboard made you look like you belonged. And besides, no one wants to talk to someone with a clipboard—carrying one was almost as effective as a see-me-not spell if you wanted to go unnoticed. Today it would serve a different purpose, giving me an excuse for questioning the neighbors.

I walked to a neighbor's house and knocked. No one home. I tried the first house across the street, an older home nearly identical to the abandoned home, albeit in much better condition. It was a narrow, single-story cottage, painted bright pink with light blue trim, and well-maintained.

Before I could even knock, the door opened and I was greeted by an elderly Hispanic man.

"What do you want? I'm not selling, if that's what you're asking, no matter how much you offer. *Pinche buitres*. Now, get off my porch."

He began to shut the door in my face.

"Wait! I'm not here to try to buy your home. In fact, I'm taking a survey of homeowners for the Save Our Austin Neighborhoods alliance. If you might answer a few questions for me, it would be a big help."

His scowl softened slightly. "Save Our Neighborhoods, eh? *Bueno*, I suppose it can't hurt. Ask your questions—but be quick, my *telenovela* is on."

I smiled and pretended to read from my clipboard.

"May I have your name?"

"Nope. Next question."

I nearly laughed. I was really starting to like this guy.

"That's okay, you can answer anonymously." I proceeded to

ask him innocuous questions about how long he'd lived here, increasing taxes, and so on—pretty much all the hot button issues longtime local residents were in tune with. Then, I got to what I really wanted to know.

"Sir, have you noticed any strange people or activity around lately? Anything that might indicate that your neighborhood has changed for the worse?"

"Lots more *gringos* moving in, if that's what you're asking. Driving the property values even higher. I can barely pay my taxes now. *Pendejos.* But at least they increased the police presence since the whites started moving in the neighborhood."

Now that was interesting. "Really? How so?"

"Well, it used to be that the only time the law came around, it was to bust a drug dealer. Couldn't get them to patrol for nothing. But lately, I've seen more cops around. Unmarked cars mostly. One cop in particular keeps checking on the house across the street. I figure he's looking for *narcos* or something."

"That's good to know, sir. That's the end of my survey. Thank you for your time."

"That's it? You made me miss seeing Jorge catch Maria with Alfonzo. Thanks for nothing. *Pinche gringo.*"

He slammed the door in my face, departing with a muttered string of obscenities in Spanish. I understood most of what he said; a year of working the junkyard had expanded my Spanish vocabulary considerably. I didn't take offense to any of it, because in my opinion you earned the right to be a curmudgeon once you hit your retirement years.

The thing about the cop stopping by the house across the street piqued my curiosity. If a cop was working with the necromancer it would explain a lot, including why they'd fingered Hemi for that murder. Hemi's skin color automatically made him an easy target for a frame up, at least to a dirty cop. But what if a cop *was* the necromancer? If so, they could cover their own tracks by losing evidence or misdirecting any investigation that might blow their cover.

The more I thought about it, the more it made sense. I hopped on my scooter and drove around the corner so I could sneak inside the house for another look. I triggered my see-me-not cantrip and took the same route as before, catching my pants on a loose nail and falling through the window on my way in. Thank goodness I was working alone, because Bells would never let me live that down. Once inside, I used my phone as a flashlight, shining it in every corner in search of something I might have missed.

For the most part everything was as I'd left it, except for where Finn had cleaned up after me. If you looked closely, you could tell the floorboards in that room had been pulled back. But there was no sign that a decomposing corpse had been there —not even a lingering whiff. The old man was good at covering evidence, that was for sure. I made a mental note to have him teach me the spell he'd used. I'd been working on something myself since I'd first stumbled on this whole necromancy thing, but his way seemed a lot less messy.

I continued to search the house, opening cupboards and pantries, checking closets—the works. After leaving the room where the ghoul had been, I entered the ritual room. No one had disturbed the area since we'd been here last, nor had anyone attempted to repair the runes and markings that I'd destroyed. I sniffed the air, if only to see if I could detect the stench of necromancy. Nope, still wasn't getting it. *Weird.*

I shifted into second sight and examined the area via the magical spectrum. There was a lingering shimmer of dark magic, but nothing new. I went back into the hallway searching high and low, hoping for anything that might give me a lead in this case.

There.

I saw a flash of something, shining silver and bright amidst the trash and debris. It carried just the tiniest mark of a magic user's energy. I zeroed in on it, finding it hidden under a scrap of paper. An empty blister pack, the kind that over the counter medicine came in. I picked it up and examined it closely in the light.

The writing on the foil said *Nicotine 4mg gum.*

Bingo. Got you, you son of a bitch.

I hoofed it back to my scooter and called Belladonna.

"Bells, can you look something up for me?"

"Thanks to your smooth Irish tongue and ginormous balls, the vast resources of the Circle are at your disposal. Shoot."

I shook my head, knowing that a punchline was coming. "Please, no double entendres regarding my tongue and balls."

At that very moment a fit and attractive, twenty-something woman jogged past with her dog. Her jaw dropped, nostrils flaring as her eyes shot daggers at me.

"Pervert!" she cried with a sharp intake of breath, and hurried down the street.

I pointed to my wireless earpiece. "No, I wasn't talking to you—I mean, I wasn't talking to myself either—"

Too late. She was gone, and I felt like an idiot.

Belladonna's husky laugh echoed in my ear. "I have to say, Colin, you certainly have a way with women. Now, what do you need me to look up?"

"Thanks for that, Bells." I pursed my lips and took a deep breath. "Can you see who the detective was that took Hemi in for questioning?"

I heard typing in the background. "Got it. Two detectives, a Sergeant Erskine and a Detective Klein."

"Hmm—can you do an asset search on them both? We're looking for anything suspicious—a recent large deposit, or maybe a purchase that wouldn't make sense on a cop's salary."

"Yep, give me a sec—" I waited for what seemed like an hour, but in reality it only took a minute or so. "Nope, they both look pretty clean. Hang on, though—Erskine is listed on the secretary of state's website as being principal owner of an LLC. Looks like a shell company. County property search says the company owns a warehouse on the East Side, not far from downtown."

"That's it. Give me the address, and meet me there in twenty ready to rock and roll."

"You got it. And Colin?"

"Yes?"

"I fully expect to get a taste of that silver tongue before this case is finished."

She hung up on me before I could respond with a witty reply. *Yeah, that'll be the day.* I ignored the rush of blood hitting my cheeks and punched another number on my speed dial list.

"Sal here."

"You know who this is, Sal. Stop trying to be coy. I need some info."

"Gah, druid—I told you that we were done wit' the old man. Far as I'm concerned, that means we're through with you, too."

I chuckled humorlessly. "Not by a longshot, Sal. I still have those photos of you and Nutmeg."

"Cinnamon. The girl's name is Cinnamon."

"One spice or another. Fact is, if Mrs. Sal finds out you're screwed."

"You're a heartless prick, you know that, McCool?"

I yawned. "Cry me a river. Now, tell me what you know about a detective by the name of Erskine."

Sal paused. "You sure you want to know?"

"Sure I want to know. Why do you ask?"

The red cap laughed long and loud. "Because, some cops aren't exactly honest, and those kind don't like pricks like you sniffing around their business. Do you really want that sort of heat?"

I rubbed my forehead in frustration. "Just tell me what I need to know, Sal."

"Fine, but don't say I didn't warn you. Erskine is dirty—has been for most of his career. But he hides it well. Doesn't flash cash around, lives like any other shmuck cop, and keeps all his dealings quiet. Rocko's had him on his payroll for a while now."

Interesting. "My sources tell me he owns a warehouse on the east side. Know anything about that?"

"Look, I told you the guy is dirty already. But I ain't no rat."

"Cinnamon looks awfully bored in this picture, Sal. But you, on the other hand—you look like you're giving it your all. Your wife would be so proud to see you like this, hard at work."

Sal growled, but it lacked conviction. "Fine. He uses that warehouse to store things. Stolen merch, drugs, cash—pretty much anything he needs to hide until he can offload it or send it through the cleaners."

"Have you been there? Notice anything strange about the place?"

"Been there once, running an errand for Rocko. But did I notice anything weird? No, not unless you think crooked cops is weird. To me, that's just scenery."

"Thanks for the info, Sal. You're a real pal."

"Go fuck yourself, druid."

A few minutes later, I pulled up to the address Belladonna had given me and sat on my scooter, waiting for her to arrive. I pretended to be looking up something on my phone, but instead

I was casing the place. Each time my eyes swept over the building, the urge to look elsewhere was overwhelming. Someone had spent a lot of time or a lot of money putting a see-me-not spell over the entire property. So, either Erskine was clued in and had hired a proper wizard to do the work, or he was our guy.

Once I focused, it became easier to check the place out. The best I could say was that it was nondescript; it looked just like a million other cinder block and metal buildings in the area. Good place for a hideout—or to stash drugs, money, and stolen property.

Just the fact that Erskine owned a warehouse here was suspicious. Real estate values in this area were increasing by the week, with properties snatched up left and right by developers. These places would be torn down to become loft apartments and condos for young professionals who liked living close to downtown, but who found the new high-rise developments on the other side of IH-35 out of their reach. A million-point-five for a two-bedroom condo did seem kind of steep, come to think of it. But the views were probably breathtaking.

The throaty sound of Belladonna's Harley hauling ass down 5th Street broke me from my reverie. She pulled up behind me, stepping off the beast and tossing her hair around after she pulled off her helmet. As usual she looked stunning. Her long black hair, dusky skin, and exotic features were magnified by her exceptional figure and sultry, cat-like grace. How she managed to avoid helmet hair was a mystery to me, but I suspected she'd paid some wizard at her work to spell her helmet to prevent it. I resisted the urge to check the magical spectrum to confirm my suspicions—a girl had to have her secrets, after all.

Her mouth turned up in a crooked grin as she sauntered over. "So, McCool, I hear you're a perv? You been holding out on me, or what?"

"Ha ha, very funny. If it wasn't for your tendency to turn every conversation toward sex and nudity, I wouldn't have been embarrassed in public."

"Oh, but I don't really speak about sex, loverboy—I only *allude* to it. I leave the direct approach to amateurs and phone sex pros."

I rolled my eyes, but my cheeks flushed hotly. "Noted. Now, can we go check this place out, or what?"

"You got it, cutie. But just one thing—where's the building?"

It was my turn to smile. I had to take my victories where I could, after all. "Look hard, and concentrate." I pointed at the building.

She did so, squinting until surprise registered on her face. "Shit, McCool, that's some serious concealment magic. You think this is our guy?"

I shrugged. "Maybe. Only one way to find out." I swept my arm in a grandiose gesture and bowed at the waist. "After you."

She slapped my butt on her way past, and I didn't even bother protesting the uninvited contact. I wasn't sure whether it was because she was wearing me down, or because I liked it. Either way I was screwed, and probably would literally be at some point. Maybe it was due, but now wasn't the time to ponder my sex life—or lack of it. Right now, we had a necromancer to hunt.

I gladly followed behind Bells as she approached the building. The truth was, she was better at tactical stuff than me. Sure, my teacher had two thousand years of knowledge to pass on, but how did you distill all that down to a few years of training? You couldn't, and that meant the training I'd received was haphazard and anachronistic in many ways. Oh, I could swing a sword, cast a few useful spells, treat minor wounds with herbs and poultices, and identify all manner of supernatural creatures. But modern military and tactical skills were just not part of the program.

Belladonna, on the other hand—now there was someone with a deep and very specialized skill set. The Circle's hunter-wizard teams were trained much in the same way modern special forces troops were. They were taught to move fast, silently, and to overwhelm their enemies with shock and awe. To put it in gamer terms, I was more like a bard, while she was like a dual-classed ninja paladin. And make no mistake about it: there were few people I'd rather have beside me in a fight.

She stopped for a moment and whistled. "Whoa, that's one hell of a powerful 'look away go away' spell. Almost made me turn around and leave, even though I know what's there. Colin, I think we've found our necromancer."

I decided to withhold judgment until we had undeniable proof, but it was looking bad for Erskine. Still, I wasn't going to take out a cop unless I was sure he was both dirty and a threat to public safety. Covering up a dead cop would be difficult, and I suspected I'd need to get Maeve involved to make it work. When cops got killed, their brothers and sisters wouldn't rest until they found the killer, and rightly so. If he turned out to really be our guy, nothing about this was going to be easy.

Bells shook it off and walked up to the front as if she were there on business, so I followed her lead. The building had surveillance cameras, so I sparked them with a short-circuit spell to ensure we wouldn't be implicated later if things went sideways. Once we confirmed the place was buttoned up tight, we ducked around the back of the building.

Bells moved forward in a crouch, stopping under a dust-covered window. A quick look inside told us no one was home. I grabbed a rock, wrapped it in a discarded rag, and busted out a pane of glass. Then I reached in and unlatched the window so we could enter.

Inside, the middle of the warehouse was brightly illuminated by sunlight, but the far corners were cloaked in shadow. With the stark difference in lighting, a night vision cantrip wouldn't do us much good. We crouched just inside the window behind a large wooden crate, taking time to allow our eyes to adjust. It was deathly quiet inside the place, so we stuck to hand signals as we moved through the building, with Bells in the lead holding a tricked out Colt .45 Government model. I tapped her on the shoulder and pointed to a stairway that led to an upstairs office. She nodded and we headed that way.

I decided that when in Rome, you draw your pistol. I pulled the Glock from my bag, press-checking the chamber to make sure I was cocked and locked. That crap you always saw on TV with people racking the slide on their pistol when they pulled it out was pure nonsense. If you were going to carry a gun, you kept a round in the chamber. Didn't do you much good when you needed it if you didn't.

We made nary a sound as we stalked to the stairs and crept up to the door at the top. When we reached the office, she motioned for me to stay back. Bells chose to remain concealed behind the wall next to the door as she opened it, so I crouched and followed her lead. As soon as she turned the handle I felt a spell release. I immediately shifted my vision into second sight and witnessed the remains of an incredibly powerful glamour and stasis spell dissipating in a rush of spent magic.

Then, the moans of dozens of undead echoed up from the warehouse floor as they emerged from behind stacks of boxes and rows of crates. They noticed us immediately, and homed in on our position.

We were surrounded and trapped. And we had played right into the necromancer's hands.

13

"It's a trap!" I yelled, right next to Belladonna's ear.

"No shit, Ackbar? What gave it away—was it the dozens of undead converging on us, or the fact that we really are trapped?"

She wasted no further time in conversation, and drew another large-bore pistol from within her jacket. A split-second later Bells was taking out ghouls Lara Croft style, with both pistols blazing and missing nary a skull or kneecap.

I waited until she had to reload to begin firing, since I only had a single thirty-round magazine available to me. Unlike Belladonna, I didn't carry six spare mags on me at any given time. Sure, I had them inside my Craneskin Bag, but it'd take too long to rummage around and find them. I paused between shots to provide my retort, if only to save face.

"I just always wanted to say that in real life." I fired three more shots, taking out two of the advancing ghouls. *Blam! Blam-blam!* "But in hindsight, I realize that finding the perfect context kind of takes the fun out of it."

The slide locked back on my Glock, just as I took a bead on a ghoul advancing up the stairs toward us. "I'm out!" I yelled.

"Then duck, or start cutting—I don't care which," she replied.

I ducked. Hot brass rained down on me as Belladonna's twin pistols ate through the crowd below, as well as those who had made it to the stairs. I tossed the pistol back in my bag and drew my short sword, ready to cover for Bells the next time she needed to reload.

Belladonna might have been a much better shot than me, but few people could best me at swordsmanship. My long, lean frame and near-superhuman agility and speed, combined with years of practice under the watchful eye of Finn, made me deadly with a blade. I was supremely confident in my skills, because I'd tested myself many times. I'd trained with reenactment swordsmen, with practitioners of Western and Eastern martial arts, with machete fencers from the Caribbean and South America, and with stick and knife fighters from the islands of Southeast Asia.

And in every single instance, the simple, brutal Celtic fighting style that Finn had taught me held up. That was the thing about modern martial artists; most of what they practiced was decades or even centuries divorced from the days when practitioners actually had to rely on their skills for their daily survival. That meant many modern fighters had bad habits, derived from practicing for show or points instead of the quick kill.

Only once had a swordsman given me a hard time, and that was a Spanish fencer who'd marked the shit out of my limbs for most of our bout—that is, until I'd taken him out Rob Roy style. But for sheer utility, nothing I'd seen had compared to what I'd learned from Finn, not even the stuff they taught hunters at the Circle. So as soon as I heard Bells reaching for her last two magazines, I leapt into the fray.

I caught the first ghoul just as I turned the corner on the

stairs, dropping low under a lunging grab and slicing his quadri-ceps just above the knee. His stench almost made me choke, but I followed through cleanly and pivoted with a backhanded stroke that took the thing's head clean off. There was no pause in my movements as I stabbed the next in line through the brain, via a thrust to the nasal cavity. I kicked her in the chest and yanked hard as she fell, feeling the suction on my blade release as I unsheathed it from her head.

I lopped another ghoul's hands off as it reached for me, a tactic that meant little to the ghoul but kept it from pulling itself closer. I danced back and dropped low, severing its lead leg at the ankle. The thing nearly fell on me, but I rolled to my left to avoid it and came up in the middle of three more of the disgusting creatures. I was about to go to town on them when three shots echoed from the stairs. All three ghouls collapsed in a spatter of brains and gore.

I looked around the room; there were no more undead left standing. Bells calmly walked around the space, her face a mask as she dispatched those still groaning and twitching. I helped her in her task by severing a few more heads. Finally, we were greeted by a welcome silence, accompanied by the unwelcome stench of two dozen rotting corpses mingled with the smell of gunpowder and dust.

"You think anyone heard that racket?"

I shrugged. "Maybe. But as strong as that see-me-not spell is, I doubt they'll be able to pinpoint where it came from." I pointed to the office above. "C'mon, let's see if we can find anything useful."

"You go ahead—I'm going to call a clean-up team to take care of these corpses." She winked at me. "Gunnarson did say that the Circle's resources were at our disposal."

I nodded and returned a smile, then headed into the office. Inside, it looked just like a typical man cave or dad's den—the kind you'd find in any middle class home. There were neon beer signs on the walls, sporting collectibles and bowling trophies, and an outdated girly calendar. The desk was covered in random crap, mostly old newspapers and copies of *Sports Illustrated* and *Field and Stream*. I tossed the desk, finding nothing but a stack of porn, a half-empty bottle of Dewar's, a stained and cracked coffee mug, a woman's bra sized 36C, and a box of .40 mm rounds.

A search of the file cabinets turned up more of the same: the detritus of a middle-aged loser's life. *Who am I kidding, this could be me in twenty-five years*, I thought. The truth was, I had no idea what a middle-aged man's life should have looked like, since my dad had died when I was very young. But, something told me it shouldn't have looked like this.

I checked the place high and low and found nothing that might implicate Erskine as our necromancer. Based on the heap of dead ghouls downstairs, I couldn't help but conclude that he was our guy. All I needed was a single, damning bit of evidence to convince me he needed to be taken out. I shifted my vision into the magical spectrum and scanned the room.

The residual magic from the spell we'd triggered earlier still shone like a beacon, drowning out anything else I might have spotted. That had been some spell, to keep all those ghouls in stasis and hide them from us so completely. Whoever cast it had some major juju, and I really wasn't looking forward to tangling with them. Hopefully when I caught up with them I'd be able to let the Circle handle it.

I growled in frustration as my search ended fruitlessly. Then, just as I turned to leave, I glanced up at the ceiling. Something flashed at me, briefly, from the tiles above. I pulled up a folding metal chair and stood on it, pushing a ceiling tile loose with the tip of my sword. A small, leather-bound book fell out, landing on the floor with a smack.

I stepped off the chair and nudged it open with my blade. Magic users often trapped their personal spell books, so it was always prudent to use discretion when first opening an unfamiliar tome. As the cover fell back, it revealed pages of handwritten notes, similar to the runes and markings I'd found at the abandoned house near the cemetery.

I couldn't help but crack a grin. We'd found our necromancer.

———

Belladonna and I were both ecstatic, because now we had an actual target to go after. The question was, how were we going to handle it? Taking out a cop was not something either one of us took lightly. As we sat on the front step back at the junkyard, sipping brews, we debated how to deal with Erskine.

I took a swig and squinted at nothing in particular. "We could find a way to let the law handle it, just to get him off the street. Maybe frame him for the ghoul murders, or even plant some evidence that he's dealing drugs or something."

She shook her head. "Too risky. For one, he's probably already onto us, considering that trap he laid at his warehouse. That was meant for us—or at least for you, since you're the one who has been poking around. I mean, you've pretty much been one step behind him since this thing started. I'd be surprised if he doesn't bolt soon.

"And besides, so far he's been covering his tracks pretty good from inside the department. You really think we could make something stick? Heck, we don't even know if there are other dirty cops involved—his partner, for one. For all we know, he might find a way to make it blow up in our faces."

I peeled the label off my beer as I pondered what she'd said.

"That's if he actually knows who we are, Bells. As far as I

know, ghouls aren't smart enough to convey what they've seen to their makers. So far, the only people who can connect me to the case are the living dead. And only one of them has survived a run-in with me."

"Speaking of which, what happened to that thing? As long as Erskine's alive, it'll keep roaming the city."

"Good point. Even if we did manage to get Erskine put in jail, that super-ghoul of his will still be out there killing. No, I think you're right—we need to take him out, for good."

Belladonna's eyes crinkled at the corners as she made a duck face at me.

"Oh, I like it when you talk tough. Do it again."

I looked away, uncomfortable with her flirting. Usually it was no big deal, but lately it had been putting me off my game. To be honest, I'd been distracted by her presence more and more over the last several weeks. I couldn't deny that I found Belladonna to be attractive... very attractive, in fact.

My mind flashed back to watching her earlier, shooting those ghouls with both guns blazing, her face lit up with glee. In many ways Bells reminded me of Jesse, at least when it came to hunting. Jesse had been the peas to my carrots, the jelly on my peanut butter sandwich. Because of the bond we'd developed through training with Finn and hunting, she understood me like few others could. I missed having that in my life.

While I was still deep in thought, Bells scooted close to me. She whispered in my ear and gave it a tiny nibble.

"Don't deny it, loverboy. You want me just as badly as I want you."

A shiver went down my spine at the touch of her teeth on my skin. It was true. I did want her, more than I cared to admit. I felt her hot breath on my cheek and neck as her hand slipped under my shirt, caressing my skin. I turned to her and we kissed, hungrily. Before I knew it she was on her back on the rough concrete of the warehouse porch. I was on top of her, kissing her lips, her neck, and the bare skin of her cleavage.

She wrapped her legs around me, grinding into me, and I responded in kind. Then she pulled my arm across her body, shifting her hips and scissoring her legs in a textbook sweep that took me off my knees and onto my back instead. She effortlessly landed lightly on top of me.

She leaned in and softly kissed me. "Aren't you going to invite me in?"

"Bells, I'm not—I can't—I don't know if I'm quite ready for this," I stuttered, my voice a husky cry for warmth and comfort despite my statement to the contrary. It had been a long time, and damn it I was so lonely.

A single tear ran down my cheek, hot and wet.

Belladonna wiped it away, ever so softly with her thumb.

"Sshh, I know," she whispered.

She stood and pulled me up with her, and I followed willingly as she led me to my room. And oh, how badly did I need this.

We were already tearing each other's clothes off as we stumbled through the door. I practically ripped my shirt off, watching as she pulled off her boots and shimmied out of her pants, inch by inch. Her abs were rock hard, and the ridges they made led my eyes down to her hips and thighs.

Two thoughts crossed my mind as our bodies hit the mattress, tangled up in each other. One, that we weren't going to get much planning done tonight. And second, I hoped Jesse would forgive me for being human.

14

An hour later... okay, fifteen minutes. Did I mention that it'd been a long time? Anyway, a short while later we were lying in bed enjoying the afterglow, not really snuggling—but not heading for opposite sides of the mattress either.

That's when I popped the question. No, not that question, the other one.

"Bells?"

"Yeah?"

"Mind if I ask you a question?"

"Sure, why not? I think you earned it."

"Was I—any good? I mean, I only ask because—"

With a sharp intake of breath, she cut me off. "Because besides Jesse, I'm the only girl you've slept with? And you think I'm way more experienced, which puts you at a disadvantage?"

"Sorry. I didn't mean to imply—"

"Stop. Colin, do you want to know how many guys I've slept with?"

"No—Bells, that doesn't matter to me. At all. You've stood by me through some of the toughest times of my life. Hell, you've practically sacrificed your career for me. So, no—I don't want to know."

Silence. Then, "Two."

I sat up in bed, pulling a sheet over me. Shrinkage, and all that. "Huh? Did you say, 'two'?"

She looked slightly hurt at my response, and pressed her lips together as she nodded her reply.

"So. Crowley and—me?"

She nodded again.

"But I thought—you always—you mean that's all just an act?"

She nodded again.

"But—why?"

It was dark, but I could see her eyes were tearing up so I grabbed her hand. "After I slept with Crowley, he boasted about it at work. Word got around, and pretty soon people started to talk. Saying I was easy, saying I was fast—the usual crap. I work in a male-dominated career field, so you can imagine how bad it soon got."

I took a sharp intake of breath. "Shit. That's why you and Crowley split up."

"Yup. Anyway, after a while I decided, 'Fuck it, I am going to own this shit.' So I did. And you know what?"

"Um, you look hella sexy in tight leather pants?"

She giggled and wiped an eye. "Well, that—but I also found out that sexually aggressive women intimidate a lot of guys. Most guys, in fact. Oh, you all talk a good game, but when it comes down to it you are scared to death of pussy. Pardon my French."

I raised my hand. "Guilty."

"Don't I know it. And when I found out it backfired on me with the one guy I really liked, I was all, 'Ha ha, the joke's on you, Belladonna.'"

I screwed my face up into a lopsided grin and pulled her close. She resisted at first, but only for a moment. "Sorry. I didn't mean to be such an ass just now."

"Meh, what were you supposed to think? I play this shit to the hilt."

I kissed her on top of the head. Her hair smelled like vanilla and lilac. "Bells, you said you intimidate *most* guys. So what do you do when a guy likes the bold, brassy you?"

"Duh. I shoot them down."

"And if that doesn't work?"

She pulled away slightly and looked me in the eye. Her eyes narrowed. "Then I kick them in the junk. Hard."

I laughed and tweaked her nose. "Did you know you're sexy when you talk tough?"

"Yup. Did you know your eyes cross slightly when you—"

I cut her off with a kiss, and after that we didn't talk much at all.

The second round was better than the first, and after Bells snuck out to the bathroom I grabbed a towel and headed to the outdoor shower. It was going to be cold as hell, but I was used to it.

I was lathering up my hair and had shampoo in my eyes when I heard the old man's voice.

"So, you finally nutted up and gave that girl what she's been wanting for—oh, the last eighteen months or so. Good for you."

I rinsed the soap from my eyes and looked over the scrap of corrugated metal roof that currently served as my shower door. "I certainly hope you weren't listening in, Finn."

He scowled. "Not on purpose, no—but by Nuada's fiery

sword, that girl can scream." He fixed me with a sly grin and a wink. "Like I said, good for you."

I groaned. "Can we not talk about my sex life—at all? There are certain things I'd like to keep private, and that's definitely one of them. Besides, a gentleman never kisses and tells."

His face grew serious. "So, you really like this one, eh? I'd have thought that the glaistig had it wrapped up, but I suppose it's no surprise you fell into the sheets with that hunter. What, with her giving you the full court press and all."

"This is me not talking about my sex life with you, old man," I said as I toweled off inside the shower.

He continued without missing a beat. "I wonder what that troll maiden is going to think. She did musk-mark you as her own." He stroked his beard and knuckled his chin. "Although, I wouldn't mind watching that wildcat girlfriend of yours in a tussle with a female troll. Now that's a cat fight I'd pay to see."

"You're incorrigible, you know that? Also, that's gross."

"Let's see you live for two thousand years, and not pick up a few exotic tastes." He rolled a cigarette as he spoke, licking it and sealing the paper between sentences. "Now, tell me where things sit with this necromancer problem you've been dealing with."

I silently thanked everything that was good and holy that he'd changed the subject, and filled him in on our progress.

"Hmm, a crooked cop you say? And a detective? I don't get it —cops turn crooked for wealth and power, but I fail to see how this detective could possibly profit from loosing ghouls on the city."

I wrapped the towel around my waist and stepped out of the shower. "I don't know. Maybe he's setting himself up to be the hero, by solving the murders and pinning it on someone else. For a homicide detective, cracking a serial murder case could mean a promotion—or a book deal. Heck, maybe even a move up to the big leagues, working at the federal level."

Finn puffed his cigarette and shook his head vigorously. "Nope, I don't buy it. There's something else at play here, something we're not seeing. Watch yourself."

"I always do."

"The hell you say."

Bells walked around the corner of the warehouse at that moment, saving me from having to deflect Finn's apprehensions. In my eyes, he still hadn't earned the right to be concerned about my well-being, and it made me uncomfortable when he expressed such feelings.

Was it petty of me? Sure, but I had good reason.

"Ah, here you are. And the old pervert too. Did you get a good listen, grandpa?"

Finn nodded and somehow blew smoke from his ears—I laughed in spite of myself. "Did I? I believe the screams I heard filled the old spank-bank for a good long while."

"And then you had to go and ruin the moment. Thanks, Finn," I said.

"Don't mention it. I'll leave you two lovebirds alone now." He paused as he passed Belladonna, resting a hand lightly on her arm. "Keep an eye on him for me—he doesn't know how much danger he's in right now."

He turned to me then, his eyes hard and glimmering in the pale light reflected from the yard lights overhead. "And you do the same for her, boy. She's a keeper."

As he walked away, my forehead crinkled and I exhaled long and slow.

"I swear, you never know what to expect from him. Sorry about that."

"Oh, I can handle a little locker room talk, believe me. Besides, I think it's kind of cute how he worries about you." She tsked as she closed the gap between us. "You're too hard on him, you know."

"Maybe." Time to change the subject. "Now, what are we going to do about Erskine?"

She leaned in and placed a hand on my bare chest, snuggling close to me. I liked it. "Well, I think we need to take him out, and make it look like a murder. Maybe a break-in gone wrong or something."

"I don't know if that's a good idea. Evidence is hard to fake."

"Meh, our clean-up team can handle it. They're very good at what they do."

"I still have my reservations about this. What if we have the wrong guy? Or, what if he's too powerful for us to handle on our own?"

She stepped back slightly, allowing her hand to linger on my skin before dropping it to her side. "I get that you're not absolutely sure about killing the guy. But look at the evidence. He was at two of the ghoul murder scenes: the one at the park, and the one behind the club. You also found evidence that links him to the abandoned house, and you found a spell book at his warehouse—where we were jumped by two dozen ghouls. What further evidence do you need?"

I sighed. "I suppose you're right. And I don't want anyone else to die. If we're going to do this we need to get to him ASAP, take him out, and destroy his focus. That should deanimate any of the ghouls he's created, and allow us to put this case to bed for good."

She growled pleasantly. "And then maybe we can spend a little more time in bed ourselves—at my place, where I have indoor plumbing."

I couldn't argue with that logic.

We hid in the dark outside Detective Erskine's home, waiting for him to show. The plan was simple. First I'd release a magical signature cantrip to make sure he was our necromancer. Once we were absolutely certain he was our guy we'd take him out, and then let the Circle's clean-up crew handle it from there.

And if he didn't show we'd break in anyway, to look for evidence that would implicate him in the murders. Later we'd point the cops to that evidence before we made him "disappear," so it would look like he got nervous and skipped town. No good cop ever avenged a dirty cop's death, and no one would keep a missing persons case open on a serial killer.

We waited in the tree line behind Erskine's house, which was a lot more swank than I'd expected based on the location. His backyard was nicely landscaped, with a pool, a built-in hot tub, and an outdoor kitchen and living area complete with a large screen TV viewable from anywhere that mattered.

No doubt about it: Erskine had nice things. Things that were a heck of a lot nicer than someone living on a cop's salary should have been able to afford. I figured he must've paid cash for everything, and paid the contractors who'd done the work under the table. Texas was rife with undocumented workers who were more than willing to take cash and tell no one. How he'd gotten around the city inspectors was anyone's guess, but a little cash payment on the buddy system could have easily kept him out of hot water there as well. Unless he planned to offload the house at some point, any unpermitted work wouldn't be an issue.

Just looking around the place got me pissed. This guy was profiting from the misery of others, killing people to get what he wanted. After a half-hour of watching his house, I wanted to throttle him.

"This is getting us nowhere," Bells whispered under her breath, rubbing her arms to fight off the cold. "I say we head inside and see what we can find."

"Alright, but be careful. For all we know he could be asleep inside."

"Naw, his patrol car's gone. He's either working, handling some illicit deal, or he's making more ghouls."

"Your optimism just fills me with confidence, Belladonna."

She winked. "It's what I'm here for—to boost your flagging confidence. Someone has to do it."

I wondered whether she was joking or serious. Was I that pathetic? I'd just slept with the girl and already I was second-guessing myself. I resolved to stop over-thinking things, to just enjoy whatever burgeoning romance Bells and I might have.

Right, good luck with that.

I followed her as she snuck along the fence line to the back door. All was quiet, both inside Erskine's place and at his neighbors' homes to either side. Lucky for us, he lived in an older area where the homes weren't right on top of each other.

I gave the door the magical once over and signaled it was safe. Bells knelt down and pulled out a set of lock picks. They were unnecessary, since I could've used a cantrip to open the lock. But any use of magic might tip him off if he was home, so I let her do things the old-fashioned way. Just as she began to insert a pick into the lock, the door swung inward slightly.

She looked up at me with concern on her face, and pointed at the door jamb. I leaned in and saw that it had been forced open. The door frame was splintered and the striker plate was missing. It surprised me that a cop wouldn't feel the need to install longer screws on his striker plates—or for that matter a security system—but then again maybe he felt like he didn't need it. Wouldn't have been the first cop I'd known to get burglarized.

I pulled my short sword from my bag, and Belladonna drew a blued-steel automatic pistol from the small of her back, to which she attached a noise suppressor. *Damn, this girl is hot.* I got my mind back on task, and listened for the slightest indication of movement from within the house as she pushed open the door.

We ghosted through the place, clearing it room by room as we went. We found lots more nice stuff, including a lot of electronics and kitchen appliances that were high end and most definitely stolen. But besides that, not much else. Despite the back door being busted open, nothing in the house was disturbed. Then, I caught a whiff of something coming from a door near the kitchen.

Blood.

I tapped Belladonna on the shoulder and motioned for her to follow. The iron-rich smell got stronger as we approached the door. I opened it using the tail of my shirt to avoid leaving prints. The door swung open into darkness. The scents of fresh blood, paint, gas, and motor oil wafted from within. I reached inside the door for a light switch and flipped it on.

There, in the middle of the garage floor, next to a very nicely restored early-seventies Corvette, was Detective Erskine. He was lying on his back, spread eagle in the middle of a necromantic circle that had been painted with his own blood. His eyes were missing, and possibly several of his internal organs as well. The markings on the walls and floor matched those at the abandoned house near the cemetery, as well as the spell book we'd found at the warehouse.

Which I currently still had in my possession.

"Son of a bitch," I said.

"I second that assertion," Belladonna stated matter of factly.

That's when we heard the sirens. We beat feet to the back door, where we could already see flashlight beams dancing across the yard and entrance.

"Shit! We are so fucked right now, Colin."

I had to think fast, because if I didn't we were both going to end up in jail. My ability to cast stealth spells was more or less limited to myself and one other person, but only if I was wearing an item of clothing that I'd previously spelled with runes. That meant one of us was going to get caught. I made a snap decision and cast the see-me-not spell on Bells.

"Colin, what are you doing?"

I grabbed her by the shoulders. "Look, if you get caught with all that hardware you carry we're both screwed. You've got about five minutes before that spell wears off. Stay hidden, and just as soon as those cops come through that door, you haul ass out the back and over the fence. Go!"

I shoved her gently toward the back door and ran to the front, heading for one of the bedrooms that faced the side of the house away from the driveway. I stopped long enough to pull the spell book out of my pocket and drop it inside my Craneskin Bag, where no one would ever find it but me. I opened a window, removed the screen, and slipped out, sneaking my way to the street without being seen. Reaching the sidewalk, I pulled Borovitz's card out of my wallet and tore it in two, then shoved it into my front pocket. I began walking at a normal pace up the street and away from Erskine's place, hoping like hell that Belladonna hadn't been caught.

I knew I'd be arrested within minutes. That would focus the cops' attentions on me and away from the house, allowing Bells a window for her to escape. Within seconds, a patrol car spotted me. Shortly thereafter, I was cuffed and in the back of a squad car.

My mom was going to be so pissed when she found out I'd gotten arrested in connection to a murder.

15

I was in an interrogation room at central booking, my hands cuffed to a metal table in front of me. A female detective with a short haircut and a serious expression sat across from me. She was in her early thirties, petite but not necessarily athletic-looking, and wore a tan long-sleeved shirt tucked into a pair of broken-in Levi's, scuffed black tactical boots, and a thick leather belt that secured a Crossbreed supertuck holster, currently empty.

She was not a happy camper at the moment.

"You know, if you don't cooperate you're only going to make it harder on yourself. We have you at the scene, we found your footprints and those of your accomplice behind the house, and I'm sure we'll find your prints inside the house as well. Why don't you just fess up, and maybe I can convince the judge to lighten your sentence? I'm sure the DA will be willing to talk a deal, once you start telling us what happened."

"I'll be happy to cooperate, just as soon as I speak with my attorney."

Detective Klein leaned back in her chair and inhaled through her nose, letting it out again slowly. "Look, Colin, your record is squeaky clean, except for that incident a few years back with your girlfriend."

I tried to keep my face neutral, but I must've let something slip. She smiled like a wolf on its way to grandma's house.

"Oh, you think I didn't know about that?"

She opened up a file folder, flipping through it and then slamming it down in front of me. She arranged several photos on the table, laying them out carefully, one by one.

"Take a look. This is what was left of your girlfriend's body, after that 'bear' was done with her. Now, I'm no expert on animal attacks, but this sure in hell doesn't look like it was done by a bear. And as far as I know, the last time a bear was seen in those parts was decades ago."

I didn't need to look at the photos; I'd seen it all firsthand.

For a brief moment I wanted to strangle her. Then I reminded myself that she was just doing her job. And if I were her, I'd think the strangely calm college-aged kid sitting in front of her had murdered Erskine, too.

I kept my eyes fixed on hers, and replied through gritted teeth. "Attorney. Lawyer. Phone call."

At that moment, Borovitz burst into the room in a flurry of motion. "Say nothing more, Colin. Detective, you have nothing to hold my client on other than circumstantial evidence. If you're not going to charge him with a crime, then we'll be leaving immediately."

All expression dropped from Klein's square, rugged face like a guillotine, and her voice showed no emotion as she responded.

"I don't think so. I get to hold your client for twenty-four hours, which is plenty of time to get the DA to file charges in the murder of Sergeant Erskine. But hey, I'll be happy to leave you two alone to figure out your story while I get the DA out of bed."

She grabbed the file folder, taking her time picking up the photos one by one, carefully tucking them inside before walking out the door. Once she was gone, Borovitz grabbed her chair and pulled it around the table so he could sit as close to me as possible.

He leaned in and spoke quietly in my ear, in sharp, clipped sentences. "Did you say anything? Anything at all?"

He may as well have been asking me, *Is it safe? Is it secret?* I shook my head no.

"Good. All evidence that might place you inside the house or on the premises has gone missing. So, all they have is circumstantial evidence. There is nothing to place you inside the home or connect you with the detective's murder.

"Say nothing else to anyone, no matter how they question or harass you. We have witnesses to corroborate your story, one that we'll discuss later at my offices. I assure you that you'll be released shortly—within a few hours at most. Just sit tight and shut up, and you'll be home in no time."

I nodded, and he stood.

"Then I'll see you at my offices in the morning. Remember, say nothing to anyone. Not even a cellmate."

Cellmate?

That night I discovered cops were relentless about questioning suspects, and that they'd say just about anything to drag a confession out of a suspect. Once they started threatening to arrest my mom, I knew they were desperate and didn't have anything on me. I guess the time I'd spent watching videos on civil rights and curbside law on YouTube had been time well spent.

I also discovered that holding cells sucked, and that there were some scary people in jail. I sat by myself in the corner and didn't get a wink of sleep. One guy tried to brace me, saying he didn't like the way I looked. So I cast a cantrip on him that caused him to lose control of his bowels. He pissed and shit himself until he was no longer a threat; it was hard to look tough when your pants were full of urine and diarrhea.

Unfortunately, it took a while for the jailers to take him to the infirmary—which meant we all had to put up with the smell. The place already reeked of vomit and urine, so let's just say it wasn't the most pleasant six hours I'd ever spent. After that guy left, I struck up a conversation with a guy wearing a Misfits shirt, and we talked classic punk bands until the early morning hours when I was finally released.

Borovitz had called it true; they didn't have anything substantial to tie me to Erskine's murder. Other than the fact that I'd been strolling through his neighborhood a few hours after the time of Erskine's death, the police couldn't actually place me at the scene. Borovitz explained all of this to me at his office later that morning, and he also explained my alibi and the "real" reason why I'd been wandering Erskine's neighborhood at that time of night.

Apparently I'd been at an acquaintance's house watching movies. Their dog had gotten out, so I was walking around trying to help them locate the missing pooch. It so happened that this same acquaintance, who I'd never actually met, lived in a neighborhood adjacent to Erskine's. Lo and behold, there were three other people I'd never met who could corroborate the story.

All of them worked for Maeve in some capacity. I met each one at Borovitz's offices, where they related the alleged events of the night to me in convincing detail, one by one. Never let it be said that it didn't pay to have a wealthy, powerful fae queen pulling your strings and watching you dance. Because apparently she could screw with me all she liked, but the Austin Police Department could piss off.

I left my meeting with Borovitz close to lunchtime, with instructions to go clean up so we could stop by the station later to answer a few lingering questions as a formality. Bleary-eyed, I nodded and took the bus back to the junkyard, napping on the way. Once home, I caught a few hours of sleep, cleaned up and changed my clothes, and met Borovitz at the police station.

He answered every question for me, and with every passing minute Klein's face grew darker and darker. Eventually she stormed out of the room, leaving her lieutenant to state that the interview was over.

Somehow, I didn't think that would be the last I'd see of Detective Klein.

Borovitz left me with clear instructions to lay low, and to call him if the police attempted to question me further. By that point I realized I was starving. I stopped by Dirty Martin's for a burger, fries, and a malt on the way home. After stuffing my face, I checked my phone and saw about a jillion texts from Bells.

I texted her back and assured her everything was fine. She insisted on seeing me, and I declined on grounds that I was about to go comatose. She relented, and I went home and slept a restless sleep punctuated by nightmares about doing hard time in a prison where the other prisoners were ghouls, the guards were necromancers, and everyone was either trying to eat my face off or sacrifice me to their dark gods.

All in all, it wasn't exactly my proudest twenty-four hours. Not by a long shot.

The next day, I woke up feeling like I hadn't slept a wink, and with a gnawing feeling in the pit of my stomach that said I was screwing this case up royally. I slammed three cups of coffee and threw on some coveralls, then headed out into the yard to get some work done and clear my mind. The coffee didn't do much for the butterflies in my gut, but I hoped a morning lost in mindless work would at least help me figure out my next move.

After a couple of hours spent pulling parts for customers, I was greasy and sweaty, but I still hadn't decided what to do next. Frustrated, I took off my mechanic's gloves and chewed my thumbnail, letting old Fionn's magical insight wash over me as I sat on the tailgate of a rusted out Ford F-150. That magic was another advantage that had been handed down to me all the way from Fionn MacCumhaill, who'd accidentally stolen it from Finnegas. I think it still rankled the old man a bit, and I felt guilty for wishing he was around so I could rub it in his face.

Thing was, I didn't like to use it because it sometimes revealed things about people that I didn't want to know. Fae magic was fickle that way. Most anything you got from the fae was going to end up becoming a burden or a curse at some point. And although Fionn hadn't gotten the magic directly from the fae, I was fairly certain the Salmon of Knowledge had been a creation of the Tuatha Dé Danann, another magical jack-in-the-box they'd left for some poor fool to stumble upon. They loved to saddle mortals with particularly capricious magics, just to see what would happen. When they did, it almost always ended in disaster.

The fae were dicks like that.

But, despite my reservations about using the magic, I didn't have much choice at the moment. I'd really thought we had things tied up and that Erskine was our guy. Instead, we'd gotten set up to take the fall for his death. Now, I needed a way forward before this case got me into even deeper trouble. The magic would make things clearer, and perhaps show me something I'd missed. I took deep, slow breaths and lost myself in it as I pondered everything that had recently happened.

Whoever our real necromancer was, it was someone who not

only knew that I was investigating the case, but that I'd been looking into Erskine. In fact, I could see how they'd been pointing us toward him all along and leading us into a trap. Sure, Erskine had been involved with the case from the beginning, but I'd bet my best longsword that he'd been working for the necromancer, covering up and hiding evidence. He must've become expendable, and at that point all Erskine's boss had needed to do was plant a few clues at the abandoned house and the detective's hidey hole, and then wait for us to connect the dots.

And as soon as the necromancer had known we'd found the spell book, they'd murdered Erskine at his house and waited for us to show up before calling the cops. If it had worked, they would've removed two pieces from the board in one fell swoop. *Boom.* Except they hadn't counted on us figuring a way out of that mess. Yet it was still going to slow us down, because now the cops would be watching my every move.

But something just wasn't clicking with this entire mess. For one, what did our mysterious necromancer gain from raising these ghouls? All they were doing was bringing attention to themselves. Then it occurred to me: maybe they weren't as practiced at necromancy as I'd assumed. What if the first few ghoul attacks had been experiments, and they had just been testing out their abilities? It'd explain why things had gone quiet, because if that were true then by now they'd have gained more control over their creations.

But no newbie could've cast that stasis spell—no way, no how.

Despite all the attention they'd brought to themselves, they were doing a hell of a job staying out of the limelight. Yet, the necromancer had to know that eventually it would catch up to them. I could only assume they expected to be found out at some point, and that they were working against the clock because of it.

But what was the endgame? What did one gain from raising an army of undead?

Army... an army of undead. *Bingo.* They weren't just randomly raising the dead for the hell of it, but instead gathering their forces and planning an attack. Against who or what, that was still anyone's guess. Regardless, if they were creating more ghouls and keeping them in stasis then they had to be hiding them somewhere. All I had to do was figure out where.

And there was still one loose end I hadn't tugged on. Elias. He'd been at the club the night of the attack, and somehow he was involved in all of this. I needed to track him down and find out what he knew. If he couldn't lead me to the necromancer, something told me that this city would be witnessing a massacre before long.

I just hoped I wouldn't be too late.

I caught up to Elias outside of CIRCE's offices, where he still worked despite the fact that I'd taken out the person funding his operation. After staking the place out, it appeared he was the only person left working for CIRCE. CIRCE stood for "Cryptid International Rescue CollectivE," and their official story was that they captured and relocated cryptids. However, a few weeks back I'd discovered that what they were actually doing was capturing those cryptids for a group that called themselves the Ananda Corporation.

Ananda had been financing them, and Crowley had somehow been tied up with them as well. CIRCE captured the creatures, Elias had delivered them to Crowley's place, and then Crowley had tortured and interrogated them to get intel on magical artifacts—one of which had been Balor's Eye. Crowley had intended to use it to kill me, but the Eye had other plans. And while Crowley had disappeared, Elias had stuck around. That meant he was probably still pulling a paycheck from Ananda. I wanted to know why.

I jumped him as he was walking out the back door, shoving him up against a van with my forearm against his throat. Yeah, I didn't like bracing people, because it just wasn't my style. But Elias responded really well to threats, and I didn't have time to follow him around for days until I figured out how he was involved in this mess. I'd gladly play the heavy if that's what it took to find and stop this necromancer.

"Hello, Elias," I said as calmly and casually as possible. His eyes first widened in shock, then narrowed into slits. He was doing his best to act unfazed.

This was going to be harder than I'd thought.

"What do you want, McCool? You already screwed up the best gig I ever had, so why don't you just leave me alone and I'll agree to do the same for you."

"See, that's the problem, Elias—you haven't been leaving me alone. The other night a buddy of mine gets picked up and questioned on suspicion of murder, and guess who was hanging around before he got arrested?"

His eyes tightened as he spoke. "Look, man, I wasn't anywhere near that club that night."

"Did I say anything about a club? You're a horrible liar, Elias. Now, I suggest you quit covering up for your bosses, and tell me what I need to know before I become impatient. Crowley found out what happens when I get impatient—I'm sure you don't want to find out as well."

"That was you? I asked what happened to him, and no one would tell me anything." His shoulders sagged, and the tension left his face as his chin dropped against my arm. "Fine, I'll tell you what I know."

I followed him inside CIRCE's offices and into the ready room, where they'd staged their capture missions. Most of the equipment was gone, and besides Elias' desk, the place was empty.

"Love what you've done with the place."

He snorted. "After you shut Crowley down, the bills stopped getting paid. I've had to sell most everything off, and I have to be out of the building at the end of the month."

"I'm finding it hard to drum up any sympathy for you right now. Why don't you spare me the sob story and skip to the part where you tell me what I need to know?"

He flopped down behind his desk and rubbed the stubble that covered his face. The guy looked like hell. Good.

"If it means getting you out of my life, I'll tell you what I know. Someone from Ananda called me a few days ago, saying they had another job for me. They wanted me to go to this bar and watch for anything unusual. I asked for further details, but that's all they wanted me to do—just watch and report what I saw."

"And what did you see?"

"Nothing, that's just the thing. Absolutely nothing. I was supposed to meet someone in the alley behind the bar to give them my report, but they never showed. I got tired of waiting, and I left."

I had to laugh. "Elias, were you aware that someone was killed in that alley later that night?"

"What do you mean, killed? Like murdered killed?"

"By a ghoul. Sounds like your bosses wanted to get rid of you, only you didn't follow orders. If you'd have stuck around a few minutes later we wouldn't be having this conversation right now."

He sagged into his chair. "Shit."

"Yeah, it must suck being you. Anything else I should know?"

He looked like he was about to have a meltdown. "Damn it, I never asked to get caught up with these people. I was fine before they approached me. Sure, I didn't have any money, but at least no one was trying to kill me."

"Focus, Elias. If you can help me take these people out, maybe it'll save your skin."

He leaned his elbows on the desk and placed his head in his hands. "Well, they're probably going to kill me anyway, so what the hell. They're after someone by the name of Maeve, that's all I know. Some sort of corporate takeover or something. I heard Crowley talking about it over the phone with someone once. And from the sound of it, they really hate her guts."

I nodded. "Any idea how they intend to do it?"

He shrugged. "That's all I know. Now, if you'll excuse me, I think I'm going to disappear for a while. A long while, in fact."

"Probably a good idea. I hear Siberia's nice this time of year."

He groaned and banged his head on the desk as I walked out. Somehow, I still couldn't bring myself to feel sorry for the guy—but I couldn't bring myself to hate him, either. Maybe he'd get away before Ananda caught up to him, and maybe he wouldn't. Right now, I had bigger fish to fry. Starting with finding out what Maeve knew about Ananda Corp.

16

I didn't trust Siobhan with the information I'd gleaned, however thin it was. For all I knew, she was in on it, and I didn't want to tip her off. It was best that I told Maeve in private, so I headed to her place. Unfortunately, Siobhan headed me off at her front door.

"Sorry, druid, but Maeve is currently indisposed. Come back to beg some other time."

She began to shut the door in my face, so I stuck my foot in the doorframe. She slammed the door with surprising force, and despite the combat boots I was wearing it hurt like hell.

"Wait! I have information for Maeve on the necromancer."

She stared at me through the space my foot had made, her face unreadable. "I can convey the information to her—what have you learned thus far?"

I shook my head. "Maeve's ears only. I don't work for you, Siobhan."

She cocked her head. "Then we have nothing more to discuss. Good day." She tilted her chin and a chill wind blew from inside the house, staggering me and knocking me off the front porch. The door slammed shut, and I was left wondering just what kind of fae Siobhan was.

This close to a gate to the Underrealms, it was no surprise that she'd have access to magic that she might not normally possess. However, I'd never witnessed her using any magic at all, besides perhaps a smattering of glamour to cover whatever alien features she possessed. The bit of power she'd just shown intrigued me, but I didn't have time to fuss about it. I still had to find this necromancer creep and shut him down.

But was it a him? For all I knew, it might've been Siobhan. It would take a huge set of balls, to be doing necromancy while living right under Maeve's nose. No, it had to be someone else.

After leaving Maeve's, I stopped by Luther's to get some caffeine in me and to update him on the situation. A barista took my order, and when I asked for Luther he told me to wait. The barista made a phone call, then motioned me to the counter.

"Luther says to come up the back way—he's upstairs." I nodded and did as requested, and Luther greeted me at the upstairs door to his apartment.

The place was much as it had been when I'd seen him there last, except Luther had company. At least a half-dozen vamps lounged around his place, drinking bloody cocktails while Billie Holliday played softly in the background. It was the middle of the day, which meant they all had to be at least a century old. Luther's personal guard, was my guess.

"Billie Holiday, Luther? Really? Next thing I know, you'll be decorating your apartment in Marilyn Monroe photos and carrying a small dog around in a handbag."

He frowned at me for a moment, then laughed. "Oh hush. You forget that I've been around for quite a while. This music reminds me of brighter times."

"You know I'm just messing with you. Anyway, I figured you'd want an update on the case."

He tsked at me. "Mmm, yes. I hear you've been quite the little jailbird lately. But no worries, I'll handle all your legal fees. Mr. Borovitz and I are old acquaintances."

"He mentioned as much, without giving specifics. Look, is there somewhere more private we can speak?"

Suddenly all conversation in the room stopped, and a half-dozen pair of vampire eyes locked in on me all at once. I slowly scanned the room, feeling like a canary perched on a low ledge in a room full of hungry cats.

Luther snapped his fingers, and they all went back to chatting amiably with each other, as if nothing had happened.

"Don't mind them. They're just a bit protective of me right now."

"Meh, I don't blame them. But I'd still rather speak in private."

"Come this way, then." I followed him down a hall and into a nicely furnished study. The room was bright, airy, and offered a wonderful view of the street below. I began to speak, but Luther held up a finger as he shut the door. He flicked a switch on a small electronic device, and the room filled with white noise.

I pointed at the sunlight streaming in through the window.

"UV blocking glass. Same stuff they use in museums. I'm old enough that the small amount that seeps through doesn't affect me."

He sat in a lovely white chair upholstered in violet fabric, and gestured that I should sit as well. "The room is sound-proofed, and the machine screws up vampire hearing. Anything we say will be between us."

"Good to know. Alright, here's the situation. I have no idea who this necromancer is, my prime suspect got killed last night, and right now every other lead I've followed has been a dead end. However, I have a reasonable suspicion that the necromancer we've been looking for is planning some sort of attack against Maeve."

"Have you told her?"

"No. I tried, but I got blocked by her gatekeeper."

He interlaced his fingers in his lap. "Ah, the *leannán sídhe*. Yes, I'm familiar with her. You should watch yourself around that one, my boy."

Leannán sídhe meant "fairy lover," but they were anything but. That kind were a sort of psychic vampire, similar to succubi. Their magic caused humans to fall madly and deeply in love with them, at which point the leannán sídhe would drain their life energies bit by bit, until their lover withered away and died of seemingly natural causes. In some cases, they'd even abandon their lovers out of spite, just to see them die of grief and loneliness.

All in all, they were a nasty sort of fae. Suddenly, Siobhan made more sense to me. That still didn't explain the magic she'd used, though. Unless she was older than she looked. Old fae studied magic like Feynman studied physics. The older they got, the more powerful they became.

"Yeah, I kind of figured out on my own that she was bad news, but thanks for the heads up. Siobhan always hovers just on the edge of anything that might work against Maeve's interests. Makes me wonder if she's not involved with this mess somehow, orchestrating events behind the scenes."

Luther tapped his index fingers together. "It's possible. The fae are nothing if not power hungry, and it wouldn't surprise me if the younger bitch was nipping at the heels of her elder. But not to worry—I have ways of getting information to Maeve that circumvent her granddaughter. I'll be sure she knows what you've discovered."

"Thanks, Luther. Other than that, there's not much to tell."

He stared at me a moment and his eyes softened. It was the

most human I'd seen him behave since this whole thing had begun.

"Just be careful out there, Colin. Whoever this person is, if they have a vendetta against Maeve it may include you as well. You've become a pawn of sorts in that old faery queen's schemes, and that puts you in the path of some very unkind and powerful individuals."

"Coming from you, Luther, I'll take that as a dire warning."

"Well, a predator knows how to recognize others of its kind. But where vampires and the fae differ is that we vampires remember what it was like to be human. And some of us are still sentimental in that regard. The fae hold no such feeble ties to humanity, because they've never been human at all."

"I'll be sure to watch my back."

He nodded. "You do that."

Luther walked me out of the room and to his front door.

"I'll keep you informed of any developments in the case. And thanks again for taking care of my tab with Borovitz."

"Pish posh, think nothing of it." I turned to go, but halted as he spoke again. "Oh, and Colin?"

"Yes?"

"It's about time you got laid. Happiness looks good on you, kid." His mouth held a barely suppressed grin as he shut the door.

I leaned against the wall and looked up at the ceiling, cracking a smile. "Feels pretty good, too," I muttered, pushing off the wall and heading to the cafe below.

I was downstairs and ordering a coffee to go when my phone rang. I didn't recognize the number, but it was local so I answered it.

"Colin? Colin McCool?" the voice on the other end asked as I picked up.

"Yup, the one and only."

"It's Brandon. We met earlier, at the morgue. I work for Maeve."

"Ah, Mr. Wolf."

His voice took on a tone of disdain. "I'm fae, not pack, as anyone with any sense could plainly tell. Seriously, I don't understand what Maeve sees in you."

"I wasn't implying—it's a reference to this movie—oh, never mind. What can I do for you, Brandon?"

"Well, at least you remembered my name for two seconds. Maeve wanted me to inform you, one of her people got a tip on a ghoul sighting at a distillery downtown." He rattled off an address. "I suggest you get over there quick, before the cops show—and don't expect me to clean up your mess if you screw this up. I only handle morgue-related incidents, you know."

Brandon hung up on me before I could reply.

"Freaking fae," I muttered as I paid for my coffee, tipping the barista two bucks even though he probably made a lot more than I did. Despite Brandon's snotty attitude, the lead he'd provided had lifted my spirits so I was feeling generous. And besides, I figured after Luther paid me for this job I'd be flush, for once. I sipped my coffee and speed-dialed Belladonna, burning my tongue as I did.

"Son of a bitch!" I swore, with Belladonna answering on the last syllable.

"I was wondering when you'd call. But if that's your idea of an apology for the two-day wait, you've seriously got to work on your game."

"No, not you—shit, sorry, Bells. Both for the unintended insult, and for not calling you sooner."

Her husky laugh was music to my ears. "I suppose you had a

good excuse, what with coming to my rescue and all. Such the white knight you are, sacrificing yourself like that. I should kick your ass for it, but it was so sweet of you that I'm giving you a pass. Next time, though, make sure you consult me before you martyr yourself on my behalf."

"Um, you're welcome?"

"I'll thank you later. Now, what's up?"

I shook my head in confusion, because I realized I had no idea how to interact with Bells now that we'd slept together. Moreover, she'd managed to express anger, disappointment, gratitude, and sexual attraction, all in the span of a thirty second conversation. Suddenly, I realized I might be getting a lot more than I'd bargained for by taking our relationship beyond the friend zone.

When in doubt, always deflect. That was the safe bet. I decided to play it cool by steering the conversation toward work, since that's why I'd called in the first place.

"I got a lead on our bad guy—or bad girl, depending on your preferred gender pronoun."

"Is that the only reason you called, because you got a lead on the case?"

"Er—no?" I answered in the form of a question, because I thought she'd told me I was off the hook for not calling earlier.

She huffed into the phone, voice frustrated. "Just tell me where to meet you and when, and I'll be there."

Yeah, I was totally screwed. "Say, fifteen minutes at the distillery on 4th Street?"

Her voice was flat as she answered. "Not a problem. Meet you there in ten." And she hung up.

The guy behind the counter shook his head as he acknowledged my plight. "Doghouse, huh? That's what happens when you sweat them too long. My sympathies, bro."

Apparently he'd been listening in on my conversation; he probably fell in the "other-than-human" category.

"Yeah. Guess I'll be stopping by the gun store later."

He looked at me like I was insane. "Dude, that's harsh."

"Oh—no. I meant to buy something nice, to make it up to her. She likes guns, and knives, and stuff like that."

He smiled and nodded. "She's a kinky one, eh?"

"You have no idea."

Belladonna was waiting for me when I pulled up in the alley behind the distillery. That told me she'd been speeding the whole way over, which boded ill for me. *Best to just get this over with*, I thought as I locked my helmet to the scooter.

As I turned around, I was surprised to find that she'd snuck up behind me. Bells was right in my face, staring at me with an inscrutable expression. I froze, unsure of what was coming, and what—if anything—I might do to influence the outcome. Finally, she grabbed me by my coat and kissed me full on the mouth. It took a moment, but I reacted in kind after I realized she meant it.

"Don't ever do that again, alright?" she breathed as she released me. She made a show of straightening the collars on my jacket, brushing away imaginary lint from my chest.

"I promise. The next time I go to jail it won't be on your behalf."

Her mouth twisted into a wry grin, but she was working hard at being stern. "I'm serious, Colin. If you ended up doing jail time to save my hide, how do you think that'd make me feel?"

"I appreciate your concern, Bells, but it worked out alright. Next time, I'll do as you say and let you take the fall."

She scowled unconvincingly. "Smart ass."

"Guilty as charged."

"You're lucky you're a good-looking guy with a nice ass. Now, what's the scoop here? Are we certain that our bad guy's inside?"

"All I know is that Maeve's guy from the morgue called and said they got a tip our perp was here. I don't think he likes me much, so he was a little vague on the details."

"Well, I guess we'll just have to play it by ear."

At that moment, a scream came from inside.

"There's our cue." I pulled out my war club. "You want to take point?"

"Naw, you'll need some room to swing that bad boy. I'll cover you."

"Alright," I replied. "Watch yourself."

I opened the back door to the distillery and headed inside, hoping like hell our necromancer was waiting for us.

17

Inside, the place had been trashed. There were smashed bottles of vodka and tequila everywhere, and drops of blood here and there as well. The fumes were overpowering.

"What a waste," Bells muttered under her breath, taking in the broken bottles and spilled liquor.

We heard another, more urgent scream. I quickened my pace as we cleared the warehouse area, entering an adjacent room with high ceilings and tall, stainless-steel vats. One of them sported a body-shaped dent, blood smeared in the depression. That vat had leaked a sizable amount of raw, unmixed liquor, and the fumes were nearly unbearable. We hurried through the room, holding our breath as we passed the alcohol spill.

"Things aren't looking good for whoever the ghoul found in here," I remarked. Thus far we hadn't seen any bodies. I knew it was unlikely, but I was holding out hope the victim had escaped.

We turned down a hall that led to what I assumed would be the front entrance of the building, only to find a large steel door chained shut. I heard a door slam behind us, and realized what was happening.

"They're locking us in. Run!" I bolted for the back entrance, only to find it secured in like manner, with a heavy tow chain and an industrial case-hardened lock barring our exit.

I looked around frantically for another exit and spotted a few high windows to our left. One stood out in the far corner of the warehouse, where a large figure balanced on the ledge. It held a lit Molotov cocktail, tossing it in a high arc in our direction.

I tackled Belladonna out of the way. The bottle shattered behind us, spreading liquid fire everywhere. I looked up, but the figure had fled out the window. I was sure it was the super-ghoul I'd tangled with at the morgue, likely being controlled directly by the necromancer from somewhere close by.

I rolled off Belladonna and pulled her to her feet. "Sorry, but there was no time to warn you."

She gave me a look that said apologies were unnecessary. "Save it for later—we need to get out of here before the fire hits that mess next door."

The flames had spread quickly. The place was basically a brick box filled with flammable liquids. In every direction, crates, boxes, and furniture went up in flames. Thankfully, the high ceiling meant we were in no immediate danger of smoke inhalation, but Belladonna was right; we had little time to spare before bad things started to happen.

A puddle of liquor had seeped under the swinging metal doors that led to the distilling area. In moments, it would catch fire and we'd be toast.

Belladonna's eyes scanned the area frantically. "Druid boy, you'd better have a plan to get us out of here, because I'm all out of options at the moment!"

The fire cut off any other route of escape, and there was no other exit in sight. I could have picked the lock on the door with a cantrip, but we were cut off from those doors now as well. Even the high windows where the ghoul had escaped were out of reach. If I boosted Belladonna up on my hands cheerleader style, she still wouldn't make it.

As the heat became unbearable, flames licking at us from every direction, I spotted an opening.

"This way!" I shouted, grabbing Belladonna by the arm to pull her along with me, ducking around flaming boxes and debris as I ran into a hall along the rear wall.

Bells looked at me skeptically. "You can't use a spell or a grenade. The blast would kill us both."

I shook my head. "I don't need to—step back and give me some room."

"I swear, if you blow me up, I'm kicking your ass."

I ignored her nervous attempt at false bravado, and placed my fingers on the wall. I reached out with my senses to feel the brick and mortar, much as I used my magic to sense what was wrong with vehicles back at the junkyard.

There.

I reared back with my war club, swinging with all my might at the weakness I'd sensed in the wall. As the club struck, a shock wave emanated from the point of impact, paired with an ear-shattering thunder-clap. The wall practically exploded outward, leaving a jagged hole approximately five feet in diameter.

My ears were ringing and I felt like I'd been standing next to a flash bang grenade as it went off—dazed and confused. Belladonna's lips were moving but I couldn't hear what she said. She was pointing behind her and then at the hole in the wall. Finally, she threw her hands up in the air in frustration. She pushed me hard with both hands, right through the hole I'd just made.

At that exact moment, the distillery went up in a ball of flames. I went airborne as the pressure wave threw me backwards across the alley. As if in slow motion, I watched as Bells spun in rag-doll fashion through the jagged opening behind me. I impacted something solid and unyielding as I landed, and everything went black.

———

I came to, groggy and with my ears still ringing. Bells was leaning on a garbage dumpster holding her side, but she appeared to be in one piece. I stumbled to my feet and staggered to her.

"Are you okay?" I asked in what I imagined was a shout.

She nodded. "Just a little banged up." I could hear her, but her voice sounded muffled. I started to fuss over her, but she shook her head. "No time for that—we need to figure out where that damned ghoul went. It'll lead us to its master, and I intend to tear that asshole apart with my bare hands."

I nodded and relented. "Give me a moment." I dug around in my bag and found a couple bottles of water, handing her one and chugging the other. Our clothing was slightly charred and we were both bruised up, but a quick check told me I still had all four limbs and most of my IQ. I'd have a heck of a lump on my head soon, and I'd be sore as hell—but I was otherwise mostly undamaged.

Collecting myself, I cast a cantrip and began sniffing around the alley. Ghouls smelled hellaciously bad, almost as bad as trolls. I knew if I could catch its scent, it'd give us a direction in which to track it. I caught a whiff of decay and rot at the west end of the alley, and signaled Bells with a whistle and a wave. Reluctantly, she pushed off the dumpster and followed me.

Bells and I tracked the ghoul on foot for a few blocks, until the trail took us down an alley behind a row of bars and restaurants. I didn't hear any shouts or cries for help, and I didn't see any broken windows in any of the buildings either. We moved on, following the scent and keeping an eye out in case of an ambush. The whine of sirens made me stop and look behind us. Smoke filled the sky as it poured from the distillery, and the sounds of emergency vehicles approaching told me we'd best keep moving.

Halfway down the alley, I found the first sign of something amiss. The strong scent of decay had led me to the remains of a cat behind a dumpster. The undead would eat anything that moved—if an unsuspecting cat were to get close enough, a zombie or ghoul would definitely have them for a snack.

I checked the cat's body to make certain it hadn't been the victim of coyotes or stray dogs, and found human teeth marks on the corpse. From the looks of it, the animal's neck had been cleanly broken, so at least it hadn't suffered. Definitely a ghoul. The kill was old, maybe a day or so. That told me the ghoul had come this way before. We were just a few blocks from Hemi's work, and I wondered if it had been hiding under our noses all along.

The farther we went, the stronger the smell of decomposing flesh became. The trail was easier to follow now, and we tracked the creature through the warehouse district and down into a construction zone. Along the way we found other animal corpses in various states of decay, most tucked under trash piles, or hidden in unobtrusive locations. We followed the trail for several hundred feet until it ended at a jagged sewer pipe jutting from an excavation site.

The pipe itself was narrow, a little more than two feet in diameter. Foul-smelling water dripped from the opening. There were signs that the creature had come this way, including foot-prints in the mud beneath. I debated going into the pipe or trying to track the creature above ground. Past experience told me that was going to be difficult, since drainage tunnels could lead anywhere in these older areas of the city.

"Looks like it's time to get dirty," I said.

Bells merely nodded stiffly.

"Are you sure you're alright?"

"I'll be fine. Let's just focus on catching this thing." She held her arm to her side, a sure sign of guarding an injury. I figured she might have busted or bruised some ribs, but I didn't want to push it. Bells was nothing if not proud.

I nodded once and crawled inside the pipe, using my phone to light the way. Chances were good this tunnel would end in a rainwater collection chamber at some point. That would give us little space to maneuver should we run into the ghoul. I wasn't concerned, since I had switched out my war club for the Glock a few blocks back. If we were lucky, we'd catch the thing off guard and I'd put a bullet in its head before it ever got wind of us.

I followed the tunnel about fifty feet before seeing the faint glow of daylight ahead. I turned off my phone to avoid giving us away and continued to low-crawl through the tunnel, which ended where it connected with one of the rainwater collection chambers that were common under Austin's downtown city streets. Faint light streamed in from a curbside drain above, revealing an empty chamber. Tracks in the mud below indicated the ghoul had headed south just a few minutes before.

I crawled out of the drainage pipe and used my phone to illuminate the space, crossing the chamber as I followed the ghoul's trail. It led me to a bare and unbroken concrete wall on the other side of the small chamber. The tracks dead-ended at the wall.

"What the hell?" I muttered aloud as I looked at the concrete in front of me. I reached out to touch it, and my hand passed right through.

"That's one hell of an illusion," I muttered. The last time I'd seen something this convincing had been when I'd tangled with the Avartagh on my first case. The Avartagh was a vampiric dwarf and a seriously powerful magician, and I'd only survived that encounter because he'd underestimated me. I hated to think I might be tangling with something that was equally as deadly, and without the advantage of being underestimated.

I waited for Bells to join me, then stuck my head through the illusion to see what was on the other side. I was looking through an irregular hole in the wall, one that had been made recently. It was pitch black on the other side. I shone the light from the phone's display into the dark beyond, illuminating a winding passage that had been dug from both earth and bedrock.

I pulled my head out and looked at Bells. She shrugged and nodded at the hole.

"After you, loverboy."

I chuckled and ducked through.

As Bells and I passed deeper into the tunnel beyond, we smelled the stench of rotting flesh. The farther we went, the stronger the smell became, so we knew we were on the right track. Besides that, there were fresh tracks in the muddy floor of the tunnel that matched those I'd seen in the chamber outside.

What worried me was that the trail we followed was accompanied by dozens of older tracks, indicating that some serious traffic had gone through here. Either this was some sort of thoroughfare being used by the ghouls, or there were a few dozen of those things hiding somewhere underground with us. I decided not to think about it and pressed on.

Within minutes, the tunnel opened into a large underground chamber, so large that the light from my phone was too dim to illuminate the entire thing. I tried to adjust the screen brightness to compensate, only to hear Bells sigh behind me.

"Don't you have some sort of magelight spell you can cast or something? Or a crystal staff you can puff on, like a magic flashlight?"

I snapped my fingers. "Flashlight! Hang on a minute." I rustled around in my Craneskin bag until I found what I was looking for.

"Ta-da!" I said as I clicked a tactical flashlight on. The space was suddenly lit by 300 lumens of LED light. What all that light revealed had us shitting our pants. The chamber had to be 150 feet across or more, a natural underground cavern carved from the limestone bedrock by tens of thousands of years of water erosion.

And across that vast underground expanse, hundreds of ghouls stood in a magical stasis, awaiting some trigger or command to snap them out of their current state.

"Ruh-oh, Raggy," I whispered under my breath.

"You have to be shitting me," Belladonna responded.

As if in answer to our exclamations of disbelief, a voice sounded from across the chamber. It was deep and sonorous, and altogether unsettling, with an ethereal quality that said it had either been magically enhanced, or magically disguised.

"Oh, believe it, children. I've been planning this a long, long time."

"Bells, I think we found our necromancer."

She deadpanned her response. "Really, Captain Obvious? What gave it away?"

I shone the flashlight beam around the room, searching for where the voice had originated. There were no shadowy figures lurking in the dark, no tall dark silhouettes staring at us from a balcony above. That's when I realized the freak was hiding in plain sight, somewhere among the sea of dead flesh in front of us.

"What I wouldn't do right now for a FLIR camera," Bells muttered.

I whispered under my breath to her. "Bells, we have to get out of here, like now. One word from this asshole, and we're going to be overrun by undead."

"But he's right there in front of us!"

I wasn't so sure it was a "he," but now wasn't the time to discuss gender assumptions. "She may as well be on the other side of the planet right now, because there's no way we can get to her."

She sighed heavily and nodded. "Points for assuming it's a she." She pursed her lips and frowned. "Run like hell?"

"Run like hell." And that's what we did, just as a palpable wave of power burst forth and a stampede of dead bodies came rushing across the space in a tidal wave of death and decay. We sprang from the chamber and back into the tunnel, with me lighting the way and Bells hot on my heels.

"Colin, what are we going to do when we get to the pipe?" she asked me with labored gasps that were altogether uncharacteristic. I glanced over my shoulder, catching a look of agony on her face that she quickly tried to hide. Even in the dim light reflected from the walls of the tunnel, I could see that her face was drawn and pale. She held one arm to her side, bracing an injury that was obviously far worse than she'd let on.

I dug around in my bag frantically as I ran, checking every so often to make certain I didn't leave her behind. She began to lag, so I slowed my pace and draped her arm over my shoulder, reaching around her waist to support her. I felt something wet, hot, and sticky under my hand. She winced away from my touch.

Blood. Bells was bleeding, and badly. And I'd missed it in my eagerness to catch the necromancer.

Despite my assistance, soon our progress slowed to a crawl. I helped as she propped herself against the wall, drawing a pistol and sighting down the corridor behind us.

"Set the flashlight on the floor, and point it that way so I can see," she gasped.

I did as she asked, all the while searching my bag for one of the spells I'd prepared. Finally I located it, and pulled it out to show her, holding it up like the Lady of the Lake wielding Excalibur.

Bells glowered at me. "An M80? You're going to save our asses with a firecracker? McCool, you'd better have a better trick than that up your sleeve."

"Don't worry, I've got this." I spoke a few words, casting a cantrip that lit the fuse to the firework, and tossed it down the tunnel as far away from us as possible. It landed just beyond the beam of light cast by the flashlight on the ground.

I moved over to shield Belladonna with my body. It occurred to me that overpressure would be a problem in these tight confines. "Close your eyes and open your mouth," I warned, and she did as I asked.

I closed my eyes, and then spoke a word in Gaelic to trigger the spell. The magically enhanced firecracker went off like three sticks of dynamite, collapsing the tunnel behind us. I continued to shield Bells for a few seconds after the blast, peppered by dirt and debris, but thankfully by nothing larger than a dime or harder than mud.

"Are you okay?" I asked loudly, wiping dust from my eyes and face. Receiving no response, I opened my eyes and blinked several times, just as Bells slumped into my arms.

18

I gently slid Bells to the ground, then stuck the flashlight in my mouth so I could see while I assessed her injuries. Her pulse was thready and her breathing steady but shallow. A rapid head to toe assessment revealed a puncture wound in her side leaking blood, with quite a bit of swelling in her abdomen.

The puncture wound was bad enough, but what really had me worried was all the swelling. That could indicate internal injuries, possibly life-threatening. Part of my druid training included first aid; I was a shitty healer and awful at healing magic, but I knew a bad injury when I saw one.

I pulled the flashlight out of my mouth and placed it so the light would reflect off the tunnel wall.

"Hang in there, Bells—I'm going to get you out of here." But first, I had to tend to that puncture wound. I pulled a first aid kit out of my bag and applied a pressure dressing to control the bleeding. Then I grabbed the flashlight and picked her up in my arms, heading for the exit to the storm drain where we'd come in.

As I half-walked and half-jogged to the exit, I noticed several things. For one, Bells felt light and insubstantial in my arms.

Whether that was just my own fears playing tricks on me, or whether I'd never really noticed how small she was compared to me, I didn't know. Bells was anything but frail, but right then I may as well have been carrying a box of pillows. Maybe it was the adrenaline, but it just felt wrong to me.

I quickened my pace as I rounded the last curve to the exit. But instead of a hole in the wall, I ran into a dead end made up of solid limestone rock.

I wondered, had I made a wrong turn somewhere? Impossible. The tunnel had been one long, singular path, and I'd noted no side tunnels or branches on the way in or out. I gently set Bells down and probed the wall ahead, hoping it was just the illusory magic playing tricks on me.

But it wasn't. The rock wall ahead felt as solid and real as my own body, and it was much more substantial. I retraced my steps, making certain I wasn't missing anything. But the trail back to the cave-in lacked any side tunnels, and the hundreds of tracks in the muddy floor below my feet said that I hadn't lost my mind. This was exactly the way we'd come in earlier.

I took a moment to kneel beside Bells and checked her pulse. She was eerily still, and the fact I could barely detect her breathing was unsettling. Her pulse grew weaker and I started to panic. I jumped up and reached into my bag for my war club; if there wasn't a way out, I'd make one for us.

Practically charging at the wall, I swung at it with all my might, right above the place where the footprints trailed to an end. I figured that was where the opening had been before it had been spelled shut. But instead of making a solid hit on the limestone wall, my club struck a magical barrier. As it connected, silver light flashed in front of me, both bright and cold at the same time. The backlash from the two magics hit me and threw me a good ten feet, where I landed on my rump and skidded across the damp muddy floor.

I popped my neck and stood. Then I walked back to the wall to examine it in the magical spectrum, which was what I should have done in the first place. What I saw shocked and worried me. The weaves that made up the spell on the wall were both complex and powerful, many degrees beyond anything I could conjure up. The last time I'd seen weaves like these I was in Maeve's treasure room, examining the spells and wards that had guarded the Eye. I couldn't break those bindings even if I had years to do so.

There was no way in hell I was getting through that spell.

As they said in the epics, this boded ill for my companion and me. As far as I knew, this was our only way out of the tunnel. I'd caved in our other exit, and even if we could get out that way there were hundreds of ghouls to fight through, plus the magician who'd cast the spell that now sealed us in. I suspected they'd triggered it soon after we'd entered the cave, which would have funneled us toward them even if we'd decided to turn back and get help.

Why did I suddenly get the feeling this necromancer was no ordinary wizard? And why did I also feel that he or she had been toying with me all along?

The way things had gone, it looked as though someone had been trying to move me off the playing field this whole time. And stupidly, I'd gotten Bells involved and put her squarely in my enemy's crosshairs.

The realization that this person was my enemy was staggering, and I chided myself for not seeing it sooner. While I'd stumbled across this stupid case while working for Maeve and Luther, it was now apparent that events had been manipulated specifically to get me involved.

I moved over to Bells and placed several large stones under her legs, placing her in a recovery position that would hopefully keep her blood pressure up until I could figure out what to do.

Then I checked my phone for a signal, thinking I might call for help. No signal. Things were looking bleak, and I was running out of options.

And so was Bells.

I looked at her and hung my head in shame. What a fool I'd been, and now a person I cared for deeply was injured and possibly dying before me. I was helpless to intervene in any meaningful way.

I sat next to her and placed her head in my lap, brushing her hair away from her face. Then, I wept silently as I wracked my brain for a way out of this mess.

I only allowed myself a few minutes of self-pity before I got up and checked the walls of the cavern inch by inch, looking for an alternate escape route. First I looked for cracks or other signs of weakness, both with my mundane sight and in the magical spectrum. Finding nothing, I used the handle of my war club to tap on the walls, thinking I could get lucky and find a spot where I might break through—one that wasn't warded and spelled against my efforts.

I worked my way around the space, from the magical barrier and down one wall of the tunnel, around to the cave-in and up the other side. I only lingered at the cave-in for a moment, both out of fear of getting trapped by falling rocks, and because I could hear debris being moved on the other side. Apparently the ghouls hadn't given up on us. Whether that was at the direction of their master or due to their inherent single-mindedness, I didn't care to speculate. All I knew was that I needed to get us out of here, and fast, before they moved enough stone and dirt to reach us.

My tapping and probing revealed nothing, and as I reached

the barrier once more I growled in frustration, slamming the war club flat against the wall. I rested my head against the cool limestone, leaning in as I looked to my left where Belladonna rested. I didn't need to take her vitals to know her condition wasn't improving. I took a deep breath and ran through my options again, desperate to find something I may have missed.

That's when I heard digging noises on the other side of the limestone wall. I pressed my ear against the rock, at once hoping I was mistaken and praying I wasn't hearing things. While I feared that it could be more ghouls trying to get at us from an adjacent tunnel, I hoped that it might be someone coming to rescue us. It was a thin hope, but one I clung to as I the noises grew louder.

Soon the digging and scraping sounds seemed just inches away from my ear. I backed away from the wall and hoisted my club, ready to bash anything that came through the wall should it not be friendly.

The clinking sounds of metal on stone grew in rhythm and intensity as I waited. Five minutes stretched into ten, and then chunks flew from a spot in the wall roughly four feet off the tunnel floor. A dark hole appeared in the wall, and the sharp end of a metal implement widened it as I shielded my eyes and face from the shrapnel.

The digging stopped, and I held my breath as an eyeball came into view, framed by the jagged hole in the limestone that had been made just moments before. It was no human eye, but one that was yellowed and bloodshot, set in lumpy gray-green flesh. A bulbous green nose soon replaced the eye, and it sniffed a few times and withdrew.

Raucous laughter and cheers erupted from the other side of the hole. A thin pair of rubbery lips set in a wicked grin filled the gap again.

"Druid, I see you okay. Trolls get you out now, no need to pray."

I sighed with relief. "Guts, is that you?"

"Hah!" he exclaimed. "Told them druid remember mighty Guts! And trolls all say Guts is nuts."

"Guts, not only do I remember you, but you might just be my favorite troll right now."

The eye jumped back into view. His words were muffled but clear enough for me to hear. "Then you tell other trolls, once you out of that hole. Guts be hero who saved Druid of Junk— who'd a thunk? Now move so can prove."

Despite the horrendous rhyming, I really was glad to see Guts. Within minutes he had made a hole large enough for us to pull Bells to safety. As it turned out, one of the troll patrols had come across the ghoul's trail and followed it. They'd called Guts in to check it out, and he'd somehow determined that we had been trapped. I didn't quite get the details of how that happened, something about unique scents was all I got. Besides, I was too concerned with getting Bells to the hospital to pay much attention.

It was well after dark when we made it topside again. As soon as I had a signal, I dialed 9-1-1 and got an ambulance headed our way. Then I called the junkyard and had my uncle relay a message to Finn that he should meet us at the hospital ASAP. From the looks of it, Bells would be headed into emergency surgery—and I figured a little druidic healing magic might turn the tables in her favor. Better to hedge our bets than rely solely on modern medicine. After that I thanked the trolls, who remained hidden in the storm drain, just in case the ghouls broke through. Guts said it wasn't a problem, and that I could count on their help any time. Good to know.

Once the paramedics arrived, they quickly performed a field assessment and loaded Bells up for transport. They asked me how the injury happened, and I muttered something about urban spelunking. The crew was kind enough to avoid making any remarks about crawling around in sewers, and they asked no further questions. I was thankful for that, since I didn't want us connected to the explosion at the distillery. I rode in the back of the ambulance in silence, watching the medic calmly and efficiently start an I.V. line and adjust the flow rate while she monitored Belladonna's vitals.

I listened in as the medic called ahead to the hospital. "Brack ER, this is medic unit 5, we're inbound code three with a trauma activation. We have a 20-year-old female presenting with acute trauma to the abdomen, blunt force and penetrating. Pulse is 120 bpm, and patient shows signs of abdominal distention—"

I tuned out the rest of her report and focused on Bells instead. Her skin was ashen and she'd been unconscious since her collapse. As far as I could tell, she showed no signs of regaining consciousness. Yet, she looked peaceful, lying still as calm waters as she breathed through the oxygen mask.

"Is she going to be okay?" I asked, raising my voice to be heard over the sirens and road noise.

The medic glanced at me while she hooked up an automatic defibrillator to Belladonna's chest. The machine would automatically try to restart her heart if she "coded." I'd learned how to operate a more basic version during my CPR and first aid training.

The paramedic nodded and spoke over her shoulder as she checked the EKG monitor and continued her assessment.

"Her vitals are stable, and we're just minutes away from

Brack. They're a level one trauma center, so she'll get the best care possible."

The answer was noncommittal and professional, but it still made me feel better.

"You can talk to her, you know. You think she can't hear, but often patients who are unconscious later say they remember what was going on around them."

I glanced at the medic, and then at Bells. She looked so frail, and it frightened me. Bells was a rock—at least, that's how I viewed her. Tough as nails and unafraid, no matter what she faced. I realized that seeing her injured had shaken me to my core. I could ruminate on that later; right now I needed to comfort my friend.

"Bells, you're going to be fine. I'll be right here, right next to you the whole time. You're going to get the best care possible, the very best." I felt foolish talking to her like that, but the medic seemed to think I was doing fine.

"Keep talking to her. It helps more than you know."

I talked about places I wanted to take her, things I wanted to show her, and people I wanted her to meet. She'd never really spent much time around my mom, and I wanted to bring her to the house to eat dinner sometime. I promised to take her to my old stomping grounds in my hometown, and show her where I used to hang out, where Jesse and I had been trained.

Jesse. I choked on her name a bit. Was it happening all over again? Maybe I was cursed in more ways than one. First the tragedy with Jesse, then Sabine's kidnapping, and now Bells. It seemed that everyone I cared for fell under my curse.

I started hyperventilating a little. The paramedic must have noticed.

"Hey, it's okay. Just breathe. We're almost to the hospital, and the doctors and staff there are going to take good care of her."

Just then, one of the machines emitted an ear-piercing alarm.

"What's wrong?" I asked in a high-pitched voice. My eyes darted back and forth, from Bells to the machine to the paramedic.

The medic adjusted the I.V. flow as she looked from monitor to monitor, then she grabbed the radio and called into the ER. "Brack ER, this is medic unit 5 with an update. Patient's blood pressure and pulse are falling. Be advised, our ETA is under two minutes, over."

A tinny male voice came back over the radio. "Message received, Medic 5. Trauma team will be on standby, over."

The rest was just a blur, as machines began beeping and going off all over the place inside the vehicle. The paramedic took Bells' pulse manually—first at the wrist, then at her throat. She listened to her chest with her stethoscope, then began chest compressions. Bells had just flatlined, and my world came crashing down.

19

I stood just outside the trauma room at the ER as they worked frantically to resuscitate Belladonna. After ten minutes, they were still doing chest compressions. I worried that if they couldn't resuscitate her soon, the doctor would call it.

I said a silent prayer, foregoing the formality of closing my eyes. The fact was, I couldn't take my eyes off the terrible scene in front of me if I tried. It felt like the day I'd lost Jesse, all over again.

Just then, someone clapped a warm hand on my shoulder. Finn's voice brought me back to the present.

"How's it looking, son?"

I blinked and wiped my eyes. "They've been doing compressions for more than ten minutes, since before we arrived. She coded on the way over."

"I'll do what I can, then. Hopefully it'll be enough."

He fixed me with a sympathetic look and closed his eyes. I felt magic peeling off him in waves as he began chanting softly in a language I'd never heard him use before, one that pierced my soul with its beauty and cadence. His fingers wove complex patterns as he spoke, and he cast his magic without concern for reactions from passersby. Surely it would've looked quite strange to anyone who might have noticed, but I was beyond caring about what anyone thought at this point. All I wanted was for Bells to be okay.

I felt a burst of energy pass between Finnegas and Bells, then Finn staggered. I caught him by the arm and propped him up, snapping my eyes to Bells to gauge the results of his spellwork.

They'd stopped doing chest compressions. She was either dead, or her heart was beating on its own again. I looked at the cardiac monitor and saw a green blip dancing a steady rhythm across the screen.

I breathed a sigh of relief, but I could tell by the pace at which the trauma team was working that her condition was still dire. I heard something about prepping for surgery, and then in a blur of activity they were moving her out of the room and down the hall. I helped Finn to a nearby chair and ran after them.

"Where are you taking her?" I asked one of the staff members trailing the gurney.

She glanced at me as she hurried along, only acknowledging me briefly as she followed Bells down the hall. "Are you a family member?"

I paused as I realized I had no idea whether or not she even had any family. "No, I'm her—her boyfriend. As far as I know, I'm all she has."

Her eyes narrowed slightly, and she slowed her pace, allowing the rest of the team and the gurney to gain some distance on us.

"I'm not supposed to be telling you this, but considering the circumstances—"

"Please, I have to know," I begged.

"Alright. We're taking her to surgery, but it's going to be touch and go. If she has any family you should do your best to alert them ASAP. There's a waiting room outside the surgical suites on the first floor near the north entrance. You can wait there while she's in surgery and someone will update you on her progress. That's all I can tell you right now."

With that, the team reached the elevators, and that was apparently as far as I could go. A nurse stopped my halfhearted attempt to board the elevator with a gentle hand on my chest. I took one last look at Bells lying there on the gurney, so frail and mortal. Then I stepped back and allowed the doors to close.

The guilt of abandonment weighed heavily on me as I watched the lights above the elevator change. I took a deep breath and headed back to the ER to fetch Finn, so we could go to the waiting room and prepare ourselves for a long, sleepless night.

***

Hours later, a short, tired-looking woman in scrubs with a surgical mask around her neck entered the surgery waiting area. She looked around until she spotted us and walked over to where we were seated. I stood up, Finn didn't. Apparently that spell he'd cast had taken more out of him than he was willing to admit.

"Are you the family of Belladonna Becerra?" the woman asked.

"I'm her boyfriend, and this man is a friend of ours. We're the only family or friends present at the moment—I don't think she has anyone else."

Earlier I'd contacted the Circle and left a message asking for Gunnarson to call me back, but I still hadn't heard from him. Which was just as well, because I didn't think I could restrain myself if he decided to get a case of the ass with me. As far as I knew, the Circle and a few close friends were all the family Bells had. She'd never spoken about her parents, and when I'd asked about her family she'd always changed the subject. I'd stopped asking in order to respect her privacy.

"I'm Dr. Coltrane, and I'm the surgeon who performed Ms. Becerra's surgery." She glanced back and forth, from me to Finn. "Understand, it's against hospital policy and federal law for me to reveal any medical information about Ms. Becerra to you. However, I can tell you that she's stable, and that once she's out of recovery she'll be transferred to the ICU."

I closed my eyes and inhaled deeply, realizing that I'd been holding my breath. I opened them again and looked Dr. Coltrane in the eyes.

"Thank you, doctor. Can we see her?"

She shook her head gently, and I saw more than a little sympathy reflected there. "Not just yet. You should probably head home, get some rest, and then come back in the morning. There's another waiting room outside the ICU. When you get back, wait there and let the nurses know you're a friend of Ms. Becerra. If you're lucky, they might let you in to see her."

I nodded reluctantly. "I understand. Thank you, again."

"I wish I could tell you more. Go get some rest and come back in the morning. That's probably the best thing you can do for your friend right now."

Finn stood and placed a hand on my arm. "We will, doctor. Thank you for your time."

Dr. Coltrane nodded, and with a tight smile she headed back to the surgical suites. I looked at Finn and sat back down.

"I'm not going anywhere."

"I know." He sat down next to me, and we passed the next few minutes in silence.

Finally, he broke the quiet by clearing his throat. "It's not your fault, you know."

I chewed my lip as I considered his words. "You're going to

tell me it's the curse's fault, right? Or Fuamnach? Just like with Jesse, and Sabine."

Finn rested his chin on his chest and sighed. "It's really not, Colin. You know it as well as me. It's time you stopped living in guilt, taking the blame every time someone around you gets hurt."

I sniffed loudly and ran a hand across my face. "Finn, it's as much my fault as anyone's. Sure, with Jesse's death I wasn't really to blame, and I know that. But since then? I've been living a life I don't deserve, trying to be normal when I'm the furthest thing from it."

Finn leaned back, clasping his hands behind his head as he crossed his ankles and looked up to the ceiling. "You deserve happiness just as much as the next person. More so, if you ask me."

I released a short, clipped laugh. "Do I? Gunnarson and Crowley both nailed it on the head, but I was too stupid to listen. I'm a damned ticking time bomb, old man, and that's the God's-honest truth. I shouldn't even be around people. Sure, things have been quiet since the Eye decided to take up residence inside my skull, but there's no guarantee that'll continue. For all I know, it might make things worse. Meanwhile this curse affects everyone around me, all while I pretend I can live a normal life."

Finn sighed through his nose and leaned forward as he looked at me, one elbow resting on a knee and the other scratching an ear. "Is that what you think, that your curse is somehow causing bad things to happen? I have news for you, kid—bad shit has a way of happening without any help from curses and magic. You're a damned McCool, for goodness sakes. Calamity and strife were your future from the moment you were born.

"Yes, you were cursed. And yes, it was my fault it happened. But if you continue to blame that witch's curse for every bad thing that happens to you or the people you love—well, you're just using it as an excuse to shirk responsibility for the life you chose."

"That *I* chose?"

He held a finger to his lips and gave me a stern look. I glanced around. People stared at us all around the waiting room.

Finn responded in a much lower voice. "You're gods-damned right, 'chose.' No one twisted your arm and made you train with me after you took out the Avartagh. That was your choice."

"I was just a kid!" I growled.

"You were a McCool—are a McCool." Finn rubbed his hands on his jeans. I noticed that his skin was pale under the rolled cuffs of the jet black Western shirt he wore. "And so we come to the truth of the matter, which is that you never really had *much* of a choice. Were you born into this work? Most certainly. But walking away from it would've been a death sentence just the same. The fae were going to follow you no matter where you went, and if it hadn't been the Avartagh it would've been something else that hunted you down and did you in.

"No, you never really had much of a choice, but you did make *a* choice. That's the reality I want you to face. You chose to stand and fight instead of burying your head in the sand. The kid I knew might have pulled the short straw, but he wasn't about to sit around and feel sorry for himself about it. That kid chose to become a warrior, and fight the good fight.

"But the young man in front of me? I don't know this person, and frankly I'm not sure I want to. Because he's too damned busy feeling sorry for himself to roll up his sleeves and make the only decision worth making—to fight to protect those he loves."

I covered my face with my hands and took a long, ragged breath. "And you call that a choice? Lady or tiger, I'm screwed either way."

He clapped a hand on my shoulder. "Yes, but at least if you

stand up and fight, you get the satisfaction of taking a few of the bastards with you."

I stared out between my fingers at him, and he fixed me with a wry grin. "You suck at pep talks, Finn. You realize that, right?"

He shrugged. "Ask Belladonna if I'm no help at all."

"Thanks for that, by the way. I don't think I said it, so thanks."

He squeezed my shoulder. "Least I could do, son. Least I could do."

We loitered in the ICU waiting area until we saw them transfer Bells from recovery. We were only able to catch a glimpse of her, but from what I saw she'd regained some color and looked peaceful, so that was an improvement. Seeing her cheered me up, but I still felt responsible for putting her in harm's way.

As they wheeled her out of sight, Finn cleared his throat and shook my shoulder gently.

"Colin, you look like hammered shit, and you smell like it too. Go home, grab a shower and a nap, and then come back when you've rested up. I'll stay here and keep an eye on her for you."

I nodded and rubbed my eyes. "You're right, I do smell like shit. I guess I forgot that we were crawling around in a sewer yesterday."

Finn wrinkled his nose. "I didn't want to say anything, but you still smell like troll musk a bit too. You might try using more of that vinegar and tomato juice concoction again—just in case."

I sighed. "How long are you guys going to keep this up?" I did my best Bill Clinton, which wasn't very good, and rasped a response as I shook my finger at Finn. "I did not have sexual relations with that troll."

It was a half-hearted attempt at humor, but the old man played along nonetheless. He winked and clapped me on the shoulder. "If you say so."

I shook my head and nodded. "Thanks. For everything."

"Don't mention it, kid. Now go see to your needs before you pass out. I'll be here when you get back."

I walked out of the hospital in a daze, and only realized I didn't have transportation after a few moments spent wandering in search of my scooter. A quick check of my funds indicated I'd be taking the bus home. I actually liked riding the bus, and I'd always found it to be a good place to think. City transit provided the comfort of being around other people, with the anonymity of being among strangers who went out of their way to leave you alone. It was the perfect environment for a lonely introvert.

But I was in no hurry to get home anytime soon, so I started walking in a random direction—head down, hands in pockets, and lost in my thoughts.

Before I knew it, I was traveling on MLK opposite City Cemetery, where this whole thing had begun. I stopped and stared at the rows of tombstones, replaying the events of the last few days in my mind. For a moment it felt as though something in the cemetery was calling to me, beckoning me to come inside. Wondering if it was just my imagination, I shrugged and stepped into the road, nearly getting hit by a car. The driver honked and yelled obscenities at me, but I just kept walking.

Soon I wandered the tombstone-lined lanes of Oakwood Cemetery. I passed what appeared to be a small chapel, with a crenelated tower attached. It had been built from the same square limestone blocks that made up many of the walls and boundary markers on the grounds. A haggard caretaker raked leaves behind the chapel as I passed, with a spare build that was all joints and sharp angles. He had wild salt and pepper hair, and a beard to match. To be honest, he looked like a slightly younger version of Finn.

The old man fixed me with a stare that was equal parts casual concern and wary regard. While I was sure the cemetery got its fair share of homeless wandering around, I was also fairly certain it was discouraged by the caretakers and staff. The last thing they needed was a bunch of homeless people setting up camp inside a mausoleum. Besides, Austin had plenty of lodging downtown at the ARCH and the Salvation Army. It wouldn't be considered cruel to chase the odd straggler away and point them toward better facilities just a few blocks south.

Plus, much of the violent crime in the area was committed by the homeless population. It occurred to me that considering the way I currently looked, he'd be a fool not to be optimistically vigilant.

"You looking for something, young man?" the old caretaker asked.

On hearing his voice, I recognized him as the same old man I'd run into during my previous visit. "Just out for a walk, trying to clear my thoughts."

Suddenly the sky darkened as a cloud passed overhead. A cold wind blew right through me, chilling me to my core. I wrapped my arms tightly across my chest and shivered. Then, as quickly as it had come, the wind abated and weak winter sunshine shone in the sky again.

The old man smiled a wolfish grin. His teeth were large and white, making his mouth a bright gash amidst the crags and crevices of his deeply tanned and wind-worn face. For no logical reason at all, I got the feeling he'd known violence and grown comfortable with it in a past life.

"Looks to be gettin' colder, and you're not dressed for it at all. Best get somewhere warm now. If you know what's good for you."

With that, the old man returned to his raking, turning his back and dismissing me. Apparently, he'd deemed me as no threat at all.

I shook my head and continued walking aimlessly, leaving the cemetery to catch a bus back to the junkyard. But instead of going home, I got off at Ben White and walked over to the Bloody Fedora, a bar owned by Sal the redcap's boss that catered to unseelie fae. I told myself I just wanted a drink to help me sleep, but in truth I felt like hurting something that deserved it. And there was always something at the Fedora that deserved it.

20

Hours later I stood outside Maeve's house, holding Sal the redcap by the scruff of his neck and yelling drunkenly at the top of my lungs.

"Maeve! Maeve, you dried up cunt, come out here so I can talk to you!"

Sal pleaded with me from where he dangled in my left hand.

"Colin, shut the fuck up and let's get outta here. You're going to get us both killed. Please kid, listen to me. I still got little mouths to feed at home."

I shook him like a wet rag until he stopped talking, but only after a parting mumble regarding heartless druids who were mean drunks.

"Maeve, come out here and talk to me like a man!" I giggled and stumbled a bit. "Well, like a fae. A female fae. You know what I mean, damn it!"

Sal hid his face in his hands. "We are so dead. Oh please, just make it quick."

Somewhere to my left, the loud grating of stone scraping on stone drew the barest sliver of my attention. After a dozen shots, a brawl with a half-ogre bartender, and turning Rocko's place upside down, I wasn't feeling my sharpest. The ground shook, staggering me and making me just a wee bit woozy. I turned just in time to see one of the gargoyles pawing the ground and glaring at me.

I tossed Sal at it, striking it in the muzzle. He bounced off and rolled a few feet, then pulled his bloody watch cap tightly over his ears and played dead.

"Go chomp on that a while, you big lug," I slurred. "I'll deal with you in a minute."

The gargoyle charged.

Despite my inebriated state—or perhaps because of it—I remained unperturbed. I'd fought dozens of creatures like it during the course of my training and career as a hunter. And often, I'd had to fight wounded, many times finishing creatures off while dizzy from blood loss or brain-addled from suffering a concussion. I was clearheaded enough to recall that Maeve had these two guardians in her garden, so I was ready for it when the gargoyle attacked.

I sidestepped the charging beast and swung my war club overhead, striking it behind the ear and driving the gargoyle's head into the dirt. Its momentum caused it to skid a dozen feet or more, plowing a deep gash into the earth with its face. Eventually it came to a stop by displacing a few flagstones from a very lovely walkway. The gargoyle remained stunned for a moment, then stumbled as it rose to its feet.

I twirled my club and whistled loudly. "Man, that looks like it hurt. You should get one of Maeve's flunkies to look at you—"

Next thing I knew, I was tumbling across the lawn. I landed in a heap against the stone foundation of Maeve's mansion.

Right, there are two of them. The one that had blindsided me now ran at me full-bore to finish the job. Unfortunately, I'd lost track of my club and there was no time to grab another weapon from my bag. I barely managed to get to my knees when the thing froze in mid-stride, mere feet from crushing me.

Maeve appeared out of nowhere in a blinding flash of magic. Behind her, I caught the briefest glimpse of a boudoir, just before she stepped out of a rift and into her garden. *Well shit*, I thought, *Maeve can fold space. Huh.*

What she did was actually a much neater trick than teleportation, which was so many degrees beyond my abilities I couldn't even imagine the forces it took to make it happen. Teleportation used magic to disassemble and reassemble the spellcaster's molecules from one location to the next. It was very dangerous, and very tricky—one misplaced syllable or gesture and you might end up with your head sticking out of your chest at the other end.

What Maeve did was much safer yet infinitely more difficult. Opening a rift between two places and stepping through it was definitely not bush league spell craft. Rumored to have once been the preferred means of magical travel in the age of the Tuatha Dé Danann, folding space was something I didn't think anyone currently living on the big blue ball could still do.

The fae queen of Austin held a hand up in the gargoyle's direction as she stepped completely out of the rift. With a slight gesture from Maeve, it settled gently down from where it had been frozen in mid-air.

"That'll be enough, Adelard—you've done your job admirably. Gather up Lothair and return to your roosts."

The gargoyle puffed out its chest and licked one of its clawed hands in a very catlike manner. It pranced slowly up to me, sniffed once and turned its snout in the air, then walked away.

"Yeah, yeah—I stink. Tell me something I don't know." At some point I'd slid back down the wall, but I hadn't a single recollection of that happening. I looked up at Maeve. "Good, you're here. Now we can talk."

She was dressed in some long white gauzy-looking thing that might have been a night gown, or perhaps an evening dress, and her normal glamour was gone. While I didn't think I was getting the full fae effect, I was pretty sure it was close. Her features were much more regal and alien than usual, and she was disturbingly, frighteningly beautiful. Her presumably bare feet were obscured from view by her gown, which was just as well. Fae were known to have freaky feet, and to be honest weird feet creeped me out. Hammertoes on a hot chick? Instant turn off. So you can imagine what seeing Maeve with bird feet or goat hooves would do to me. I'd never be able to look her in the eye again.

In a very ladylike manner, Maeve squatted down to get eye level with me. And without revealing said feet or even a single square centimeter of skin, I might add. I think that impressed me even more than seeing her create a spatial rift. But perhaps I shouldn't have been too impressed. She'd had several millennia to practice, after all.

"Colin MacCumhaill, whatever am I to do with you?"

I looked her in the eye and spoke with as much menace as I could muster, considering that I was laid out in a heap in her flower bed.

"Release me. Leave me alone to lead a life in peace, away from the fae, from the supernatural, from it all," I growled.

Then I threw up all over her pansies and snapdragons.

Fifteen minutes later we were inside her home, in a sitting room just past the foyer that I'd never seen before. As I said, Maeve's house had a way of popping new rooms into existence and rearranging itself. I suspected the rooms were a reflection of Maeve's whims and moods, and not any real sentience on the house's part. At least, I hoped they weren't—because the idea of being inside a sentient house made me hella nervous.

A few moments before, hat in hand, Sal had prostrated himself before Maeve—something I'd never thought to see from a redcap. Of course, he'd blamed the whole thing on me and said he'd wanted nothing to do with bringing me here. Which was absolutely, one hundred percent true, in fact. I didn't remember much of the evening before I'd arrived with Sal, but I did vaguely recall a brawl, tearing Rocko's place apart, and drinking half the booze in the joint—not necessarily in that order. After which, I'd forced Sal to drive me to Maeve's place.

She gave me a potion to drink, only after swearing by all that was fae it was a gift freely given, no harm to me or mine, yadda, yadda, yadda. I didn't really care at that point, since the room was spinning and I didn't want to yak on her rug. The potion sobered me up right quick, and I immediately felt like an asshole.

"Sorry for calling you a—well, a C-word."

She fixed me with a stare that was either compassionate or calculating. With her, it could go either way. Maeve was ancient and alien, and her motives were as unpredictable as Texas weather. Or so I'd heard.

Yet, for the brief time I'd known her she'd proven to be as steady and calm as anyone I'd ever known—a far cry from the capriciousness and cruelty that I expected from a faery queen. Maeve's kind were known to delight in toying with the lives of mortal men and women, and I'd always just assumed she was doing the same with me. Her machinations had pulled me back into the world of the supernatural, and I'd been in one hot mess after another since she'd first summoned me to her home.

Which is why, in my drunken stupor, I'd decided she was to blame for Belladonna's current state.

Maeve tsked and broke the silence. "If it were anyone else,

that person might be spending time with a very nasty boggart deep within the bowels of my cellars about now. But I seem to have become fond of you, Colin McCool. I must be growing softhearted in my old age."

I laughed humorlessly. "No offense, Maeve, but you're anything but softhearted. With all due respect, I believe your interests in my well-being are purely selfish. The only reason you didn't squash me like a bug is because you need me. Or, more specifically, you need the Eye."

She nodded. "I do need the Eye. But don't think that just because you studied a few years with Finnegas you have the fae all figured out. We do have emotions, although we tend to keep the better aspects of them hidden away like so much useless dross."

She made a small dismissive gesture, sweeping an imaginary bug off her knee.

"Enough about that. You mentioned wanting to be released from my service. Yet, you've never truly been held at all, have you? You're certainly under no geas or spell of my making, of that I can assure you. Every decision you've taken and action you've made over the last several months have been completely under your own volition. And if you don't want to complete the task I've set before you, I suppose there's nothing I can do to convince you otherwise."

I took a deep breath and let it out before responding. "You have my mother's paintings, which is why I currently find myself under your thumb."

She nodded slightly. "Indeed, I do. But from this point forward, you have my solemn vow that I'll not harm your mother's career or livelihood."

Fae couldn't lie. Oh they could dissemble, sure—but lying was something that was completely beyond their abilities. For whatever reason, they were incapable of speaking falsely.

That's why I was taken aback by Maeve's words.

I squinted and pursed my lips, both due to a pounding headache and disbelief. "What's the catch?"

She sat back in her chair and crossed her legs, one knee over the other. Somehow, she still managed to keep her feet hidden under the hem of that gown of hers, and I silently thanked my lucky stars for that small favor. I really had no idea if she had goat feet, but I didn't want to find out.

Maeve steepled her fingers in front of her chest. "There is no catch, Colin. I am simply looking out for your interests."

"Maeve, who are the players behind the Ananda Corporation, and why do they seem to want your head on a platter?"

She took her time before answering. "For your own safety, I refuse to answer that question."

I held a hand up in protest. "Enough. I'm sorry for insulting you and getting you out of bed, but I'll believe you're looking out for me when pigs fly."

She tilted her head slightly. "You've obviously never spent time in Underhill."

I stood, holding one palm to my forehead in response to the sharp stabbing pain behind my eyes. "Your potion was very useful. I'll be going now."

She stared at me over those steepled fingers, like a spider waiting to see if its prey would escape or tangle itself further through struggle. The front door was within my line of sight, so I decided to see myself out. Maeve uttered not one word until I was almost out the door. She spoke at a conversational volume, but despite the distance it sounded as if her lips were right next to my ear.

"We still have much work to do, Colin. When you're ready to continue, I'll be here."

I woke up fully dressed, still in the filthy and blood-stained clothing I'd been wearing for two solid days. I sat up and licked my lips, but my tongue was too dry to make a difference. Thankfully my headache was gone, probably due to that potion Maeve had given me. No telling what side effects I'd suffer from it, but nevertheless I was glad to have avoided a serious hangover.

The night previous I'd taken a cab back to the junkyard, wasting my grocery money on the fare because I was too weary and hungover to care. It was close to four in the morning when I'd arrived, and a look at my phone told me I'd slept for ten hours. I had a voice message from Finn, calling from the hospital to say that Bells was awake and asking for me, along with several texts from Sabine and Hemi asking about Belladonna's condition.

I felt like an ass for leaving her at the hospital, and for not being there when she'd come around. So I took a quick shower, rode the bus downtown to retrieve my scooter, and made a beeline for the hospital. I found a space in visitor parking outside the ER, and practically sprinted to the ICU.

When I hit the desk, a nurse stopped me cold before I could run in. "Just a minute there, young man—where do you think you're going?"

"Belladonna Becerra—is she awake?"

"Yes, but you've missed visiting hours." She looked me over and tapped a pen on her chin. "You must be Colin. She's been asking for you. Right now we have her sedated so she can rest, but wait here and I'll see if I can let you in to see her."

She disappeared around a corner. When she came back she waggled a finger in my face. "You can only see her for a minute or two. The only reason I'm even letting you in is because I think it'll help her rest. You're to get in, say 'hi' and 'bye,' and that's it. Am I understood?"

I nodded quickly, looking past her shoulder to see if I could catch a glimpse of Bells through the doors to the ICU.

The nurse rolled her eyes. "C'mon, before you run in there without me and I have to get security to take you down."

I was pretty sure she was serious, but the only thing on my mind was getting in to see Bells. The nurse walked me through the doors, past a few other rooms with patients who all looked to be in bad shape. Some were on ventilators, most were unconscious, and one was strapped into a bed that reminded me of something out of a late night horror movie. The poor guy had this circular metal thing around his head, and there were screws going through the circle and into his skull. I must've stared too long, because a male nurse inside the room noticed and pulled a curtain to block my view.

I felt a hand on my chest and stopped walking. The nurse's brow furrowed as she whispered. "Two minutes, that's all you get."

I nodded quickly and entered in the room. Belladonna was sleeping—or at least her eyes were closed—and she was still hooked up to everything, just like when they'd brought her in. Some color had returned to her cheeks, and she'd been cleaned up as well. I noticed a bruise and a scrape on her forehead, and her lip had been cut slightly in the blast.

I walked over and grabbed her hand, ever so gently.

Her eyes fluttered open halfway and she spoke softly, her voice raspy and her speech slurred. "Mmmm. You're here."

"Shhh. Just rest. The nurse told me you need it."

"Ah, you met Nurse Ratched."

I smiled. "She said she'd cut me off at the knees if I stayed too long."

She squeezed my fingers. "Probably just has a crush on you. Wants to keep you to herself." She closed her eyes, and her lips curled up slightly. "Tell her I'm onto her."

I leaned in and kissed her on the forehead. "You don't have a thing to worry about."

"I know," she replied. Then she was fast asleep again.

I wiped my eyes, squeezed her hand, and planted a soft kiss on her lips for good measure. Then I walked out of the room, being careful not to disturb her as I left. I stopped at the nurse's station, where the nurse typed away.

"When can I see her again?"

The nurse finished what she was writing and turned to face me. "She should be transferred out of ICU tomorrow morning. You can see her as much as you like then. In fact, she'll probably need someone to help her once she's moved to the post-surgical floor."

I thanked her and went out to find Finn. He was sitting in the ICU waiting room, chatting up an attractive middle-aged black woman. At first I thought he was flirting, then I realized he was comforting her. *Wonders never ceased.*

I waited for a lull in their conversation before I approached. Finn patted the lady on the hand, and handed her a box of tissues. She took one and wiped her eyes, smearing a bit of her mascara.

"Thank you for the kind words, Mr. Murphy." She spoke with an accent that might have been Caribbean or African; I couldn't identify it.

"Don't mention it, Mrs. Akinjide. Your husband will be fine, I'm certain of it."

Finn squeezed her hand, then begged to be excused when he saw me approach. She smiled kindly as he left. I led Finn into the hallway so we could talk away from the quiet of the ICU waiting room.

He pointed a thumb over his shoulder. "Lovely woman. Husband was in a car accident, sole provider for the family.

Cervical injury. They'll end up with a hell of a settlement from the insurance, but doesn't do them much good until then."

I squinted one eye shut. "Not to be a downer, but are you sure it's the best thing to be giving her false hope?"

Finn frowned. "False hope? I snuck into the guy's room and spent the better part of thirty minutes healing him. Doctors will say it's a miracle, but you and I will know better."

I shook my head. "Glad to have you back, old man."

He sneered and waved my comment off. "It was nothing. Makes me sorry I can't do it for everyone, but magic always has a price. Speaking of which, I am dead on my feet and famished, so if you're alright by yourself I'll be taking my leave. There's a bag of breakfast tacos and the back seat of a van calling my name."

"Thanks, Finn. And sorry for leaving you here so long."

His eyes narrowed with a frown, then he smiled and winked. "Blew off some steam, did we? Well, I heard about it already. Maeve has people everywhere, you know. One of her goons came by to give me an earful, something about you disrespecting their queen. Bah! Back in my day a druid could give anyone a good verbal drubbing, kings and queens included. We were respected back then. I told him to stuff it, but don't be surprised if they hold it against you."

"Noted. Now, go get some rest, and thanks again."

He began to walk off and gave me a parting glance over his shoulder. "Don't do anything stupid. I mean, nothing that's more stupid than calling out a faery queen on her own turf."

"Double-noted. I'll see you back at the junkyard tomorrow, after Bells gets transferred out of ICU."

He tipped an imaginary hat and left. I took a few deep breaths to settle the impotent rage I still felt. On the one hand, I was relieved that Bells was going to be alright. But on the other hand, saying I was pissed was an understatement. If I'd had a line on whoever our bad actor was, I'd have been long gone and on my way to do some damage.

But I was still just as clueless as I'd been when this whole thing had begun. So I stuffed my rage way down deep and walked back in the ICU waiting room, knowing my time would come soon. And when it did, I'd be ready to square things up with the responsible party—on my terms.

21

I must've dozed off, because when I woke the shadows in the waiting room were longer, and Sabine was sitting across from me.

"Welcome back to the land of the living."

I wiped a hand across my face and rubbed my eyes. "How long you been here?"

She shrugged. "A few hours. You were asleep when I got here, so I spoke with one of the nurses and snuck a look at Belladonna's chart."

"How'd you manage that?"

The corner of her mouth turned up slightly as she tilted her head and arched an eyebrow. "She's one of Maeve's. After the stunt you pulled last night, she decided to plant someone here. I'm guessing it's both to keep an eye on you, and to keep Belladonna safe—you know, so the walking magical A-bomb doesn't start a countdown."

I nodded and took a deep breath. "Huh. I don't know if I should be thankful or upset about that."

She squeezed one eye shut and pulled her lips sideways. "I'd go with thankful, considering you insulted the local faery queen and managed to escape with your life."

"Okay, point taken." I chose my next words carefully. "So are you here checking on me, or on Belladonna? I know you two don't exactly see eye to eye."

She crossed her legs and adjusted the loose floral peasant skirt she was wearing, placing both hands on a knee as she leaned forward and looked me in the eye.

"Let's just clear the air right now, okay?" She marked each item by ticking off her fingers, one by one. "One—I know you slept with Belladonna, and I'm not mad at you about it. Two—that being said, you should have told me, instead of waiting around for me to hear about it through the grapevine. And three—we're friends, we've always been friends, and we're always going to be friends. Nothing is going to change that. Even if you were being a bit of a shit, and borderline leading me on."

I forced myself to maintain eye contact, even though I didn't want to. "Okay, I deserved that. Worse, in fact. Sorry."

"Colin, what you fail to see is that I have a different perspective on our friendship than you do. Yes, I'm attracted to you, and I'm not going to deny it. But the fact is, you'll be dead and gone in 60 years or so, and I'll still be around. So, while I care about you deeply, there's no way I'd allow myself to fall in love with you. None."

I really didn't know what to say to that, so I didn't say anything. Sabine said it convincingly enough, but I'd be a fool to miss the hint of longing in her voice.

Then, she cracked a smile and winked at me. "Besides, you really, really needed to get laid."

I laughed and bowed my head. "No comment. But thanks for being here, Sabine."

"Where else would I be? Like I said, friends, now and

always." We both looked at each other, then away. An uncomfortable silence followed.

I decided to change the subject. "So—what did you find out when you looked at Belladonna's chart?"

"Well, I'm no doctor, so I had to ask Maeve's plant to decipher it for me. According to what she told me, a thin piece of metal had entered Belladonna's abdomen and pierced her liver. She had severe internal bleeding, and it was a miracle she made it."

"A druid miracle. Finn showed up and worked his juju while she was coding. I'm pretty sure that's what saved her."

Sabine chewed her lip. "That had to be some heavy-duty magic, Colin. Nothing like that comes without a price."

"The old man mentioned something to that effect. He healed some dude with a spinal cord injury too. Makes me wonder what's gotten into him."

She shook her head. "How much do you really know about druid magic? I mean, I know you trained under Finn, but how deep did your training go?"

"Not very. I always preferred bashing skulls over casting magic, so we focused most of my training there. Besides, that's pretty much how the druids have always trained hunters, or so I'm told."

"Makes sense. So you never trained in any advanced magic —not even in theory?"

"Nope. I mean, I know about that stuff, and we discussed some high-level magical theory, but just in the general sense."

She nodded. "I think you need to talk to Finn. Something's not right if he's throwing around magic like that. Especially in his current condition."

"I don't get what the big deal is."

"C'mon, Colin. You know where fae magic users get their power."

I rolled my eyes. "Sure, from the Underrealms. Every two-bit hedge wizard knows that."

"And human magic users don't have access to that pool of magic, so they have to gather and store magic in foci and power sinks."

"Yeah, or barter for it with powerful supernatural creatures, if they're really that dumb. So what?"

"Colin, think! How much power do you suppose it takes to bring someone back from the brink of death? Like, a crap-ton. That's why almost all serious necromancy requires animal or human sacrifices. And even then, the best they can manage is the semblance of life. All fae know this, which is why hardly any of us mess with that stuff. Even with access to the Underrealms, we still can't create life—we can only exchange it. Do you see what I'm getting at?"

"Sabine, be for real here. You're telling me Finn used his own energy to heal Belladonna and the guy with the spinal cord injury?"

"Maybe not the guy—as old as he is, he could probably manage that using an external power source. But saving Belladonna? Definitely."

I sat back in my chair, dumbstruck.

Sabine nodded slowly. "Now you get why it concerns me."

"Shit. But why?"

She shrugged. "I don't know, but you need to talk to him to find out what's up."

"I feel like an idiot for not knowing this."

She smiled. "Yes, you're an idiot, but I don't hold it against you. Now, let's go find the cafeteria. I seem to be experiencing an inexplicable craving for lime Jello."

We sat across from each other in the hospital cafeteria. I had destroyed two burgers and an order of fries, and was close to finishing a bowl of ice cream. Sabine, on the other hand, was still picking at her lime Jello.

"I don't know why they think adding pear slices improves the flavor. Lime Jello is perfect all on its own."

I ate my ice cream in silence. I'd been thinking about Belladonna for most of our meal, and how it'd been my fault she'd been injured.

Sabine placed a warm hand on my wrist. "Colin, you need to stop blaming yourself for what happened. It's not your fault."

I tossed the spoon into the bowl, suddenly realizing I was no longer hungry.

"That's what everyone always says. But you know what? If I hadn't taken that job from Luther, Belladonna wouldn't be lying in the ICU right now. And if I had just marched my happy ass away from everyone after what happened to Jesse, you'd never have been kidnapped, Bells would be fine right now, and you all would've been a lot better off. Not to mention safer.

"It all boils down to choices, Sabine. And I keep making the wrong ones."

"Colin, everyone makes mistakes. And in your case, I don't think the mistakes you've made have been that bad, considering the circumstances. So you're cursed—totally not your fault. And so you're dangerous, too. Big whoop! As far as I can tell, after that first event the only time your curse has kicked in was when you were on the brink of death."

"Yeah, so?"

She pinched me on the wrist, hard. "So, dummy—maybe you're not as dangerous to other people as you think. All this time since Jesse died, you've been convincing yourself that you're a mortal danger to everyone around you. But I don't think that's the case. Sure, you're dangerous as all hell when your curse kicks in, but I think you're more like a nuclear warhead than nitroglycerin."

"Meaning?"

"Meaning, until someone flips your switch, you're perfectly inert. Think about it. The first time it happened you were facing down a demon that turned out to be way out of your league."

I propped my head on one hand and trailed my finger through a drop of melted ice cream. "Yeah, but I don't see what that has to do with what happened."

Sabine shook her head and rolled her eyes. "You seriously never worked this out on your own? Colin, you were set up from the start. Fuamnach cursed you right before you went into that cave after the Caoránach, precisely because she knew you were outmatched. She knew the fight would trigger the curse."

I pushed myself away from the table. "I don't want to talk about this."

"You'll need to face up to it eventually, Colin. Not only did Fuamnach place that curse on you, she also manipulated events so you'd immediately transform. The question you really need to ask yourself is why."

"Isn't it obvious, Sabine? She was trying to get back at Finn. I mean, those two have been feuding for millennia."

She tapped her spoon on the edge of the styrofoam bowl. "It has to go deeper than that. Why curse you? She could have just tracked you down and killed you outright. No, there's some reason why she needed you to be cursed. I think there's a much bigger game going on here, but we simply don't have enough information to see what it is.

"And besides that, I think it's time you stopped playing the victim. What's done is done. You need to quit feeling sorry for yourself, and start thinking about how to get in front of what she has planned. It's time to stop being the pawn and get your head in the game—otherwise the people around you are just going to keep getting hurt."

I sat, stunned, and processed what she'd said. She was right; I had been playing the victim. It was a role that I'd accepted, and one that I'd grown quite comfortable playing. But all it had gotten me was trouble and pain, because by playing the victim I'd fallen into passivity. And nobody ever won a fight by playing defense.

I pulled my chair close to the table again, placing my elbows on the surface as I leaned in. "You're right, I'm being a total pussy about this. About everything."

She smiled and crossed her arms. "Well, I wasn't going to say it."

"Yeah, well—maybe you should have."

"Meh, you have enough to deal with without being insulted. But you've been hiding from this thing long enough. You need to stop allowing yourself to be manipulated, and start controlling your destiny again."

"Time to become the hunter instead of the prey."

"Exactly."

"The cat and not the mouse."

"Sure—"

"The windshield instead of the bug."

"Colin—"

"The boot instead of the butt—"

She reached across the table and slapped her hand over my mouth. "Enough already! I can see you get the point."

I winked at her and peeled her hand off my face. "Since you seemed to want to drive your point home, I figured the least I could do was reciprocate."

"You're a dick."

"All part of my boyish charm."

Sabine flicked a glob of green Jello at me, and it splatted

right in my eye. I licked a stray fleck off my lip, and she giggled as I made a face.

"Man, you weren't kidding about the pears."

———

Maeve's undercover nurse-slash-spy found us in the ICU waiting room a few hours later, and let us know that Bells was being transferred out of the ICU. She was friendly enough with Sabine, but snide and short in responding to my questions. Apparently, by insulting Maeve, I'd pissed off the entire fae contingent, save Sabine. *Fantastic.*

We waited around for a few minutes while the staff got Bells settled into her new room. Then we headed up the stairs to the fifth floor, foregoing the elevator because Sabine said she hated them.

"Enclosed spaces and strangers? No can do," she explained. So, the stairs it was.

I opened the door to the stairwell to find Gunnarson and two of his goons waiting for me. As usual, they were dressed in the latest "tacti-cool" fashion—cargo pants in muted, neutral colors, tight lycra shirts, and digital camo field jackets with lots of pockets and zippers. Combat boots rounded out the look, but at least they hadn't gone so far as to tuck their pants in their boots. I had to give them credit for showing at least some restraint.

I glanced over my shoulder and addressed Sabine. "You can head on up—I'll be right there."

She nodded and broke eye contact, rushing up the stairs to get away from Gunnarson and his Iron Circle cronies as fast as she could. Gunnarson and one of the goons watched her go, while the third just looked confused. Since he couldn't see through Sabine's see-me-not spell, I figured he was either their muscle or a newb.

Gunnarson spat tobacco juice toward the far corner of the stairwell. "Fucking fae. I don't know why you hold truck with those faery bastards, McCool. Being as how they ruined your life and all."

"Oh, I don't—she's about the only one I can stand."

He tongued a molar. "'Cept Maeve. From what I hear, you're developing quite the cozy relationship with her. After that stunt you pulled, well—I'm surprised you're not a lampshade in her parlor."

I leaned against the wall of the stairwell and crossed my arms. "You heard wrong. So, to what do I owe the pleasure?"

"How's Becerra?" he asked.

"Fine. I take it you know she was just transferred out of ICU, since you knew I was headed up to see her."

"And you're wondering how I knew you'd take the stairs? We keep intelligence on most of the fae in the city. Every single one is a threat, so we make it our business to know their strengths, weaknesses, and quirks. Which brings me to why I came here in person."

He reached into a leather briefcase and handed me a file folder that was a good two inches thick. It was labeled "Eyes Only" and warded with sigils against prying eyes and sticky fingers. Instead of reaching out for it, I glanced at the folder and cocked my eyebrow at him.

"For fuck's sake, McCool, you think I'd do something that obvious if I wanted to take you out? The protective spells have been deactivated. It's safe to read."

I took the file and opened it, glancing at the cover sheet:

SUBJECT NAME: *Fear Doirich*

KNOWN ALIASES: *The Dark Man, The Dark Druid*

A quick flip through the folder revealed that most of the information was redacted. I handed the file back to him.

"Everyone knows who the Fear Doirich is—so what? No one

has seen him since he turned Fionn's wife into a deer. Nobody ever saw Sadhbh again either. Are you going to tell me you have a file on her, too?"

Gunnarson frowned so deeply that the ends of his prodigious mustache nearly met.

"And I thought you were at least halfway sharp, McCool. You really think the Circle keeps files on entities that are long dead? The Dark Druid is as alive and well as you and I. In fact, we've been keeping tabs on him for centuries, mainly because every couple hundred years or so his work shows up in connection to some calamity or tragedy. We can connect him to several plagues and natural disasters over the years, and to many of the worst serial killings throughout history."

I rolled my eyes. "Next you're going to tell me that the Fear Doirich was Jack the Ripper."

"And maybe worse."

I had a hard time believing that there was another two-thousand-year-old druid running around. For one, Finnegas never mentioned him except in the context of myth and legend. Which were, of course, history to us. Second, if a druidic serial killer had been running around for the last two millennia, it seemed like Finnegas and the fianna wouldn't have found a way to bump him off.

Still, I couldn't just write it off. Gunnarson might have been a dick, but he was a dick who cared about protecting the populace from supernatural threats. He probably had selfish reasons, but he still had an interest in keeping supernatural entities from preying on humans.

"So, the Circle thinks this guy is behind all the necromancy?"

Gunnarson nodded. "Bingo. Give the druid a cookie."

I ignored the jab. "But what makes you think it's him?"

Gunnarson spat tobacco juice on the wall, near my feet.

"Because it fits his past M.O., that's why. Far as we can tell, his hobbies are necromancy, spreading death and destruction wherever he goes, and being really fucking vindictive when he gets turned down for a date. In every instance where he's shown up in the past, necromancy was involved. And based on the photos you showed me, we think he's our guy—the runes and symbols match records we have in our archives of his past work."

"If that's the case, what's his motive? I mean, why just turn up in town and start making ghouls all over the place?"

Gunnarson tucked the file back into his briefcase and made a show of avoiding my gaze while looking smug.

"Well, that's the million-dollar question, isn't it, McCool? What would make a nearly immortal, evil druidic magic-user just pop up in Austin and start sacrificing kittens and unicorns? Seems like an awful waste of time, unless there was something here he wanted."

He looked at me and smirked. "But you wouldn't know anything about that, would you? No, you're just as ignorant and innocent as a newborn babe. Anyway, now you know. What you do with this info is up to you."

"I'm damned sure not going to sit on it. And if the Fear Doirich is our guy, I'll still need back up when I track him down."

Gunnarson looked at me with a half-squint and exhaled heavily through his nose. "You'll have it, much as it pains me to agree to it. I can't have this fucker running around my city killing civilians and turning them into the undead. Just don't get any more of my people injured. Becerra's a loose cannon and a cowboy, but she's ours. And we don't like losing our own."

I felt bad enough about Bells as it was, but I wasn't going to share any of that with Gunnarson. "I can't promise anything. Especially not if it's really the Dark Druid. He was bad news two thousand years ago. I can't imagine he's mellowed much in all that time."

"Fair enough. My people know the score, and no one in the Circle thinks it's going to be puppy dogs and rainbows when they hit the streets. But if you make a mistake that gets any of my people hurt, I swear I'll lock you up in a dungeon so deep, they'll need to call to China to bring you back."

I chewed my lip. "Um, China's not—never mind. You got a picture of what this guy looks like now?"

"Might not do any good—we suspect he's a body jumper. Last time he showed up was in Nazi Germany, and he wasn't doing photo ops. One of our operatives got a glimpse and drew this." He dug around in the briefcase and handed me a photo of a charcoal drawing on a yellowed page. "Here."

I took the photo and flipped it around to get a good look.

"Son of a bitch." I folded the photo and tucked it into my jacket. "Gunnarson, have a strike team or SWAT team or whatever the hell you call them ready to go. I think I know who our mysterious necromancer is, and where to find him."

22

I took the stairs two at a time on my way up to Belladonna's room, gasping for breath by the time I staggered in. Sabine was sitting in a chair facing Bells, and they were both laughing about something. Well, Sabine was laughing. Bells looked like she was resisting the urge, and failing miserably.

"Oh, don't make me laugh, you bitch—it hurts too much!"

I stumbled to the foot of the bed, hunched over with my hands on my knees. Whatever conversation they'd been having stopped the moment I walked in. Sabine sat prim and proper, looking like the cat that ate the mouse. Bells wiped her eyes, holding a pillow to her side.

"Damn it, but that hurts. Hi, Colin."

I looked between them as I caught my breath, because this was not how I'd pictured this going down. In fact, part of the reason I'd sprinted the whole way up was to intercede in what I thought would be an awkward situation.

"You two—but I thought—aw, forget it. Just got some big news on the necromancer front."

Sabine fixed me with a scowl. "That's it? Basically, your girlfriend just woke up from coma, and that's how you greet her?"

"Um—" I didn't know what to say. What I'd wanted to do was walk right up and kiss Bells, but I didn't want to make anyone feel uncomfortable... including me. It's not that I was a coward; I just didn't have a grip on how all this stuff worked.

Sabine looked at me expectantly, then her jaw dropped open with a tsk. "For goodness sakes, kiss the girl already!"

Bells just laid there, staring at me with a beatific expression. While she looked a bit groggy, her eyes were bright, and she was smiling at me like a dope. So I walked up and kissed her, full on the lips.

I closed my eyes and leaned my head in to gently touch hers. "You really scared the shit out of me, you know that?"

"Sorry," she whispered. "But I wasn't about to puss out after that ghoul tried to kill us."

"Bells, you almost died. *Did* die, in fact, briefly."

"Merely a flesh wound. I've had worse, you pansy."

Sabine snickered. I sat down on the bed, apoplectic.

"Bells! Your heart stopped beating—I watched them pump your chest."

"Jealous?"

I tried to stammer a reply and failed. Sabine tittered and wiped her eyes again.

"Colin, she's on drugs. Heavy duty drugs. You couldn't get a serious answer out of her right now if you tried."

Bells narrowed her eyes at me. "He's being overly sensitive. Don't know if I like it."

Sabine chuckled. "You'd best get used to it. Manly man that he is, he has to be the weepiest guy I know."

"Okay, I get it. Bells is high and you two just formed the newest chapter of The Sisterhood of the Traveling Pants. Now that I'm up to speed, why don't I fill you in on the latest shocking news?"

Bells wrinkled her nose at me. "Now he's just being surly." She reached up to pinch my cheek, and missed so she pinched my arm. "You're cute when you're angry." She looked at Sabine and grinned. "Sabine, tell him he's cute when he's angry."

Sabine raised both hands in protest. "Don't look at me—I got him to kiss you, my work is done."

Bells stuck her tongue out and gave Sabine the raspberries.

I clapped my hands on my knees. "Okay, so—I think I know who the necromancer is."

Sabine sat up straight. "Commander Gunnarson dropped you a tip, did he? Do tell."

"That prick," Bells mumbled.

"No arguments here, but he did just provide some info that suggests our necromancer is—get this—the Fear Doirich."

Belladonna's eyes snapped open. She'd been drifting off a little, but that woke her up. Sabine covered her mouth with one hand.

"Tell me you're not going after him, Colin."

"Sabine, honestly—"

She stood up, livid. "Damn it, Colin, look at Belladonna. Look at her! If it's true, he did this to her. Legend says back in the day even the fae gave him a wide berth. You'll end up like Belladonna, or worse, if you confront him."

Bells nodded in an exaggerated manner, slurring her response slightly. "She s'right, you know. Don't do it."

"Gunnarson says he'll provide me with back up."

Sabine stamped the floor. "Really? You're going to trust him to have your back? Colin, for all you know he's steering you toward this confrontation in hopes that the Dark Man takes you out. Have you considered that at all?"

Belladonna's hand slapped down on my wrist. "She's totally right." She turned her head lazily to look at Sabine. "Hey, you're not all bad, Sabine. I totally take back what I said about your choice in clothing and that rat's nest you call a hairstyle."

"It's just her glamour," I quipped.

"It's what she chooses to show the world. Fair game, in my book."

Sabine sighed, maintaining eye contact with me. "I'm going to ignore her right now. Colin, promise me you won't go after him before you speak with Finnegas."

"Sabine, I can't let him get away."

"And if you end up like her, or worse?" She gestured at Bells, who waved back at us lazily.

"Still here, people. And I feel great."

I looked at Bells, who despite being three sheets to the wind and banged up looked more lovely to me than she ever had. I turned my eyes back to Sabine, making the effort to see through her glamour, past the frumpy illusion she presented. Her preternaturally beautiful, almond-shaped eyes pleaded with me, and the look on her face spoke of desperation and fear.

But I was tired of playing defense. Doing so only put my friends in danger. It was time to go on the offense, and show this old bastard just who he was messing with.

"I'll talk to Finn, I promise. But then I'm going to kick this guy's ass."

Sabine rolled her eyes. "Fine, do what you want. But just remember that it's everyone else who'll have to deal with the consequences if you get yourself killed."

Bells opened one eye and looked at me. "What she said. Don't get killed."

I leaned down and kissed her on the forehead. "I'll be back."

She grinned, eyes closed. "I'll be waiting. For you to take me to a good brawl, I mean. Once I'm out of this hospital bed. Being as I'm missing the fight, and all."

"Sure thing, Bells. It's a date."

Sabine remained silent, mouth curled in disapproval as I headed to the door. I returned the look with a sheepish grin and a shrug, and hauled ass for the elevators as soon as my feet hit the hall.

I looked at the artist's rendering several times, both on the elevator and on my way to the parking lot. There was no mistaking it: the guy in the drawing was a dead ringer for the cemetery caretaker. If I was right, the necromancer had been right under my nose this whole time and I'd failed to see it. And, he'd been playing me for a fool since the moment I'd first set foot in that cemetery.

I considered the implications and my next steps on the way back to the junkyard. My first question was fairly obvious: why hadn't he crushed me like an insect the first time we'd met? If he was as powerful as everyone said, surely he could've prevented me from tracking down his ghouls and interfering with his plans. Instead, he'd let me discover his activities, leaving me a clear trail to follow at each and every turn.

But to what end, I hadn't a clue. I only knew I was tired of playing the unwitting pawn, and seeing my friends get hurt because they were useful for leverage or in the way. And, I was tired of playing the victim, of being a game piece instead of a player. The time had come for me to go on the offensive. I was ready and willing to dole out some consequences, and the Fear Doirich was currently at the top of my shit list.

Problem was, I didn't know how I was going to take him out. At least, not without hulking out on him. And I wasn't just worried about the ríastrad; I was also worried about the Eye. I'd done quite a bit of reading up on it since the events at Crowley's farm, and from what I understood it was capable of leveling a small city. I couldn't imagine the amount of damage that could be done if I let my Hyde-side loose while in possession of a magical weapon of mass destruction.

That meant I needed to figure out another way to catch or subdue him, one that didn't involve a magical or physical confrontation. I had no idea whether he could harness powers that were equivalent to what I'd experienced when Crowley used the Eye on me. But if so, it could conceivably trigger my dark side to come out—and that was something to be avoided at all costs.

When I got back to the junkyard I immediately ran to Finn's van. I knocked and heard a muffled response from inside. I opened the door and found him bundled up on a bench seat, sipping a cup of tea in front of a Coleman stove.

"Come in, and shut the door if you don't mind. Takes forever to get this thing warm."

I clambered in and sat on the floor across from him. "Don't you think it's time to move into an apartment or something?"

"Maureen is trying to find me a place outside the city, somewhere with some space to stretch my legs. All this concrete and metal—bah, don't know how you can stand it."

"You get used to it." Finn looked gaunt and pale. "Are you alright?"

"Magic," he replied, between sips of tea. "Takes it out of me these days."

"Sabine seemed to think it was dangerous for you to perform those healing spells. Maybe even suicidal."

"Pah! She can't be more than a few decades old. Still a child. What does she know about magic, and especially druid magic? I'll be fine. Just need some time to recharge my batteries, is all."

I turned the flame up slightly on the camping stove. "I

thought that's what you were supposed to be doing in the first place. You know, after going cold turkey?"

"Like I said, I'll be fine."

I left it at that. Finnegas was two thousand years old. If he said he knew what he was doing, I believed him.

"Fair enough." I waited for a moment before jumping into the next topic of discussion. "Finn, why didn't you tell me about the Dark Druid?"

He pursed his lips into a wry grimace. "It's him, huh? Hmph. Should've known."

I nodded, watching him to see if I could spot any sign of deception. He'd lied to me, again. Or at least withheld information. And that was pretty much what had gotten Jesse killed, which was why I wanted to make sure he wasn't going to make this a regular thing again.

He pondered the depths of his tea cup, averting his gaze. "I suspected he might be involved the moment I walked in that room. Magic looked like his work, but it's been centuries. That prick always did favor brute force over finesse though. His spell work was ugly, harsh stuff. We ought to have known he was a bad seed, by the way he expressed himself in his magic."

"Wait a minute—you knew him?"

"Sure I knew him. Hell, I taught him, for Lugh's sake. He was my first student, before I met Fionn. Smart, but headstrong and prone to anger and violence. Him and Cúchulainn were cut from the same mold, I think, 'cept the Hound wasn't near as mean. Even so, I always said Cathbad should never have trained him."

He poured the dregs of his tea out in a nearby coffee can. "But I guess we both made our mistakes. Only problem is, mine is still running around killing people."

"He hurt Belladonna, Finn. And he's been pulling my strings

this whole time. The least you could have done is warn me about him."

He glowered at me and gestured animatedly with his tea cup. "And what, have you go chase him down like you're going to do now? He'll kill you—or worse, trigger your ríastrad and let you go on a rampage, a real killing spree. And he'll use the death and destruction you cause to further his powers."

"Or I'll kill him."

"Boy, you're about as likely to kill the Fear Doirich as you are to sprout wings and fly. Colin, hear me out. You're smart, and a damned good fighter. And you have a greater talent for magic than I've ever let on, although I steered you away from it for fear you'd turn out like me. Or worse, like him. A little magic, a man can stand. But great power? It changes you, in more ways than I care to admit. I was never meant to walk this earth for as long as I have, and someday I'll pay for it—for all my crimes."

"Crimes? What are you talking about?"

"Stolen power, boy! The greatest temptation of all—to steal for oneself a power that mortal men should not possess. When I was young, I was a fool. I wanted wisdom, knowledge, and a life-time to acquire it. But a lifetime wasn't enough, so I began extending my years a little at a time. Oh, there are various ways to do it—all great wizards and druids know what they are. But they all come at a price. And I've been paying that price for the last two thousand years."

I shook my head. "I don't see what the downside is to being nearly immortal."

He laughed bitterly. "That's because you're young. Life is still new and wonderful to you, despite the pain you've experienced. But me? I'm old, and tired. I grew weary of life centuries ago. But yet, I can't move on."

"And the Fear Doirich? What's his deal? Did he use the same magics you used to extend your life?"

"No, he took a much darker path. He's a body thief."

"Gunnarson mentioned something about that," I said. "Is that like possession?"

"Worse. With possession, the entity lives within the host alongside the host's own spirit and soul. This makes it possible to perform an exorcism, and get the person back.

"But a body thief uses dark magic to force someone else's soul out of their physical form. That puts them in a state of limbo, unable to move on to the next life, and unable to reenter their own body. Many hauntings are caused by just such magics."

Then, it hit me. "You think he's here to get a new body."

"Not just any body. I have a strong suspicion he wants yours."

That threw me for a loop. "Why me? Can't he body-snatch whoever he wants?"

Finn pulled the covers closer around him and gave a barely perceptible shake of his head. "It is because of who you are, of what you are—and what you possess."

"He wants the Eye."

Finn lifted his shoulders an inch or so, then dropped them with a sigh. "Without a doubt. But he likely also sees you as a bonus, a sort of package deal that he just can't pass up. Even so, the joke's on him."

"Really? How so?"

Finn reached for a thermos, which I handed to him so he wouldn't have to get up. He poured himself another steaming cup of tea, and I waited while he collected his thoughts.

"How much do you know about the Eye?" he asked.

"I've been reading up on it, ever since it embedded itself inside my skull. But the records are vague about what it is, how it was made, and why Balor had it in his possession."

Finn sipped his tea. "Hmmm. Yes, I suppose they are. The Fomorians of Irish folklore might be compared to the Titans of

Greek legend. In fact, I think they were probably the same people, if you could call them that. But in reality, they were more like demons than anything else, monstrous creatures that never truly belonged to this plane of existence. Some were beautiful, all were terrible, and they were powerful enough to oppress the Tuatha Dé Danann for a time.

"That alone should tell you everything you need to know about the Fomorians. They were powerful, monstrous creatures who enjoyed conquest and destruction. Like the fae, the Fomorians drew their power from other worlds, but they were craftier. When Balor saw how men were using foci to store and wield magic, he decided to use such a device to make him that much more powerful."

"The Eye."

"Just so. The Eye was—and still is—a pure construct of Fomorian magic, crafted by Balor to focus and enhance what power he was already able to wield. But there's a difference between it and, say, an amulet or staff that a human might wield. The Eye has the ability to tap directly into the Fomorian plane of origin for power."

It was all starting to gel for me now. "So, the Eye has the potential to make any human the equal of the fae in magical power. No wonder he wants it. That could make the Fear Doirich the most powerful human magic user on earth."

"Exactly. In essence, he'd be god-like in the powers he could wield, much like the Tuatha and Fomorians of old. And there aren't very many fae left who wield that sort of power."

I pondered the implications, and asked the obvious question. "Finn, if that's so, then why haven't you and Maeve whisked me away and locked me up where the Fear Doirich can't find me?"

He extended a finger in the air. "Ah, now we come to the heart of the matter. See, Maeve can't use the Eye herself. The magic is anathema to her kind, in fact. It's why Lugh never used it either, even though he was half-Fomorian and Balor's grandson. Too much Tuatha blood. But Cúchulainn? He inherited many Fomorian traits from his true father. Do you see where I'm going with this?"

"I think so. You're saying that Cúchulainn's ríastrad was caused by his Fomorian ancestry, which he inherited from Lugh."

"Yes, and that's why the Eye chose you—or rather, your alter ego—to wield it. When Fuamnach cursed you with the ríastrad she somehow altered your physical make-up, giving you those same Fomorian traits that Cúchulainn possessed. Call it a sort of magical gene splicing, if you will.

"And that's why I'm not concerned about the Fear Doirich taking the Eye from you. For one, he could never wield it, and second, it wouldn't have him."

I took a deep breath and blew it out through pursed lips, gathering my thoughts after the revelation I'd just received about my curse.

"But Finn, aren't you forgetting something? If he takes my body over, then can he wield the Eye?"

Finn nodded. "Yup. But it ain't gonna happen."

"Why not?"

"Because the Eye makes you immune to necromancy, his most powerful magic!" The old man cackled and slapped his knee, spilling a small amount of tea as he did so. He set the cup down and wiped his eyes. "Ah, serves the dumb sumbitch right. He was always an asshole."

"I still need to take him out, Finn. And if I'm immune to most of his magic then I'm home free, right? I can just run in and kick his ass. Boom, done."

"Ah, but I said *most*. Meaning, not all. And what he can bring to bear without his necromancy is still enough to squash you flat. No, you can't fight him head on, that's for sure. You're going to have to be crafty about it.

"Good news is, I've been preparing for this. I knew eventually you'd figure it out and insist on going after him. So I came up with a plan. Here's how it's going to work—"

23

F inn and I spent the better part of an hour painting my body with runes in a complex spell that was designed to be nearly undetectable—at least until it was triggered for its intended purpose. When we were finished, I admired the old man's handiwork in the bathroom mirror. Finnegas might have been currently weakened by years of drug and alcohol abuse, but he was still a master of the druidic arts. Marking these runes on my skin and setting up this spell was pretty much child's play to him. It would have taken me months just to figure out the spell, and weeks to draw up the runes correctly.

"You ever consider taking up a career as a tattoo artist?" I asked with a wry grin. "I know a few studios in SoCo that would kill to have you slinging ink for them."

He scowled at me. "Bah. Probably have me doing bad Celtic knotwork and kanji tattoos." He stroked his beard and cocked an eyebrow. "Of course, it might not be a bad way to meet young, attractive women with daddy issues."

I chuckled as I craned my neck to get a look at the runes on my back. I wanted to remember how he'd done this, in case I needed to use this spell again in the future. I doubted I could pull the whole thing off myself, but there were components of it that might come in handy. The only downside was that it was pure druid magic, which meant I couldn't wear armor over it, or it would interfere with the spell. I'd have to go commando on this one... and I had a feeling it was going to hurt.

"Be careful not to smudge that. It still needs a few minutes to dry."

"Alright already. Get me a fan or something, will you? I'm kind of getting antsy."

Finn rolled his eyes at me and mumbled something about young people being impatient, but he shuffled away to grab a fan from the shop. While I waited, I pondered what he'd told me while he'd worked on the spell.

He'd explained that the Fear Doirich used an ingenious method that allowed him to jump from body to body and extend his lifespan. Each person consisted of three components or elements: the soul, which was basically a person's thoughts, emotions, memories, and personality; the spirit, which was literally the spiritual power supply for each person; and the body, obviously the corporeal shell that housed the soul and spirit while on this plane of existence.

According to Finn, the spirit served as a sort of metaphysical glue, melding the soul and body together as one. However, the Dark Druid had transferred his spirit into a phylactery, which freed his soul to jump from one body to another. When he wanted to do his body snatching thing—typically when his current vessel was nearing the end of its usefulness—he'd find a suitable and usually unwilling donor, cast some major necromantic juju, and force their soul from their body.

At which point the Fear Doirich would take up residence in said body, using the host's spirit to bind him within, until he needed to find a suitable replacement yet again. Finn's plan hinged on discovering where Darky Darkerson kept this phylactery of his. I'd need to find it before I confronted him, otherwise the whole plan was moot. In which case I'd either be squashed like a gnat, or the Fear Doirich would trigger my curse and then do a disappearing act, leaving me to tear up the city. All that death and destruction would power him up with death magic, which he'd eventually use to come back and kill me anyway, in order to take the Eye.

Either way, I was royally screwed. Everything hinged on me finding that phylactery. And I was pretty sure I knew exactly where it was—or, at least, who had it in their possession. All I needed to do was track that person down. And for that, I was going to need some supernatural assistance.

By the time Finn had returned with a shop heater, the ink was nearly dry. A few more minutes under the furnace blast of a forced air propane heater and I was all set. The old man flipped off the heater, and we stared at each other in the awkward silence.

He raised his chin at me, a universal male sign of regard and greeting. "If you die, don't worry—I'll be standing by to console your girlfriend."

"Hmpf. Like she'd go for a shriveled up old coot like you."

He crossed his arms and sniffed. "Daddy issues, my boy—it's every old man's ace in the hole. And I'm pretty sure your girl has them in spades."

"You're a horrible person, you know that?"

He winked and clapped a hand on my shoulder in what would have been a fatherly gesture, had he not just ruined the mood.

"Just trying to give you some last minute motivation, kid. Now, go have fun storming the castle."

I called Sabine before I left the junkyard, and asked her to relay a message to Chief Ookla and Guts through Maeve's people.

"Way ahead of you, druid boy. No way was I letting you take this guy on with just Gunnarson and his goons at your back. The trolls are going to meet you at the graveyard in thirty minutes."

"Thanks, Sabine. How's Bells doing?"

"Sleeping beauty is doing just fine. I'll keep an eye on her while you're gone. Just make sure to come back in one piece."

Sabine wasn't clued in on what was really going on, and I didn't feel the need to worry her with the details. Little did she know that I might not come back at all, if the Fear Doirich found out I was immune to his necromantic mojo before I was able to put the whammy on him.

"I'll do my best," I mumbled.

Sabine sighed. "Just don't get killed." Then she hung up.

Guts and his crew were waiting for me when I pulled up to the cemetery, decked out in their full battle rattle. They were wearing magically enhanced bone armor, and carried an assortment of war clubs, axes, and other fighting implements made from bone, bronze, and some sort of volcanic rock. This bunch were all stink-free, thankfully. I admired their gear as I walked up, reminded of both ancient Aztec and Maori weaponry. Hemi would've been pleased.

"Oy, mate—you starting the party without me?"

As if on cue, Hemi sauntered out of the shadows to join me. I greeted him with a fist bump and a bro shake.

"Man, I am glad to see you. I take it Sabine told you what was going down?"

"Sure enough. Whatever you need, bro. I got your back."

"Thanks, man. Just so you know, it's probably going to get hairy once the fighting starts."

He smiled. "That's why I came."

I greeted Guts as well, made introductions all the way

around, and looked over my crew. It consisted of about a dozen of Ookla's warriors, Guts, and Hemi. I'd called Gunnarson on the way over; he agreed to have a team in position to move in after the fighting started. I'd just have to keep my fingers crossed that he wouldn't bail on me and leave our asses hanging in the wind.

But, first things first. Once Finn had told me his plan, something that Madame Rousseau mentioned had clicked. I was pretty sure I knew exactly where to find the Dark Druid's phylactery, and that was our first order of business.

"Listen up, fellas. We're tracking a particular ghoul that's going to have a peculiar scent, like two humans in one body. Guts here knows the one we're looking for, because he's the same ghoul that led Bells and me into an ambush at the distillery and the sewers. Has your team picked up the trail yet, Guts?"

He smiled a crooked, lumpy grin. "We on the scent, know where he went. We find where he be—hunt good, you see."

"I have faith that your people will get the job done," I replied sincerely. These were the same warriors who'd rescued Bells and me. As far as I was concerned, they were worth twice as many of Gunnarson's people, because I trusted them.

Guts nodded enthusiastically, his muscles flexing in anticipation beneath gray-green lumpy flesh. "We bring tribe and Druid glory, no worry."

I turned to Hemi, who was stoically indifferent to the presence of the trolls. Despite the cold, he was dressed in board shorts and a t-shirt. His jade battle club was tucked into his waistband, and he held a six-foot whale bone spear in his right hand. I suspected it was incredibly old and rare. Runes carved along its length pulsed with magic.

"Hemi, we're going to let the trolls take the lead in tracking this ghoul down. He has something I need, and once we retrieve it we're going to proceed with the assault on the graveyard. I just need you guys to run interference so I can get close to our main target."

I glanced around the group, making momentary eye contact with everyone. "Under no circumstances are you to engage with the old man. He might look weak, but he's not, and it's my job to put him down. Even if it looks like he's about to take me out, do not interfere. Everyone got that?"

No response.

"Look, I need everyone to be clear on this. My plan hinges on taking a beating from this guy so I can get close to him. It's unavoidable. The last thing I need is someone playing hero and screwing up my plan. Am I understood?"

They all nodded, reluctantly. For this group, taking on the baddest dude would mean gaining honor for their tribes and families. When the time came, I hoped they'd resist the urge to attack the Dark Druid. I didn't need them getting in the way, and I'd feel terrible if any of them died needlessly.

Hemi raised a finger. "What if you're killed?"

I laughed. "Thanks for the vote of confidence. Look, if I go down don't try to avenge me. And if I start—*changing*—run. I won't be able to tell friend from foe after that. In either case, get as far away as you can, and alert Maeve's people or Gunnarson so they can evacuate the immediate area."

I guess my reputation had preceded me, because everyone nodded their assent.

"Alright, Guts. Go find me a super-ghoul."

We tracked the creature deep into the cemetery, staying away from the chapel to avoid alerting the Fear Doirich of our presence. I knew that once we took out his super-ghoul, it was on.

However, if things went according to plan, he wouldn't realize I'd snagged the phylactery until it was too late.

After a few minutes of tracking, Guts and his people had led us to the oldest part of the grounds. We'd made reasonably fast progress to this point, but suddenly the trackers slowed, finally coming to a halt in a cluster of old gravestones and rusted wrought iron fences.

Guts convened with his troll trackers and turned to me with a shrug. "They say trail end here, just disappear. So, ghoul must be near."

I shifted my senses into the magical spectrum and spotted a series of magical runes painted in blood on nearby grave markers and statuary. The spells were designed to keep undead creatures concealed by hiding all trace of them from the living. I recognized it as the Dark Druid's handiwork, since it matched the rune work I'd discovered at the condemned house.

I hated what I was about to do to these historic markers, but there was no avoiding it. I pulled a magic marker from my pocket and drew a circle around one of the runes. Then I drew several counter-runes inside that circle. Finally, I triggered my counter-spell with an incantation and a few small gestures.

Whoosh. The rune inside my circle dissolved, like smoke drifting into the darkness. I did the same to the other runes I found, and soon the smell of death and rot became so strong that even Hemi could smell it. The trackers signaled for us to follow, and they soon led us to a mausoleum tucked in the far corner of the grounds. The structure looked ancient, and was covered in an authentic patina of filth and decay, the kind only centuries of neglect can produce.

As we approached, the smell of rotting human flesh became overpowering. It was all I could do to keep from gagging. Hemi looked a little green around the gills as well, but Guts and his people appeared none the worse for the wear. I supposed they were used to it, and was glad they had been using magic to cover up their stench while on patrol for Maeve.

However, I'd come prepared this time, and pulled a small canister from my pocket. I rubbed some of the contents under each nostril, and handed it to Hemi so he could do the same.

"What is this, a magical cream or something?"

I shook my head. "Vick's Vaporub. Should help cover some of the smell."

He slathered the stuff liberally all over his upper lip. "Right then, let's get this done," he said. "Lead the way, Colin."

I pulled my war club out of my Craneskin Bag and headed through the opening in front of us. I paused inside to allow my eyes to adjust to the dark, and saw that the room was empty except for a granite sarcophagus in the middle of the space. I motioned for help, and Guts, Hemi and I lifted the lid and set it to the side as quietly as possible. Inside, a tunnel entrance had been dug through the granite floor of the tomb.

I signaled for Guts to leave his trolls outside to guard our retreat, and traded out my war club for a long knife and my Glock. I also strapped on a headlamp that had red LEDs in place of standard white bulbs. I possessed a very limited form of night vision, but even with a cantrip I still couldn't see in complete darkness. The red glow from the headlamp would be less likely to give us away, and would give off just enough light to allow me to see in the inky blackness below.

I climbed in and lowered myself to the bottom, crouching and shuffling out of the way to make room for Guts and Hemi. The smell of death inside the small tunnel was overwhelming, and it almost made me wish I could smell the trolls instead. Almost.

I followed the tunnel for about 30 feet with Hemi and Guts on my heels, until I heard something moving around ahead. I brought us to a halt and sheathed my knife, reaching into my bag for a little surprise I'd been working on since this whole thing had started. I pulled a mason jar from my bag, quickly drew a rune on the lid and another on the side, and hefted it in my right hand, keeping the Glock in the left. I could shoot equally well with either hand, but throwing was another matter; the last thing I wanted was to flub a toss and get this stuff on us instead of the ghoul.

I motioned for Hemi and Guts to stay back, then crept forward as quietly as possible. Soon I saw a bulky shadow shuffling around in the murky darkness, about twenty feet ahead. I muttered an incantation and threw the jar as hard as I could at the thing, flipping the switch on my headlamp to give us more light at the same time.

The jar hit the ghoul on the left leg, shattering and splashing the contents all over its lower body. The contents of my magical "grenade" had an immediate effect, and the ghoul's flesh began bubbling and smoking like nobody's business. The ghoul howled in anguish and headed straight for us, making me wish I'd prepared another jar.

After my first encounter with this ghoul, I decided I didn't care to tangle with it again if I didn't have to. That's when I went to work on a spell that would allow me to take it out from a distance. I settled on a sort of "acid bomb," based on a mixture of lye and water. Lye was the stuff farmers and mobsters used to get rid of dead bodies, but it normally took a while for it to work. That's where the magic part came in; lye dissolved flesh, and the spell I'd paired it with simply sped up the process.

My acid grenade spell did exactly what I'd intended, and the ghoul's legs deliquesced before it reached us. Even a magically-animated corpse needed muscles and tendons to move, and the thing stumbled and fell flat on its face. Fortunately, my aim had been true and the spell hadn't killed it, instead only serving to slow it down. It pulled itself along with its arms and hands, roaring furiously at us in either pain or anger; I couldn't tell which.

As it neared, Hemi stepped forward and aimed the sharp end of his staff at the ghoul's head.

"No, don't kill it!" I shouted. "We need to keep it alive, so its master won't know we're coming."

He stepped back and relaxed. "You might have mentioned that before we came in here."

I shrugged. "Didn't know if my spell would work or not." I reached into my bag and pulled out my short sword, then went about the grim work of hacking the thing's arms off. A minute or so later, a squirming, limbless torso was the only thing left.

Guts looked on in approval. "Druid right. No arms, no legs, no can fight."

Hemi rubbed his chin. "Can these things regenerate?"

"A little, but not from something this serious. And not without dead bodies to eat, or their master's help. Guts, can you hold this thing down for me?"

Guts complied, pinning it facedown with a knee in its back. The ghoul struggled desperately to crane its neck around and take a chunk out of the troll.

"Now for the fun part." I glanced at Hemi. "If you have a weak stomach, you might want to look away."

I cut a hole in the ghoul's back, right under its rib cage, and stuck my hand inside up to the elbow. The smell was enough to make me sick, and it felt just as I expected it would—like I was digging through putrefied human organs. I felt resistance as my hand reached the thing's diaphragm, the muscle that separated the chest cavity from the abdomen. I leaned in and pushed until my hand pierced the thick layer of dead muscle. Once through, I dug around a bit more until I found what I needed.

"Hell yeah. Now we're in business."

I pulled out my find and held it up in the red light of my

headlamp. It was a crystal, roughly an inch in diameter and four inches in length, possibly quartz or some kind of gemstone. It pulsed gently in my hand, almost like a beating heart—but much, much more slowly. I wiped it off on the ghoul's hoodie, and a closer examination revealed something moving and swirling inside.

I nodded at my companions and stood.

"Alright, fellas. Time to go ruin a necromancer's day. Just as soon as I get some alone time with a pack of baby wipes."

24

Guts was shocked that I wouldn't want the scent of dead ghoul all over me. He insisted it would be a turn on for the troll maidens back at his camp, and that I'd have my pick if I'd only leave it on. I tactfully explained how much I appreciated his advice, but that my mate wouldn't understand if I took up with a troll maiden.

He gave me a puzzled look in return, and said something to the effect of, "Druid is nuts, but more for Guts."

But Hemi just wouldn't let it go, and kept razzing me about it as we made our way closer to the chapel.

"I dunno, Colin. I'd think you'd like the idea of having a couple of half-troll ankle biters around, to pass on your druidic knowledge to and what-not."

"That's not in the cards for me, Hemi. But, I'm sure Guts here can put in a good word for you with the ladies back at the troll camp."

Guts scowled at me. "Pah! Troll girl no can like until see how man fight."

I chuckled. "Looks like you already struck out there, big guy. What a shame."

"Meh, it's alright. My mum probably already has a nice Maori girl picked out for me back home. A fine, strong woman with lots of meat on her bones. Just my type."

We were close to the chapel, and I gave the signal to end the chatter. I gestured for Guts to gather his warriors around. We remained hidden behind a low wall, and once everyone was within hearing range I whispered my final instructions.

"I just texted Gunnarson that we're ready to make our assault. Once we go in, expect heavy resistance—"

At that very moment, a hand burst from the ground and grabbed one of the troll warriors around the ankle. Then two hands shot out of the ground—then ten, and within seconds we were under a massive surprise attack by the Dark Druid's ghouls.

"It's a trap!" Hemi yelled with a grin on his face, slashing and stabbing left and right with glee as he waded into the attacking undead.

I yelled at him as I decapitated a ghoul coming up on Guts' six. "Damn it, Hemi, you beat me to the punch. I almost got to drop an Ackbar reference twice in one week."

Guts was busy hacking away at two ghouls with an obsidian hand axe, but found the time to chime in and surprise us both.

"Trolls look up to Admiral Ackbar—he real hero of War of Stars, and best-looking by far."

I ducked a lunging ghoul, sweeping its leg and causing it to brain itself on a tombstone. I pivoted and shot another under the jaw, blowing its brains out the top of its skull. By this point, the fighting was too fierce to engage in any more casual banter. Even so, I muttered a shocked response under my breath.

"Trolls are fans of the greatest space opera ever. Who knew?"

I vaulted a low cast iron fence to avoid three ghouls converging on me, and climbed on a low-roofed mausoleum to gain a tactical advantage. I shot two of them through the tops of their skulls, and buried my short sword in the neck of the third. The thing fell, wrenching the sword from my grasp.

"Damn it to hell," I muttered.

Thankfully, I'd come prepared with spare ammo. I emptied the mag into four or five ghouls in an effort to help my companions out, then quickly swapped out a fresh mag as I surveyed the battleground. We were holding our own, but just barely. Despite the dozens of ghouls scattering the ground, more kept coming.

That's when I realized the huge tactical error I'd made. As a powerful necromancer, the Fear Doirich had an unlimited supply of dead bodies to animate here in the graveyard. And while most were in a sorry state and easy to destroy, he could simply overrun us with the sheer numbers at his command. Where he was getting the necromantic power to raise them was beyond me, but the fact remained that if this kept up, we were done for.

I holstered the pistol and reached into my Craneskin Bag for my war club. I had to get to the chapel and take the Fear Doirich out, otherwise every single one of us was going to die. Two of Guts' warriors were already down, and the way those ghouls chewed on their rubbery hides, I didn't think they'd regenerate fast enough to get back into the fight.

I searched briefly and spotted Hemi. He was backed against a low wall, spinning that whalebone spear like a plane propeller, crushing skulls and making frightening faces as he fought. His tattoos glowed a bright blue-green, the color of the ocean on a warm sunny day. He looked happy, of all things, but I knew he was aware of our current predicament. He took out the last two ghouls in front of him, gaining a momentary reprieve. The big man cast his eyes about until he spotted me atop my perch.

"Colin, where the hell are Gunnarson's people?" he yelled.

"I don't know," I replied. "But I need to get to the chapel. I'm going to hop off here and wade through these bastards so I can make it to the back door. Gather up the trolls, cover my back, and follow me so we can make a stand there."

"Understood," was his only response. He went into whirling dervish mode, mowing his way through the throng of ghouls ahead of him to rejoin the remaining trolls.

"On me, mates!" he yelled, smashing his way into the midst of the trolls, rallying them to form up on him and Guts. They quickly circled their wagons. I counted eight trolls remaining, including Guts.

There was a slim chance we'd draw away the ghouls feeding on the downed trolls when we advanced on the chapel, but I wasn't hopeful. I wished them a speedy journey to the troll version of *Tír Tairngire*, the Promised Land, and vowed to make their sacrifices count.

I bashed away the few ghouls trying to join me atop the mausoleum, then got a short running start and jumped over the rest. I rolled as I hit the ground and came up in a sprint, making a beeline for the chapel and swinging like mad at every ghoul who got in my way. I had no time to see if Guts, Hemi, and the rest were at my back or not. I just kept mowing down ghouls in hopes they were right behind. Soon I saw the dimly lit windows of the old building ahead.

As I neared the chapel, the ghouls thinned out. It was apparent the Fear Doirich had known the direction we would come from, and had planned his ambush accordingly. I only hoped he didn't suspect I'd stolen his phylactery, and that I could keep it secret long enough to get close to him and activate Finn's spell.

Finding the back door unlocked, I burst into the chapel, scanning the area inside for threats. Surprisingly there were none, so I turned to see how the trolls and Hemi had fared.

Several trolls filed in after me, looking exhausted but already healing from their wounds. Guts and Hemi formed the rear guard, holding off the undead while the rest escaped to the chapel. As the last troll entered, the Maori and the troll warrior smashed a few more skulls, then we pulled them inside and locked the door.

The back entry was made of heavy wood, with bars over its window. It wouldn't hold for long.

"Guts, get your boys to barricade this entrance and the front entrance, and the windows as well. But make sure you leave an escape route, because if things go south with the druid you'll need to leave quickly."

He nodded at me and started barking orders in trollish. Hemi stood guard at the door, bracing it with his back until the trolls shored it up with a few church pews. Once they appeared to have things under control, I headed to the sanctuary and began looking in earnest for stairs, a trap door, or anything that might lead to a crypt below us. Searching in vain for several minutes, I remembered a scene from an episode of Blacklist and pushed on the lectern. It tipped over on a hinge, revealing a laddered stairway down.

I gave Hemi a half-assed salute before slipping down the steps. "Wish me luck."

"Warriors make their own luck, mate. Kick his ass."

I smiled and headed into the darkness, tripping my night vision cantrip when I hit bottom. Dim light streamed through cracks in the floor above, revealing a small stone room and a sturdy wooden door opposite the steps. I opened it and headed down a short hall, which led to another door. This one was covered in glyphs and runes, which from the looks of them had been written in blood. I wondered how many people had been sacrificed down there in order to animate all the undead above. The very thought angered me, and it took an effort to regain my composure before examining the wards on the door.

"The wards won't harm you, boy," a muffled voice proclaimed from the other side of the door. "You and you alone are free to enter."

I decided to check for myself, and shifted my vision into the magical spectrum to examine the wards, just in case.

"You sure went through a lot of trouble to get me here," I shouted. As far as I could tell, the old druid was telling the truth. The spells were nastier than an incubus with the clap, but they were specifically designed to recognize druidic magic. I muttered a short incantation and gestured rapidly with both hands, and the wards temporarily released.

The old caretaker's voice replied as I placed my hand on the door knob. "When you're as old as I am, you get bored. Watching you chase my ghouls around the city was a much needed distraction. And you turned out to be so full of surprises! Quite unlike Finn's other pupils."

I hesitated, then turned the knob and pulled the door open, ducking out of the way in case he was waiting with a spell or some other attack. When nothing happened, I peeked around the door frame.

A tall figure stood in the shadows on the other side of a room that was roughly twenty feet square. The space was more or less a smaller version of the sanctuary and nave upstairs. However, this worship area had been defiled by all manner of foul magics and desecrations.

The old caretaker frowned as he stepped into the light. "Oh, do come in. If I'd wanted you dead, you'd already be one of my ghouls."

I took in the scene before me, aghast in spite of myself. The pews had been moved from the center of the room and now lined the walls, making space for a huge necromantic circle that adorned the floor, easily fifteen feet across. It and the runes within and without had been painted in thick lines of blood. Whether human or animal, I couldn't tell—but I suspected human. I saw no corpses or signs of sacrifice beyond the massive amount of dried blood on the floor, but the smells of fresh blood, vomit, feces, and urine were overpowering.

Fear, I thought. *That's the smell of absolute, mind-rending terror.* Someone had recently lost their life in this room. Perhaps several someones.

I made eye contact with the druid, observing his every detail. He was now dressed in a dark hooded tunic over jeans and black boots. A thick leather belt secured his tunic. A sword hung from one hip, a dagger from the other. He held a tall carved staff that appeared to have been made from bone and some dark stained wood. As I approached the circle I paused, stopping a few feet short of the edge.

Not yet, I thought. *Let him think his magics repel me.*

"Your entertainment almost killed my girlfriend."

His face barely registered any emotion at all, except perhaps distaste. "Mortals come and go, Colin. That's something you learn, once you've lived a few centuries. What's one girl's life in the grand scheme of things?"

"Is that why you killed Erskine, even after he'd served you faithfully?"

The old man nodded. "Erskine was a tool who had served his purpose. Besides, I needed his spirit to power more ghouls."

"That's cold."

"Please, spare me the maudlin crap. Humans are cattle, an

expendable resource. I'm sure your vampire friend would tell you the same. Such a shame you'll never experience the freedom that comes from realizing everything around you is transient, but you."

"Finn doesn't seem to think so."

His face darkened. "Yes. But Finnegas was always too senti-mental to accept that truth."

I took note of how he rankled at the mention of Finn's name. Definitely bad blood there.

"Do you intend to kill me?"

He laughed. "Kill you? Of course not. On the contrary, I don't want to harm a single hair on your head. You see, my young healthy friend, I intend to inhabit that magnificent body of yours. And then I'm going to march my undead into Maeve's demesne and secure it for a very close friend of mine. In fact, you're my prize for taking the bitch queen out of the picture."

"Maeve's no easy target."

He rubbed his hands slowly. "She will be, once I have you. And the Eye."

"And if I resist?"

He considered the possibility, for a second or two at least. Maybe he was just humoring me.

"Oh, you don't want to do that. It'll only cause you pain, Colin. Needless, senseless pain. Besides, it might force me to harm your physical form. And to be honest, I've always been horrible at healing magic. So please don't resist."

I pursed my lips and nodded. "So that's how it is, huh?"

"That's how it is." He extended his gnarled hands in front of him and examined them with interest. "And how it was for the McCool whose body I currently inhabit. What was he, four generations removed from you? Five? I forget now. But for some reason, it seems your line is particularly suited to necromantic possession. Thank goodness that old fool Finnegas is so invested in keeping you McCools alive."

What the hell? How long had this guy been body-snatching my ancestors, anyway? And did Finn know? If so, it meant that once again Finn had failed to reveal the entire story, leaving me to be blindsided by the truth. The old bastard looked up and flashed a long-toothed grin at me.

"Would you believe that you weren't my first choice for a replacement? I should be wearing your father's skin right now! That is, if he hadn't died before I could transfer my soul into his body. He put up quite a fight, and then decided to take his own life before I could complete the transfer. Such a waste."

"Bastard!" I screamed at the top of my lungs, simultaneously drawing my Glock and snapping off three shots, two aimed at his chest and one at his head. All three rounds melted into slag as they reached the invisible barrier made by the Fear Doirich's mage circle. They hung in the air for a second, maybe two, then were vaporized into nothingness.

"Wondering why Finn never told you? It's because he doesn't know, my boy. And oh, he's suspected as much, and tried to hunt me down himself a few times. But while his magic has faded over the centuries, mine's as strong as ever. He couldn't find me unless I wanted him to. Perhaps that day will come soon, yes?"

I fumed where I stood, still pointing the pistol at the druid's face. I was on the balls of my feet, and it took everything I had to keep from charging into the circle to take him on.

I felt a slight breeze on my cheek and heard a voice in my ear —the softest whisper, far too low for the Fear Doirich to hear.

Not yet, my love. Wait.

"Jesse?" I asked, forgetting everything else at the sound of her voice.

The Dark Druid rolled his eyes. "She speaks to you, eh? I've seen her following you everywhere over the last few weeks, moping along behind you while you ran all over town with that painted whore. Imagine, Colin—she was right there all the while, suffering while you humped that trash."

The druid must've have seen something register in my eyes.

"You weren't aware. I see. Well, this evening is turning out to be just full of surprises for you, isn't it?"

He crossed his arms and tapped a finger on his lips. "You could be with her again, you know—once I inhabit your body."

"Liar." My response simmered out in a low whisper.

"I assure you that I speak the truth. Your soul will be trapped on this plane, just as hers is right now. You'd have centuries to spend together. Perhaps millennia. That's what you want more than anything, isn't it? It's written on your face, Colin. Why not make this easy on us both?"

I narrowed my eyes and nodded slowly. "You want me? Fine, you can have me then."

I whipped the gun up to my head and pulled the trigger.

25

I knew I couldn't kill myself. I'd tried in the months after Jesse's death; oh, how I'd tried. But each time I had, my curse would kick in. My "Hyde-side" turned out to be resistant to just about every physical insult imaginable. Gunshot wounds, thirty-story falls, drowning, drug overdoses—there was virtually nothing that could kill me, short of perhaps complete immolation at ground zero of a nuclear detonation. Which I'd considered, by the way. But I couldn't come up with a means of stealing a nuclear warhead that didn't involve killing a ton of people.

However, the Fear Doirich didn't know that. I was certain that he knew about my ríastrad, the curse that caused me to morph into a twisted, deadly version of myself that was apparently one hundred percent Fomorian nightmare. He also knew I had Balor's Eye lodged inside my skull. Oh, he wanted his hands on that bad boy, I could tell.

But he had no idea I'd survive a bullet to the skull. None at all. I banked on the fact that he'd be ready and waiting in the event I attempted self-harm.

I was right. In an instant, dark inky tendrils rose from between the flagstones beneath my feet, whipping about and wrapping around my arms like the limbs of some great dark octopus—or perhaps the deadly appendages of an eldritch nightmare. They felt fairly solid, but I was certain I could break the bonds with little effort. Just as Finn had said, I was mostly immune to the druid's necromancy.

Yet, the druid's magic proved sufficient to alter my aim, and the bullet missed completely. The Fear Doirich closed the gap in a heartbeat, moving with nearly the alacrity I'd seen in ancient vampires and fae.

"Ah, ah, ah—naughty of you to try that. Fortunately, I learned my lesson with your father. Unfortunate for you, I suppose. But you'll be with your ghost girl soon, never fear."

I allowed the tendrils of inky black to lift me up and draw me into the circle with the druid. He floated back to the center as his magic pulled me in, closer to where I wanted to be. His death magic held me a few inches off the ground, roughly three feet from where he stood.

Just a bit closer, I thought. *C'mon, you decrepit son of a bitch, come closer and get me.*

He spared me one more glance and tsked.

"This might hurt a bit," he said.

He closed his eyes and began chanting. More shadowy necromantic magic rose from the floor beneath us, weaving itself in complex patterns around his body and arms. Then those tendrils shimmered as the magic concentrated in thin tight bands, crawling like little snakes to coalesce in a dark ropy mass around each of his hands, until they pulsed with an eerie glowing darkness.

That is, if you could call it a glow. It was more like the absence of light, as if the magic was erasing the warmth and energy from the space around it. Watching it was incredibly disconcerting, and the evil emanating from the old druid repulsed me to my core.

His eyes snapped open, revealing pupils large and black. He began floating toward me, extending his arms and that dark evil magic toward my chest.

"Now, I will have a new vessel, one that will last me thousands of years. And you will be with your beloved." His eyes swam with the same inky blackness that surrounded his hands, until it obscured both the pupils and whites. "Everyone wins, Colin. Relax and it will all be over soon."

I waited until I could smell the stench of his breath, to the point when his dark magic had nearly touched my chest. His breath smelled of clotted blood and flesh. Now I knew what had become of the missing organs from the bodies he'd sacrificed. Disgusting.

His hands touched me. I felt the cold, writhing pulse of his magic against my skin. Then, it just stopped, like it hit a wall of glass. The druid's face registered confusion and disbelief.

"What? What is this?"

"Problems? I guess I forgot to mention—side effect of the Eye. I'm immune to your death magic bullshit."

His face contorted in fury. "No! I've slain dozens of people to power this spell. This cannot be happening!"

"Oh, it be happening." I strained against the shadowy bonds that held me and snapped my right hand into my Craneskin Bag, grabbing the phylactery and pulling it free.

I swung as hard as I could, punching him in the chest and smashing the phylactery in my fist with the impact, driving shards of the crystal deep into my hand as his spirit released. I extended my arm to the side, letting the remaining shards fall as I spoke the trigger words to the spell Finn had prepared.

"*Póg mo thóin*, bitch."

The trigger words to the spell could've been anything, but Finn had wanted to send a message to the Fear Doirich. For my part, I was more than happy to deliver it for him. "Kiss my ass" in Gaelic seemed appropriate at the moment.

There was a *whoomp* and a burst of light as the runes on my body flared. Green druidic magic flowed out from my hands and into the Dark Druid's chest. The light of Finn's spell combined with my own magic was designed to do one thing, and one thing only: to bind the Fear Doirich's spirit and soul to his current body, for good.

"No!" he screamed as he realized what Finn and I had done. He struggled against the bonds of my teacher's spell as it entered his body. Tendrils of bright green magic displaced his own necromantic energies, snuffing them out as they wrapped around his arms and legs to hold him tight.

White and green light suffused the Fear Doirich's form, until it shone from his mouth and chased the darkness from his eyes. The magic flared brightly, bright enough to nearly blind me and illuminate the room. As it did, every necromantic rune and glyph, and every last trace of the necromantic circle, vanished in an instant. It was as though every trace of necromancy had been purged from the Dark Druid's body, and from the room.

Because that's exactly what Finn's spell had done.

Then the magic released him and the Fear Doirich slumped to the floor, catching himself on his hands and knees. I fell as well, struggling to one knee, drained of energy by the spell.

The druid looked up at me, his eyes human once more but full of menace.

"What have you done to me, boy? What have you done?"

I stumbled to my feet and ran.

I slammed the door to the crypt behind me and tossed a simple cantrip at the door to jam the lock. It wouldn't stop him, but it might slow him down for a few more seconds. I needed time to get in the open before he caught up to me. Plus, I needed to give Hemi, Guts, and the remaining trolls time to evacuate. Things were about to get ugly.

I scrambled up the steps to the chapel and slammed the lectern back in place. Hemi, Guts, and four troll warriors stood dazed amidst a sea of ghouls. Some of them were intact, others in various states of dismemberment. None moved. My people looked like shit.

Hemi turned to me and waved, looking slightly shell-shocked. "They just collapsed, all at once. We were about to be overrun, and they all fell like their strings had been cut. Is he dead?"

"We should be so lucky. Help me move something against this thing, now. Then you guys need to haul ass."

The trolls, Hemi, and I managed to roll a dilapidated church organ near the lectern. We flipped it on its side, wedging the lectern in place. I knew it wouldn't hold for long.

I grabbed Hemi by the arm. "Help Guts gather up his survivors, and then you guys get the hell out of here, just as far away as you can. Once the druid gets hold of me, it's going to get messy fast."

Hemi screwed his mouth up in consternation. "I can't let you take this clown on by yourself. He'll kill you, Colin."

I shook my head. "Trust me, he can't kill me. But once he starts in on me, I'll be as much a danger to you guys as he is. Now go—get out of here before he recovers from Finn's spell."

Guts clapped me on the shoulder. "Honor to fight with druid of might."

"The honor's all mine, Guts."

I watched as he and his trolls made their exit, moving like a bunch of green, lumpy extras from *The Last of the Mohicans*.

Those guys were rubbery ninjas that healed like Deadpool. Just as ugly, too, but damned handy to have in a fight.

Hemi clapped me on the shoulder and followed after them.

"I'm buying the beer after this," he shouted as he left the chapel.

If I make it out of this alive, I thought. *And I give myself 50/50 odds, at best.*

Finnegas had warned me I'd have only a minute or two to prepare once the spell had taken effect. What the Fear Doirich was experiencing right now was the feeling of mortality, along with all the aches and pains that age and decrepitude brought with it. Unlike Finnegas, who had slowed his aging process through magic, the Dark Druid had been jumping from body to body for two thousand years, discarding his hosts when each "vessel" was no longer of use.

He'd also used necromancy to sustain his physical hosts when they started to wear out, much in the way that necromancy preserved the dead. Strictly speaking, the body he was using was dead, but it had been kept in a state of suspension through magical means. That meant he'd never really experienced what it felt like to be old. Now that I'd removed the magical effects from his current body and locked him inside, it'd take him a few minutes to get his bearings.

But he was still hella dangerous. I needed to be ready for him when he recovered. Mundane weapons would be no good against him, because he'd be magically warded. And my magic was no match for his, that was for sure. I'd have to rely on treachery and the few magical weapons I had at my disposal. A loud crash from below told me he was on his way. I ran out the back door of the chapel, digging through my Craneskin bag.

My main fear was that he'd catch me in the open, trigger my curse, and then I'd get loose and rampage all over East Austin and the campus, which was just across the highway from here. I couldn't let that happen, and thankfully I knew just the place to finish this once and for all. I headed there at full speed, casting small spells and cantrips left and right. They were traps that would mostly be minor annoyances to him—but they would lead him straight to me.

There was a huge explosion behind me, and I looked over my shoulder to see the organ flying through the air, headed my direction. I dove to the left between some headstones, and it crashed to the earth right where I'd been a split-second before. Organ shrapnel pelted me as the thing shattered on impact. I rolled to my feet and sprinted on.

The mausoleum where we'd found the druid's super-ghoul was just as we'd left it. I wasted no time diving into the sarcophagus, tumbling down the hole at the bottom and into the tunnel underneath. I reached to flip on my headlamp and cursed when I discovered it was missing. Scrambling on all fours, feeling my way ahead in the dark, I followed the tunnel as quickly as possible to its terminus in the room where we'd left the ghoul.

Once I heard the groans of a struggling, limbless ghoul, I paused and pulled out my phone so I could use the glow from the screen to lay my trap. I pulled out my final surprise in the dim light, shoving it into the soft earthen ceiling of the tunnel above me. I set the fuse on my spell with a rune I hastily scratched in the dirt, and then I walked to the other side of the cavern, kicking the now helpless ghoul in the ribs for the hell of it along the way.

I turned off my phone, and waited.

I didn't have to wait long. The tunnel soon lit up with a soft silver glow, the kind that came from ancient druid battle magic. Finn had demonstrated some of it for Jesse and me, once. It was mostly elemental magic—lightning, fire, and the like. But he'd refused to teach it to us, saying it was too dangerous for us to learn just yet.

Damn it if I didn't wish I'd tried to steal those spells from him now. I didn't have a lick of warded clothing on at the moment, nor armor or kevlar of any kind. Just my old Army trench, combat boots, jeans, and a now bloodied and filthy white dress shirt.

But what I did have I held at hand, ready for the druid to appear. As he strode into view, his eyes all aglow with silver light, lightning dancing off his fingertips, I hurled my magic spear with all my might. It flew true and straight, right at the druid's heart.

He caught it just as it reached his tunic. I'd never seen a human move that quickly. The old druid turned the spear over in his hands, as if admiring the craftsmanship.

"Not bad work, I have to say. Not good enough to kill me, but not bad."

He thrust the spear into the ground, halfway up the shaft, then snapped the rest of the handle off like a dried twig.

"Now, my turn," he said, and smiled a devilish grin.

Lightning shot out from his right hand, catching me in the chest and blasting me into the dirt wall behind me. I hung there for a moment—not suspended by magic, but held by the suction of the impression my back had made in the dirt. It felt just like you might think—like I'd just been struck by one hundred million volts of electricity, and thrown back by a shockwave caused by instantly super-heating the air in front of me to 20,000 degrees Fahrenheit.

I was completely stunned and unable to breathe, like I'd had the wind knocked out of me by a giant, invisible hand. I slid off the wall and collapsed. Finally my body recovered and I began taking in short, gasping breaths.

It's now or never, I thought. I muttered the words that would trigger my own spell, and the tunnel behind the druid exploded —not quite with the force of his lightning bolt, but with enough force to knock him flat.

And to collapse the tunnel.

I struggled to my knees, still wheezing. There was a huge black hole burned into my shirt, and the flesh underneath was charred and smoking. I couldn't feel a thing, but that was because I was in shock.

"You're trapped down here with me now, bitch," I mumbled.

He brushed himself off and floated to his feet. I'd just hit the guy with a spell that had basically been a magical demolition charge, and he *floated* off the ground. This was not good.

He sneered at me with contempt and floated closer. The light of his magic dappled the walls, floor, and ceiling of the small cavern like moonlight dancing on water.

"Stupid boy. Do you think me trapped? Think I can't destroy you and escape this hole?" He landed in front of me, and squatted in order to get in my face. "I *will* have what I came for. Well, the other thing I came for. Obviously you're damaged goods now, even if I could make the transfer. But once I have the Eye, I'm sure it won't matter."

He grabbed my jaw with his left hand, lifting my chin as he drew his right hand back, fingers extended into a claw. I watched as a ball of lighting grew to fill his hand.

"Prepare to be with your beloved."

The druid slammed his hand into my head with tremendous force. I felt searing pain, then everything went black. In an instant all was dark and silent. It was as if I'd been transported to a place where nothing existed—a perfect void.

It was peaceful, yet frighteningly vast and empty.

I saw her approach from out of the nothingness, like she'd just walked into the room with me. Except there wasn't a room, there was nothing—not heat, sound, light, or pressure. She was just there, all at once, and the warmth of her presence filled the space around me.

Jesse.

She smiled. *I can't stay for long, because your other self is coming.*

No, Jess, don't go. Stay with me.

She strode up and touched my cheek. I felt her caress in my core, at the seat of my being. I could only describe what I felt as pure love.

You can't stay here, either. Your time isn't done yet. But don't worry, my love. I won't be long gone from you. She kissed me lightly on the lips. *Now, go kick his ass.*

26

The transformation was already taking place when I came back to consciousness. But this time was different. As always, I felt disconnected from myself, from that other side of myself—like a passenger on a roller coaster ride from hell.

As I watched my body transform, warping into that massive, hideous beast, I tried to figure out what was different. Then I realized what it was; I wasn't alone.

I heard a voice inside my head. Which was weird, because *I* was inside my head.

I calculate an eight-in-ten chance that the druid will destroy your Fomorian form. This is unacceptable.

By this point, my Hyde-side was battling it out with the Dark Druid. And, the druid did appear to be winning. Yet, no matter how many times I—we—got pounded into the dirt by the druid's magic, we popped right back up again and came at the old bastard one more time.

But that couldn't last forever. At some point, the damage would be more than my magically-altered cells could heal.

I gave a mental shrug. "Well, I don't know what you expect

me to do about it. It's not like I can just eat a Snickers and regain control of myself."

If you die, the druid will gain possession of me. He cannot wield me properly, and my purpose will not be fulfilled. This outcome is unacceptable.

"Again, it sounds like tough titties to me, Eye. If you wanted to help out, you should have piped up before the evil druid started kicking my ass."

I cannot. Your human form will not allow me to communicate with you. It is only when you transform that I can speak to you in this way.

"You know what? For a sentient magical object of unimaginable power, you're no flipping help at all."

I am a transdimensional being trapped within a physical object that binds me to this plane of existence. The object is merely my anchor to this world. I am not a rock.

"Whatever." I remembered our first encounter, and mentally frowned. "By the way, what the hell happened to your great big booming 'I channeled the power of a god!' voice?"

I am speaking directly to you, consciousness to consciousness. Sound volume has no meaning here, as the laws of physics do not apply.

I watched through the eyes of my other self as the druid sliced off my arm at the elbow. It was a nifty spell—a thin sheet of hyper-compressed air moving at tremendous speed, basically the mass of an elephant compressed down to the width of a razor blade's edge. Damn it but this guy was good. Except, he'd been aiming for my neck. My other self was too fast for him. But only just.

You will soon die.

"He will. But from the looks of it, I won't feel a thing."

And actually, I didn't. For some reason, I wasn't as present in my other form as I had been in the past. The pain was still there, somewhere, but I just wasn't receiving it at full volume. I felt helpless, sure, but only in the way you might feel helpless to stop a car accident happening right in front of you. Was it upsetting? Yeah, but I'd just been with Jesse. In a few seconds, I'd be back with her. Seemed like an even trade.

I cannot allow it. I need you alive.

"Wait a minute—I thought you wanted the *other* me to wield you? Wasn't that the whole point of this Vulcan mind-meld thing you did?"

The other half of you will not listen. While I find its destructive nature to be appealing, and while its genetic code allows me to connect with your mind through my anchor, it is too feral to be of use to me.

"Can't you just fly out of my head and blast the Fear Doirich yourself?"

There is not sufficient time to do so. It took a tremendous amount of energy and several hours to completely anchor my magic in your Fomorian form. I cannot instantly leave this body. By the time I did, the druid would already have defeated you.

"Huh. Sounds like you screwed yourself when you anchored yourself in my skull. Well done."

If you were in control of your Fomorian form, we might work together. Our desired goals are aligned, although you cannot see that yet.

"Again, Eye—you screwed yourself. I'm as much of a passenger here as you are."

Not so. My magic is sufficient to allow you control over your Fomorian form, at least for a short time. Long enough to defeat the druid, certainly.

"Hmmm—nah, I think not. I have somebody waiting for me on the other side."

Unacceptable. I cannot allow your physical form to perish. Prepare for transposition of astral consciousness in three—two—

"No, wait! I don't want to—"

—one.

The sensation of returning to consciousness in my altered physical form hit me like a truck. All at once I felt more physically powerful than I ever had. I felt absolutely superhuman, at least for the span of a millisecond or so.

Then the pain hit. The Fear Doirich was frying me, from the inside out. I had no reference point for this level of torment. The agony was something I'd never imagined possible. And the bitch of it was, I couldn't even scream. All I could do was crouch on my knees and my remaining hand, virtually paralyzed.

The druid's current magical attack is super-heating the air inside your lungs and boiling the fluid within your body. While your Fomorian cells can renew organ tissue relatively quickly, we must counter-attack immediately if you are to survive.

I felt the Eye shifting inside my head, coming to rest somewhere behind my eyeballs.

Lift your head.

I did, although it took a tremendous effort.

Now, open your eyes.

I strained to open my eyes, fighting against the desire to pass out from the inferno raging inside my chest. As I did, a huge torrent of magical energy burst forth from each orbit, striking the druid square in the chest. The force of it threw him across the small cavern.

Holy shit, I thought. *I am freaking Darkseid.*

I have no knowledge of this entity. Again.

I locked my eyes on the druid, who was struggling to his feet on the other side of the cave. Once more, the Eye's magic focused and released through my own body, practically immolating the druid's tunic. The old bastard was magically shielded, so the blast didn't outright kill him. But even a hack druid like me could see that his wards wouldn't hold much longer.

I rose to my feet, which took a superhuman effort considering I was barely able to take air into my lungs. The pain was still there, and I was nearly paralyzed with panic by my inability to breathe properly. Honestly, who thought up spells like that? I concluded that this bastard was one evil son of a bitch, and he *really* had to die.

Finally, my lungs started working again. I took a huge breath, perhaps the sweetest I'd ever taken. I focused my gaze on the Fear Doirich again and felt the Eye's magic gathering behind my eyes. The druid swayed back and forth, and it looked like he was barely holding it together. He held one hand extended in front of him, fingers weaving in complex patterns as he chanted. That hand was readying his ward for the coming attack. But his other hand was doing something behind his back.

Was he casting two spells at once?

A ragged oval sprang into existence behind him, the space beyond reminiscent of the nothingness where I'd met with Jesse moments before. The druid spared me one last look of hatred, then stepped through the portal. It winked out just as the Eye's blast struck one final time.

"Impossible," I wheezed. I'd never seen a spellcaster weave two complex spells at once. No one was that good.

The blast struck the wall of earth behind where the druid had stood, and the concussive force of the magic threw earth and stone everywhere. A deep rumbling soon followed, and dirt and debris began falling all around.

The roof of the cavern fell in on me, and then everything went black.

I came around just as the trolls and Hemi were dragging me out of my earthen grave. Apparently, they'd followed the druid at a distance, then had stuck around after he and I had entered the mausoleum. Hemi and Guts had tried to follow us in, but when the tunnel caved in they'd backed out and sent the trolls for more help.

Once the mausoleum had collapsed, they figured I was done for. However, a brilliant red beam of energy came blasting through the wreckage, leaving a crater that revealed my bloody, dirt-covered face at the bottom. After that, it was just a matter of digging me out from under the remaining debris. The troll warriors cheered when they pulled me out. Unfortunately, only seven of them had made it.

I hurt worse than a bare ass on a bed of nails, but at least I was alive. And whole again—whether due to my Hyde-side's ability to heal or the Eye's magic, I wasn't certain. Despite my good fortune, I felt more than a twinge of regret that I couldn't be with Jesse. And, I felt guilty that Bells hadn't even crossed my mind, not after the prospect of being with Jesse presented itself.

The deep rumble of Hemi's voice brought me back to reality.

"I thought you'd bought the farm for sure, bro."

"Isn't that a purely American colloquialism?" I asked as I spat out dirt and blew mud from both nostrils.

"Well, I have been working on my American—since you drongos can't seem to understand plain old English."

"Do I even want to know what a drongo is?"

"Eh. It's a debatably useful term."

Guts pointed at one of his warriors. "Drongo."

The warrior turned and looked at us with a "Who, me?" expression. Hemi and I shared a laugh, then Gunnarson turned up with his goons to spoil the moment.

"Commander, nice of you to show up, oh—two hours late."

He cleared his throat. "We ran into some undead activity on

our way in. Had to clear it up before we could provide assistance. But you heroes seem to have handled things well enough."

"You seem a little disappointed, Gunnarson. Upset that I didn't die on schedule?"

He placed his hand on his hips and scowled. "Well, there's always the next time. I'm sure you'll find a way to get your ass in a sling before the month is out."

I accepted a hand from Hemi, and he hauled me to my feet. "Not this month. After this mess, I'm taking an extended vacation."

Gunnarson raised an eyebrow. "Out of my city, I hope?"

I resisted the urge to slug him. "Maybe. Look, I'd love to stay and chat, but I have a friend to visit at the hospital. Since we took care of the necromancer and the undead, I'm sure your boys can handle the cleanup."

I turned my back on him without waiting for a response. "C'mon, Hemi. Let's go help Guts and his crew gather up their dead."

Hemi had a full cooler of Lone Star in his car, so we all drank one to honor the trolls who had fallen, then watched as more trolls showed up to carry them away to their camp. They'd proven to be a much more complex and honorable people than their reputation gave them credit for, and I for one was glad to have seen another side of them. I promised Guts I'd be there for the burial ceremony.

"They died well, Guts."

"Ditto at that, mate." Hemi raised his can in reverence, then downed it all at once.

Guts nodded in agreement, but looked sad. "Much crying back at camp tonight, and much to do before daylight."

"I understand, Guts. I'll see you in two days." He'd explained that troll custom required two days for mourning and one for burial. Apparently, trolls died so rarely that every funeral was a major event. This one would be unprecedented in troll history. I just hoped they didn't start associating me with all the recent deaths in their tribe. Truth was, I liked having Guts around.

Hemi held out his hand. "I'll leave you to it, mate. Get a bath so you can go see that girl of yours."

We shook hands and bro-hugged, then agreed to meet the next day for a game of pool and some brews. I watched him leave before I hopped on the Vespa to head to the junkyard. On the way I thought about Jesse, and how quickly I'd forgotten about Bells when she'd shown up.

Sure, this thing with Bells and me was new. But was that how it was going to be? I'd get involved with someone, only to have Jesse's ghost show up and throw a wrench in the gears?

I loved Jesse, and I always would. But if I was going to fulfill this great mission I supposedly had ahead of me, I needed to be able to move on. I was sure she understood that, just like I was sure she'd be waiting for me on the other side.

But what would that mean? If I fell in love with someone, got married, had kids, and grew old with them—would that mean I'd forget about Jesse? Would I be a polygamist in the next life? Could I even fall in love with someone else?

And was it even fair to do so, when I was a danger to everyone around me?

It was all too much to think about. The truth was, I needed some alone time to work out everything that had happened. The Eye, my curse, the Fear Doirich, finding out how my Dad had died—everything.

But now I knew there was a way to control my alter-ego.

Knowing that possibility existed provided me with a small glimmer of hope. At least now I felt that I might have a shot at a normal life, sometime in the future.

But what was it, really, that the Eye wanted? It had said it desired revenge on the Tuatha Dé Danann, but I got the feeling there was a whole lot more to it than that. And besides, if all I needed was the power of its magic to allow me to control my Hyde-side, didn't that mean I could do it on my own if I gained more power?

Finn could help me make sense of all this. I goosed the throttle on my Vespa, eager to get back to the junkyard where I could get some answers.

When I got back to the junkyard, there was a set of car keys on my bed, and a note:

Sorry, kid. I know you have questions, but I need to get some answers of my own before it's too late. I hate being cryptic, but for right now it's best you don't know what's going on.

I know, I know—I kept you in the dark about the Fear Doirich, and now I'm withholding more information. I'll reveal all in good time, but recent events require me to seek answers to questions that you don't even realize exist.

Yet, I know you do have questions. Talk to the Alpha, and the Queen. You can trust the Alpha, and Maeve knows much more than either of us combined. But don't trust her, no matter what she tells you.

It's small recompense, but I've left you the keys to the Gremlin. I was going to give it to you anyway on your next birthday, but since I might be gone for a while I figured I'd better let you have it now. No sense in letting it sit.

Watch yourself, and listen to the Alpha. He'll steer you true.

-Finnegas

I grabbed the note and nearly crumpled it, then thought better of it and set it on the shelf. I picked up the keys, twirling them around my finger. Then I left them on the bed and grabbed some towels, heading out to shower.

Once dressed, I walked around the yard to the place where I'd found Finn working on the Gremlin several days past. There it sat, but in much better condition than it had been the last time I'd seen it. The body work had been completed on it, the windows had been tinted, and he'd hired someone to paint it flat black. It sat on original rims, there was plenty of good rubber on the tires, and it had an aggressive stance that spoke of suspension work and upgraded shocks.

I opened the door, and found the interior had been replaced. There was new carpet, a fresh reproduction dash and gauges, and recently reupholstered seats. I shook my head and slid into the driver's seat behind the wheel, running my hand across the steering wheel and dash.

I popped the key in the ignition and cranked the engine over. It fired up immediately, greeting me with the throaty rumble of a five-liter V8, naturally aspirated and blowing smoke through a set of high-performance exhaust headers and glass packs on the back.

He'd even replaced the stereo with an updated model.

"Finn, you sneaky son of a bitch," I whispered. "You knew you were leaving all along."

I shut the door, put the car in gear, and pulled out the back gate. After I'd locked the place back up again I hopped in the Gremlin, dropped the hammer, and roared off into the night.

27

I arrived at the hospital in time to catch the tail end of a heated conversation between Bells and a tall, well-dressed woman with long dark hair and striking gray eyes. They spoke in what I thought was a dialect of Spanish or Portuguese, but it was hard to tell. I didn't have a talent for foreign languages, and with the exception of learning some Gaelic for spell work, I'd never had the time or inclination to pick up another.

I had the good sense and decency to wait outside the room, and within a few minutes their conversation ended and the woman stormed out. She stopped in front of me as she passed, regarding me with those haunting grey eyes. That's when I realized I was standing in front of Belladonna's mother. Despite the difference in height, there was no mistaking they were closely related. This woman was strikingly beautiful.

Needless to say, I was taken by surprise when she grabbed me by the lapels of my coat and slammed me against the wall.

"Don't get my daughter killed. If you do, you won't live long enough to regret it," she threatened, in English that only carried the slightest of accents. She released me and walked off before I could gather my wits to reply.

Well, I see which side of the family Bells takes after, I reflected. I blinked once or twice, took a deep breath, and entered the room.

I pointed over my shoulder with my thumb as I entered. "Was that—?"

Bells looked furious, but her face brightened immediately when she saw me. Which, of course, made my stomach twist up in knots. Hopefully I didn't look as guilty as I felt.

"My mother. She flew in from Spain to see me, just to say I told you so. Probably flying right back out again tonight."

"Hi, Colin." Sabine sat curled up in a chair, reading a trashy gossip mag and pointedly minding her own business. She didn't bother looking up as I entered.

"Hi, Sabine. Bells, I thought you were Portuguese?"

"Galician. The dialects are similar. Did she threaten you?"

I nodded. "With bodily harm."

"Well, she didn't break you, so she must like you." Bells patted the bed by her side. "Come, sit with me."

Sabine looked up from her magazine. "If you two lovebirds are going to start smooching, I believe I'll take my leave."

Bells cocked her head at Sabine, her brow creasing. "You can stay, Sabine. No one's chasing you away."

"No, I think it's time to go. I'll leave you two to—well, whatever you're about to do." She walked out without another word.

"Bells, give me a second." I followed Sabine out, jogging to catch up to her. She didn't slow as I fell in step at her side. Finally, she pulled to a halt at the stairwell exit. "Thanks for keeping an eye on Bells."

"I did it for you, not for her. Although she's not nearly as annoying as I remembered. By the way, there's something off about her mother. She's not fae. But she's not exactly human either, that's for sure."

"Hmm, good to know. Just in case she attempts an impromptu beheading or castration the next time I see her."

"Just watch yourself around her."

"Are you going to be okay?" I tried to ask the question without making it sound pathetic. I failed.

"You're not very good at any of this, are you?" she asked.

"Uh-uh. Not one bit."

She smirked. "Well, it's a damned good thing you're cute, McCool. Because charm just isn't your thing."

Sabine stood on tiptoe to kiss me on the cheek. "I'll be fine."

She opened the door and headed into the stairwell, and my brain caught up too late to say something meaningful and appropriate. *Smooth, Colin. Real smooth.*

I yanked the door open just as it had almost closed, and blurted out the first thing that came to mind.

"I'll call you tomorrow. Maybe we can meet for coffee or something."

"Maybe," she replied, without turning around. I watched her head down the stairs with her eyes focused anywhere but on me.

"Damn it," I muttered, to no one in particular.

Bells was both happy and relieved to see me. She didn't remember much of our previous conversation, but she had recalled enough details to be concerned about my safety while I was gone. Sabine had only barely kept her from jumping out of her hospital bed to gear up and come help.

"So, you solved the city's necromancer problem, all by your lonesome. I bet Gunnarson was pissed when he found out you didn't get killed."

"Not quite all alone. I had a squad of trolls and a quarter-ton of angry Maori at my back. But yeah, Gunnarson was visibly disappointed when he saw me."

She wrinkled her nose and squinted. "What's the deal with

Hemi, anyway? Ever find out why he's all magically tattooed and stuff?"

"When I ask about it he says, 'It's family business, eh?' and changes the subject. So I've stopped asking."

"Seems like something you'd want to know, being as you two are best buds now and all."

I chuckled. "Speaking of which, what's the deal with your mom?"

She dropped her eyes and tugged on a snag poking up from the bedspread. "Next topic, please."

"Fair enough. I think I owe you an apology."

I proceeded to explain about what had happened with Jesse, and how that made me feel. I was completely honest with her about everything. About how good it felt to see Jesse, how in the moment I wanted so badly to give up so I could be with her again, and how guilty I felt about the whole thing.

Bells just sat there and listened the entire time, not saying a word. She didn't look angry, but tears welled in her eyes by the time I finished.

"Well, thanks for sharing that with me. For a while there I was sure I wouldn't have to compete with a ghost anymore, but I guess I was wrong."

"Shit. I'm sorry, Bells. Maybe I shouldn't have said anything."

"The fact you did says a lot. And it's to be expected that you still have feelings for her. I mean, this girl was your first love, and from what I gather she was meant to be the love of your life. I'm jealous, sure—but it also hurts me to know you had that taken from you prematurely. Don't forget, I was there for most of the aftermath."

I squeezed her hand, gently. "I haven't forgotten. You helped keep me sane, Bells."

Her mouth screwed up in a crooked smile. "I wouldn't

exactly call it sanity. More like a day by day struggle to hold it all together."

"Yeah, that about sums it up." I held onto her hand, refusing to let go. "I really do care about you—you know that, right?"

"I know. But until you complete this great mission or whatever you and Jesse were supposed to fulfill, I'm always going to be competing with her memory, real or imagined. And just how am I supposed to compete against that?"

I stayed with Bells until after visiting hours, and we talked until I got chased from the room by the nursing staff. But as far as the topic of Jesse was concerned, there wasn't much else to say. I knew something delicate and precious was at risk between us, but I had no idea how to stop loving Jesse.

I thought about it as I drove around town in the Gremlin, and finally decided to stop by Luther's. I knew he'd be up—and besides, I wanted to give him an update on how things had gone.

When I entered the coffee shop, he was behind the counter with one of his staff, serving drinks for the late night crowd. He noticed me immediately and pulled off his apron, laying it on the counter.

"Already heard about your heroics last night. C'mon upstairs, I have something for you."

I followed him up to his apartment, now empty of guests and spare and spotless as usual.

"You look troubled, my friend. Beer or whiskey?"

"Whiskey."

"Coming right up."

Luther didn't really drink it, but he always had the good stuff on hand. I watched as he pulled out a bottle of Hirsch Reserve, pouring me a generous two fingers. I gasped, and he patted my hand as he pushed the glass into it.

"Trust me, you've earned it. And besides, I know girl trouble when I see it, honey. Now, have a seat and tell me all about it."

"Well, the necromancer is gone now," I said as I took a seat at his breakfast bar. I explained the entire gory episode, with Luther only interrupting once or twice to clarify the odd detail. It took the better part of a half-hour to tell the whole story. After I finished my account, Luther poured me another $250 shot of bourbon, commenting as he poured.

"Hmmm—I'll need to send a rep to the troll funeral. Those things can get pretty wild. By the way, don't drink their grog. You'll wake up married to a troll maiden."

I held my tongue, recalling how everyone had been razzing me this whole time. *Could it be? Naw.* I chased the thought from my mind.

"Now, tell me about your girl problems," he said.

So, I did.

Five minutes later, Luther let out a low whistle. "My my, but you've gotten yourself in one fine pickle. Mercy, mercy, me."

"Any advice?"

He graced me with a sympathetic look. "Sugar, I've been alive for a long, long time. Not as long as Finn or Maeve, but long enough. And you want to know what I've learned?"

I waited, and he took a sip of my bourbon before he continued.

"Rule one—you take love where you can find it, if it's real. Rule two—when it's time to go, you always leave your lover better off than when you found them. And rule three? You never break a young girl's heart. Not if you can help it."

I slugged the rest of the bourbon, immediately regretting that I hadn't taken the time to savor it. It'd be a while before I drank something that pricey again.

"Thanks, Luther. I appreciate the advice."

He walked me to the door and gave me a quick hug.

"You'll be fine, and I'm sure you'll do right by that girl. Now, I almost forgot." He handed me a thick envelope. "Your fee, in cash. Don't deposit it or you'll end up in trouble with the law. And don't get pulled over with it, or else you'll lose it to the cops —and then I'll have to get it back for you."

I resisted the urge to look inside the envelope, and instead pocketed it inside my coat. "Thanks, Luther."

"Austin's vampire community thanks you. Now, go get some rest, kid, you look like hell."

Just as Luther had promised, the troll wake was rowdier than the party after my fight with Guts. Thankfully, Luther sent a rep, along with a few cases of top shelf vodka, so I was able to avoid drinking the troll's grog. Still, after three rounds of individual toasts to each troll who had fallen, I was well and properly hammered.

That's when Guts came walking up with a troll maiden, who carried a small bundle swaddled in leather and burlap. She smiled at me demurely, and Guts clapped me solidly on the back as he walked up, causing me to spill my drink.

"Druid! Now good time to show you wife and son. You look, see how handsome half-troll become."

"Aw, Guts, I didn't know you were married? And a kid, too?"

He smiled broadly. "No. Not my wife and babe. Is one you and she made."

Guts grabbed the troll maiden gently by the arm and pushed her toward me. By now we'd gathered a crowd, and I was standing in stunned silence, not sure what to say or do. I'd fathered a troll-child? How fast did troll babies gestate? And how in the hell was I going to explain this to my mom?

"Um—I—well. Ahem. I don't know what to say." I felt my face burning. The sky started spinning, and suddenly I wanted to puke.

"What, you no like troll wife?" Guts asked, crossing his arms and pulling himself to his full height. "Maybe you not know, we mate for life."

"I really don't mean any offense by this, Guts, but I think I'm going to be sick."

The trolls standing around me all stared, with plenty of furrowed brows and fingers tapping weapons menacingly. Then, Guts and his crew burst out laughing.

"Ha ha, joke on you. You no have troll wife, she too pretty for you!"

The entire crowd joined in, and soon they were all laughing, pointing, poking, and prodding. The troll maiden turned out to be Guts' sister, who had been in on the joke the whole time. Guts had wanted to prank me as a way to regain tribal honor after his lost fight. It seemed that trolls liked a good prank, and they appreciated the long game as well.

I puked in the bushes nearby, for good measure. Then I found Guts as he was jabbering in trollish with his buddies and yukking it up.

"Okay, okay—I can be a good sport. But how did you get everyone else in on it?" Guts scratched his head in confusion. "You know, the whole thing about the troll musk, and marking me as her mate?"

His eyes widened as he nodded slowly. "Oh, you really get troll musk on you. But you no remember kissing Guts' sister. Too much troll brew."

With that revelation I immediately ran for the bushes again, which the trolls found unbelievably hilarious.

Two days later, I pulled the Gremlin up in front of the local pack's clubhouse. I had a score to settle with the Dark Druid, and to do that I needed to be able to control my dark side. That would give me access to the Eye's power, if only temporarily. But the next time we met, I swore it would be enough.

And I knew of one person who could help me in that regard.

Samson was sitting on the front steps when I arrived. Somehow, this didn't surprise me at all.

He remained seated as I walked up, sipping a Shiner despite the cold. "So, you ready to take me up on my offer?"

"If the offer still stands."

He took a slug of beer. "It does. What's good for the druids is good for the Pack. Always has been, always will be. But it ain't gonna be easy, I can tell you that."

"Figured as much."

He chuckled. "You only think you know, but you don't. Pack life ain't easy. Let me give you another chance to back out. Are you ready to suffer, like you've never suffered before?"

I thought back to my training with Finnegas. Some of it had been absolutely brutal. Then I thought back to the pain I'd felt after losing Jesse. Honestly, how hard could whatever he had planned for me be?

"I am."

He finished off his beer. "One last chance. Because once you start this, there's no quitting. You either learn to control the beast, or you die. Are—you—certain?"

I nodded.

"Say it. You have to say the words."

I hesitated, but only for a second or two. "I'm certain."

"Good, then it's done." Samson set his bottle down on the concrete steps.

Three questions, three chances to back out. *Well, that was encouraging.* I kicked a rock with the toe of my boot.

"When do we start?"

On cue, the pack walked out from behind the building, flowing out in a half circle around me. Cutting off all escape. Samson chuckled and grinned.

"We start now."

NEWSLETTER

This concludes the second volume in the Colin McCool Junkyard Druid series... but there's more Colin waiting for you at my website! Go to MDMassey.com now to download your FREE novel, Druid Blood: A Junkyard Druid Prequel. When you do, you'll be subscribed to my newsletter, and you'll be the first to find out when the next Colin McCool novel, Moonlight Druid, hits bookstore shelves.